Violence, Terror, Genocide, and War in the Holy Books and in the Decades Ahead

Violence, Terror, Genocide, and War in the Holy Books and in the Decades Ahead

New Psychological and Sociological Insights on how the Old Testament, the New Testament, and the Qur'an Might Influence Violence

Timothy Philip Schwartz-Barcott

<teneo> //press
AMHERST, NEW YORK

Copyright 2018 Teneo Press

All rights reserved.
Printed in the United States of America

No part of this publication may be reproduced, stored in or introduced into a retrieval system, or transmitted, in any form, or by any means (electronic, mechanical, photocopying, recording, or otherwise), without the prior permission of the publisher.

Requests for permission should be directed to
permissions@teneopress.com, or mailed to:
Teneo Press
100 Corporate Parkway, Suite 128
Amherst, New York 14226, USA.

ISBN: 978-1-934844-38-0

TABLE OF CONTENTS

List of Tables vii

Dedications xi

Acknowledgments xiii

Opening Epigraph xvii

Preface xix

Chapter 1: Introduction and Profiles of Some Terrorists and Groups 1

Chapter 2: Violence, Terror, and War as Portrayed in the Qur'an 27

Chapter 3: Portrayals of Violence in the Old Testament 91

Chapter 4: Portrayals of Violence in the New Testament 179

Chapter 5: Summary of Findings, and Claims of Other Authors 225

Chapter 6: Suggestions for Reducing Religious Violence Worldwide 287

Appendix: Systematic Content Analysis and Coding Procedures 307

Bibliography 311

About the Author 317

Index 319

List of Tables

Table 1: Some Key Events in the Life of Muhammad and Islam 37

Table 2: Estimates of the Number (Percentages) of Words and Phrases Presented as Physical Violence in the 114 Surahs and 6,220 Verses 42

Table 3: Portrayals of Violence, Battles, or War in Parts of the Qur'an 46

Table 4: Surahs in which 25% or More of the Verses Convey Violence 51

Table 5: Who Performs, Threatens, or Demands Violence in the Qur'an? 53

Table 6: The Targets of Allah's Violence in 612 Verses of the Qur'an 60

Table 7: Physical Violence in the "War and Battle" Surahs 74

Table 8: Violence and War as Portrayed in Genesis 103

Table 9: Violence and War as Portrayed or Referred to in Deuteronomy 125

Table 10a: Verses in the Old Testament That Convey Violence 171

Table 10b: Verses in the Old Testament That Convey Violence (Cont) 172

Table 11a: Summary of Portrayals of Actual Physical Violence against Humans in the Books of the New Testament 184

Table 11b: Summary of Portrayals of Actual Physical Violence against Humans in the Books of the New Testament (Cont.) 185

Table 12: Violence as Portrayed in Matthew's Gospel 187

Table 13: Portrayals of Violence in Mark's Gospel 191

Table 14: Violence Portrayed in Luke's Gospel 194

Table 15: Violence Portrayed in John's Gospel 197

Table 16: Violence Portrayed in Acts of the Apostles 199

Table 17: Violence Portrayed in Paul's Epistle to the Romans 202

Table 18: Violence Portrayed in Paul's Other Twelve Epistles 204

Table 19: Violence Portrayed in Hebrews 208

Table 20: Violence Portrayed in the Epistle of James 210

Table 21: Violence Portrayed in Peter's Two Epistles 211

Table 22: Violence Portrayed in the Epistle of Jude 213

List of Tables

Table 23: Violence Portrayed in John's Three Epistles 215

Table 24: Violence Referred to or Portrayed in "The Revelation of Jesus Christ to John" 219

Table 25: Summary of the Quantities and Qualities of Violence Portrayed in all Books of the New Testament (as presented in the previous fourteen tables) 220

Table 26: Verses that Convey Violence in the Old Testament, the New Testament, and the Qur'an 227

Table 27: Percentages of Verses in the Three Books that Convey Terror, Genocide, Wars, and Battles 228

Dedications

This book against violence is dedicated in the memory of my beloved parents, Delma Marianna Favro (1914-1999) and Philip John Schwartz (1910-2002). They were caring, faithful parents who avoided violence and tried their best to live peacefully with the people they encountered anywhere in the world. They did not criticize or discount other religions. To my parents, their Catholic religion helped them live this way—peacefully.

Requiescat in Pace.

This book also is dedicated to all people who have been the victims of violence due to their religious beliefs or to the religious beliefs of other people. In the decades ahead, let us encourage religions and religious people to become much more effective in reducing misunderstandings, conflict, and violence throughout the world.

Acknowledgments

A number of people have helped me complete this book over the five years I have worked on it, including one year of extreme illness. As with my other books and many of my published articles, my lady, Donna Schwartz-Barcott, has allowed me to have the time to think, research, and write. She also has commented on many of the findings and interpretations that are presented in this book. For this, I am most thankful.

The late Emeritus Professor Gerhard Lenski of the University of North Carolina, Chapel Hill, was a loyal and astute mentor to me for more than forty years on many topics, including the sociology of religion, from hunting and gathering societies to the most contemporary spiritual belief systems. Over the last forty years, he provided incisive comments on almost all of my research that has been published. In the final months of his life, in 2015, he continued to do so with his usual brilliance and grace.

Mohammed Taheri-Azar, a very devout and intelligent Muslim man, graciously helped me to understand how various verses in the Qur'an can influence peoples' behaviors. He also read through my statements about Islam and the Qur'an and made very helpful suggestions to increase the accuracy of my statements.

Emeritus Professor Richard Cramer of the University of North Carolina, Chapel Hill, helped improve the accuracy of a number of statements in Chapter 3 about the history of Judaism and about various verses in the Pentateuch. Also providing relevant comments on a version of the manuscript was Katherine Meyer, Emeritus Professor of Sociology at the Mershon Center for International Security Studies at Ohio State University, and Director of Social and Economic Sciences at the National Science Foundation in Washington, D.C. Professor Mark Juergensmeyer provided helpful comments regarding my work. He is Founding Director of the Orfalea Center for Global & International Studies at the University of California, Santa Barbara.

Helpful comments on various parts of the manuscript also were provided by Reverend Charles Barrett, Pastor of Wayside Presbyterian Church in Signal Mountain, Tennessee, and by my dear niece, Bridget Barrett. Patricia Metzger Livingston of Sunland, California, provided a very careful and astute reading of the manuscript to make it more valuable to open-minded people, regardless of their orientation towards religions. Reverend Timothy T. Rich, Pastor of St. Luke's Church in East Greenwich, Rhode Island, shared with me his interpretations of a number of verses in the Old and New Testaments that were rather ambiguous or troubling for me.

While I was writing this book, I benefited from many conversations with Kamal, Husam, Haval, and Evan Elias. They helped me appreciate their harrowing experiences in northern Iraq—between 1990 and 2016—as members of the indigenous Yazidi ethnic-religious minority group. The Yazidis were subjected to persecution, terror, and genocide by members of other religions. Fortunately, the Eliases now reside safely and legally in the U.S. They are gainfully employed and hope to become U.S. citizens as soon as possible.

Alan Greco of Alan Greco Design in East Greenwich, Rhode Island, helped me design the cover. Ashley Atkinson of Atkinson Editing in Tampa, Florida, was absolutely superb in helping me prepare the manu-

Acknowledgments

script for publication. Editor Paul Richardson at Cambria Press and Teneo Press provided timely guidance and support throughout the publication process.

I thank all of these people. Of course, I am the only person responsible for any errors, omissions, or oversights in this book.

Opening Epigraph

Religion seems to be connected with violence virtually everywhere. The September 11 assaults were only the most spectacular of a series of bloody religion incidents. In recent years, religious violence has erupted among right-wing Christians in the United States, and Muslims and Jews in the Middle East, quarrelling Hindus and Muslims in South Asia, and indigenous religious communities in Africa and Indonesia. Like the activists associated with Osama bin Laden, the individuals involved in these cases have relied on religion to provide political identities and give license to vengeful ideologies.

Religion is crucial for these acts, since it gives moral justifications for killing and provides images of cosmic war that allow activists to believe that they are waging spiritual scenarios. This does not mean that religion causes violence, nor does it mean that religious violence cannot, in some cases, be justified by other means. But it does mean that religion often provides the mores and symbols that make possible bloodshed—even catastrophic acts of terrorism.
 —Mark Juergensmeyer in his book *Terror in the Mind of God* [1]

Notes

1. *Terror in the Mind of God. The Global Rise of Religious Violence.* Third edition. Revised and Updated. Berkeley: University of California Press. 2003. P. xi.

Preface

As indicated by its title, this book analyzes *all* of the verses in the most "holy" books of Judaism, Christianity, and Islam that portray or refer to physical violence and war against human beings. I analyze these verses as objectively as possible, based on my training and my years of teaching and research as a sociologist. Along the way I offer many warnings as to how these verses might be used and misused by some people now and in the decades ahead to plan, commit, and try to justify violent acts, including terrorism, by themselves and by others. In the final chapter, I offer some suggestions for reducing these risks.

Of course, it is true that the vast majority of violent acts in the modern world are not religious in nature; nor are most of the terrorist acts in the modern world predominantly religious in nature, despite what we hear often from some political leaders, news commentators, and interest groups. Even when violent acts are prompted by religions and by religious beliefs, it is not always or necessarily because of verses in the "holy books" of these religions.

But *sometimes* they are. Sometimes violence, terrorism, and war are related to the religions of the perpetrators and the victims. And sometimes verses in one or more of the holy books have inspired violence and terrorist attacks. Certainly, this was the case in the terrorist attacks organized by Osama bin Laden on 9-11-2001, as presented in several parts of this book. This also has been the case in quite a few of the terrorist attacks by Jewish zealots and by Christian fundamentalist-extremists in recent decades, as indicated by Mark Juergensmeyer in the epigraph at the beginning of this book. But those events are in the past, as were the Muslim invasions into Spain, France, and Eastern Europe after Muhammad's death, the "Christian Crusades," and so many other "holy wars" by adherents of so many different religions and religious factions within the same religion.

The purpose of this book is to deepen our understanding of how and why some of the passages in the holy books can be used and misused to inspire and motivate some people towards violence, terrorism, and war now and in the years ahead—especially in the next few decades. Another purpose is to alert us about this prospect. An additional purpose is to suggest some ways to reduce the likelihood of the holy books being misused to promote violence and war. Unfortunately, not all of the encouragements toward violence in the holy books are in the past tense. It is naïve and dangerous to try to dismiss them simply on the grounds that they are obsolete anachronisms or that they are taken without regard to historical context. In the contemporary world, as in the past, persons need not take "historical context" into account if and when they decide to try to kill someone because of a passage in a "holy book" that says "kill them"—or that they interpret that way.

And this is exactly what some people do, have done in the past, and are likely to do in the years ahead. I hope that new insights in this book will lessen this likelihood of violence in the future, although I cannot say that I expect this to be the case.

Violence, Terror, Genocide, and War in the Holy Books and in the Decades Ahead

Chapter 1

Introduction and Profiles of Some Terrorists and Groups

Epigraph

If the Qur'an urges believers to fight, as it undoubtedly does, it also commands that enemies be shown mercy if they surrender. Some frightful portions of the Bible, by contrast, order the total extermination of enemies, of whole families and races—of men, women, and children, and even their livestock, with no quarter granted....

The Bible overflows with "texts of terror," to borrow a phrase coined by American theologian Phyllis Trible, and biblical violence is often marked by indiscriminate savagery....

But in terms of the violent and unacceptable faces of their fundamental scriptures, differences between the faiths are minimal.
—Distinguished religious scholar Philip Jenkins in his book *Laying Down the Sword: Why We Can't Ignore the Bible's Violent Verses.*

VIOLENCE, TERROR, GENOCIDE, AND WAR

AN UNDERSTANDING: VIOLENCE, TERROR, AND WAR USUALLY ARE *NOT* DEPENDENT ON RELIGION OR ON "HOLY BOOKS"

Countless books have been written about whether various religions and their "holy books" influence the amounts and the types of violence, terrorism, and war. It seems to me that a vast amount of highly credible research indicates that the answer is "yes—sometimes"—but with many qualifications, caveats, and conditions that are very important. There is no doubt that some religions and their holy books have influenced the quantities and qualities of violence in some places and at some times in the course of human history. There also is little doubt that the influences often have been to *restrain* violence, perhaps far more often than to promote or justify violence.

It is rather clear that violence, terrorism, and war often occur without any linkage to religion or religious books. We know from archeological evidence that there was plenty of violence and warfare before any books were written and before the emergence of the religions of Judaism, Christianity, and Islam. And there is no doubt that violence, terrorism, and war have occurred in many places of the world where these religions are absent or are relatively rare or weak politically. But there are exceptions to this. And, unfortunately, it seems as though exceptions will continue in the decades ahead in many parts of the globe, if only because it is so much easier now for so many people across the globe to use and misuse religions and passages in the "holy books" to promote and to justify violence.

AN HISTORICAL CASE OF A "HOLY BOOK" DIRECTLY INFLUENCING VIOLENCE

Here is one example of how passages in a holy book supposedly had a direct bearing on a very violent event—in this case, the First Battle of Kosovo in the Balkans in 1389 CE.

Profiles of Some Terrorists and Groups 3

Murad I, The Grand Vizier of the Ottoman Empire, marched towards Belgrade with an estimated 10,000 cavalry and Janissaries. His march was blocked at Kosovo by Serbian Prince Lazar I and some 25,000 Bosnian, Serb, Albanian, Bulgarian, and Wallachian troops. The armies confronted each other for days as their leaders tried to determine how and when to engage in battle. As required by Islam, the Qur'an was recited repeatedly each day in the Muslim camp. It is said that Murad consulted it several times in deciding when to attack.

> The grand vizier opened the Koran at random, seeking inspiration. His eyes fell upon the verse that said, "Oh Prophet, fight the hypocrites and unbelievers." "These Christian dogs are unbelievers and hypocrites," he said. "We fight them." He opened the Koran a second time. This time he read, "A large host is often beaten by a weaker one." "They are the large host. We are the weak one," he said. "We fight them." [1]

SOME CURRENT TERRORIST GROUPS AND PEOPLE

Violence against humans obviously occurs in many forms besides organized warfare and terrorism by groups and individuals, and for many different reasons besides what some people might believe is based on passages in a "holy book." However, as indicated in the opening epigraph by Mark Juergensmeyer, warfare and terrorism are two of the most controversial and concentrated forms of violence against human beings, particularly when the warfare and terrorism seem to be inspired, directed, and justified by religious beliefs and passages in books that are considered to be holy.

Let us consider some of the groups and organizations that are alleged to engage in terrorist activities.

According to a number of sources, there are more than two hundred terrorist organizations in the world.[2] Some of them do not seem to be affiliated with Judaism, Christianity, Islam, or other religions. Examples include the Communist Party of India, the Irish National Liberation Party, the Kurdistan Democratic Party, and the Revolutionary Armed Forces of Colombia. About ninety of these organizations have been designated as "terrorist groups" by the U.S. government. These include al-Qaeda Worldwide, the Army of Islam, the Palestine Liberation Front, and the Islamic State of Iraq and Levant. The U.S. State Department also has a list of Foreign Terrorist Organizations (FTOs). Of the sixty-one FTOs, the ones that are alleged to be strongly associated with Islam include ISIL Khorasan, ISIL Libya, al-Nusra Front of Syria, Army of Islam-Palestine, al-Qaeda Worldwide, and several dozen others.[3]

Now, as to "domestic terrorism in the U.S.," relatively few of the alleged terrorist groups and organizations are strongly linked to religions by name or in their operations. Of the five that are, one is Jewish in name (Jewish Defense League), several are Christian in name or affiliation (Army of God, The Arm of the Lord, Ku Klux Klan, Phineas Priesthood), and none are Muslim (notice that al-Qaeda is not on the list).[4]

- Animal Liberation Front
- Alpha 66 and Omega 7
- Army of God
- Aryan Nations
- Black Liberation Army
- The Covenant, The Sword, and The Arm of the Lord (possibly inactive since 2012)
- Earth Liberation Front
- Jewish Defense League
- Ku Klux Klan
- May 19th Communist Organization
- The Order
- Phineas Priesthood
- Symbionese Liberation Army

Profiles of Some Terrorists and Groups

- United Freedom Front
- Weathermen

Of course, we also know that there has been an increase in violence by so-called "lone wolf" terrorists. These are individuals who do not belong to an organized group per se, but who are attracted to and inspired by the propaganda of foreign terrorist organizations, such as al-Qaeda and ISIS, to commit violent acts on their own.

Now let us briefly consider some alleged terrorists and terrorist organizations that are sometimes considered to be strongly related to Judaism, Christianity, and Islam—and possibly to the holy books of these religions.

SOME JEWISH GROUPS AND TERRORISTS

According to religious scholars Ami Pedahzur and Arie Perlinger,[5] probably the first example of post-Biblical terrorism by Jews was by a Jewish religious and political movement called "Zealotry" in the 1st Century CE. It often incited the residents of Judea Province to rebel against the Roman occupiers and use armed force to expel Roman legions from the holy lands. Mark Juergensmeyer and other scholars of religious violence point out that, in contemporary times, there are many similarities among Jewish, Christian, and Muslim terrorists and terrorist groups and networks. They tend to be alienated and isolated from the values and the people who participate in the majority, mainstream culture. They view secular governments "as an existential threat to their own community." Often their ideologies are not only religious but political as well. However, Juergensmeyer contends that some of the newer Jewish groups tend "to emphasize religious motives for their actions at the expense of secular ones." He claims that "most networks consist of religious Zionists and ultra-orthodox Jews living in isolated, homogenous communities."

More than a dozen groups have been identified as "Jewish terrorist organizations."[6] Two of the most notorious ones are Kach and Kahane

Chai. Both groups are banned in Israel, although they continue to operate there. They have been classified as "terrorist organizations" by Israel, Canada, the European Union, and the United States. The Jewish Defense League (JDL) in America, founded by the late Rabbi Meir Kahane, also has been classified as a terrorist organization. The National Consortium for the Study of Terror and Responses to Terror reported that JDL members attempted at least fifteen terrorist attacks in the U.S. since 1980.

One of the most well-publicized "Jewish terrorists" was Baruch Goldstein, an American-born Israeli physician. In 1994, Goldstein committed the massacre at the Cave of the Patriarchs in the city of Hebron. He shot and killed twenty-nine Muslim worshippers inside the Ibrahim Mosque, and wounded one hundred twenty-five others, before he was shot and killed. Goldstein was a supporter of Kach, the Israeli political party that was also founded by the late Rabbi Meir Kahane. Kach advocates the expulsion of Arabs from Israel and the Palestinian territories. By the way, in 1990, Kahane was giving a speech to Orthodox Jews at the New York Marriott East Side Hotel in Manhattan when he was assassinated by a Muslim extremist, Egyptian-born American citizen El Sayyid Nosair, who had been residing in Jersey City, N.J.

Among other violent events that have been determined to constitute religious terrorism is the killing of four Israeli Arab civilians by Eden Natan-Zada in August 2005. Prime Minister Ariel Sharon decried the killings and announced that Natan-Zada was a "bloodthirsty Jewish terrorist." Author Ami Pedahzur determined that Natan-Zada's motivations were religious.

The Jewish "Revolt" terror group supposedly plans "to create a Jewish Kingdom in Israel" that will replace the State of Israel. The group's members have been blamed for at least eleven arson attacks against Palestinian and Christian churches.

The Duma arson attack in July 2015 killed a Palestinian baby and injured a number of family members in what the Israeli Prime Minister termed a "terrorist act." Graffiti in Hebrew left at the scene proclaimed,

"Long live the messiah!" This is the motto of the messianic wing of the Chabad-Lubavitch Movement. Members of the Movement are said to believe that the messiah is Menachem Mendel Schneerson, a rabbi who died in 1994. "The messiah is expected to return, rebuild the ancient kingdom, and redeem the world."

SOME CHRISTIAN GROUPS AND TERRORISTS

The Crusades and the Spanish Inquisition are two of the most famous cases of widespread generalized violence by Christian entities. Christian religious terrorism dates back to at least 1605 and the Gunpowder Plot in England. It was a failed attempt by a group of English Catholics, including Guy Fawkes, to assassinate King James I and to blow-up the Palace of Westminster. Their purpose was to stop the spread of the Reformation and of Protestant state churches. "Fawkes and his colleagues tried to justify their violence in terms of religion." [7]

Mark Juergensmeyer categorizes contemporary Christian terrorists as part of

> ...religious activists from Algeria to Idaho, who have come to hate secular governments with an almost transcendent passion. They dream of revolutionary changes that will establish a godly social order in the rubble of what the citizens of more secular societies regard as modern, egalitarian democracies.[8]

In the U.S. alone, there are reports of more than a dozen so-called Christian terrorist organizations allegedly including the Order, Phineas Priesthood, and the Ku Klux Klan. The Army of God is one of the most prominent ones.

"The Army of God (AOG) is a Christian terrorist organization" that has engaged in the use of a wide variety of violent threats and actions in the U.S. to fight against abortion, homosexuality, and other behaviors considered to be condemned by Biblical passages. According to the

Department of Justice (DOJ) and the Department of Homeland Security's Joint Terrorism Knowledge Base,

> The Army of God is an underground terrorist organization that has been active in the U.S. since 1982. In addition to numerous property crimes, the group has committed acts of kidnapping, attempted murder, and murder.[9]

Here are some of the violent actions attributed to the AOG or to people supposedly inspired by it:

- In 1993, Shelly Shannon, a very active member of the AOG, was found guilty of the attempted murder of Dr. George Tiller, a physician who performed abortions. Buried in Shannon's backyard, police found an "Army of God Manual" and a guide to arson, chemical attacks, invasions, and bombings.
- The AOG also claimed responsibility for the murder of Dr. John Britton and clinic escort James Barrett, by Paul Jennings Hill.
- Clayton Waagner claimed to be a member of the Virginia Dare Chapter of the AOG. He mailed over 500 letters containing white powder to 280 abortion providers in 2001, claiming that the powder was anthrax.
- The AOG also claims responsibility for Eric Rudolph's bombing of abortions clinics in Atlanta and Birmingham and "The Otherside Lounge," a gay and lesbian bar in Atlanta.

The AOG website encourages acts of violence against abortion clinics and surgeons who perform abortions. It also includes a number of Biblical passages as justifications for this kind of violence. Here are a few of them:

- *"Arise, cry out in the night: in the beginning of the watches pour out thine heart like water before the face of the Lord: lift up thy hands toward him for the life of thy young children." (Lam. 2: 19)
- *"Oh that my head were waters, and mine eyes a fountain of tears, that I might weep day and night for the slain of the daughter of my people." (Jer. 9: 1)

Profiles of Some Terrorists and Groups

- *"Who will rise up for me against the evildoers? Or who will stand up for me against the workers of iniquity?" (Psalm 94: 16)
- *"Let death seize upon them, and let them go down quick into hell: for wickedness is in their dwellings, and among them." (Psalm 55: 15)
- *"Yea, they sacrificed their sons and their daughters unto devils, and shed innocent blood, even the blood of their sons and of their daughters." (Psalm 106: 37, 38)

The website also lists passages from the New Testament in an effort to justify violence against abortionists:

- *"And Jesus said unto him, No man, having put his hand to the plough, and looking back, is fit for the kingdom of God." (Luke 9: 62)
- *"Verily, verily, I say unto you, Except a corn of wheat fall into the ground and die, it abideth alone: but if it die, it bringeth forth much fruit." (John 12: 24)

The AOG website also commends the violent actions of more than a dozen people who have been convicted and imprisoned for violence against abortion clinics. These include Paul Jennings Hill, Robert Dear, Scott Roeder, Shelley Shannon, and Eric Rudolph.

The Case of Eric Rudolph

Eric Rudolph committed at least four bombings, including the bombing at the Centennial Olympic Park during the Olympic Games in Atlanta in 1996. He also claimed responsibility for bombing the "The Otherside Lounge" in Atlanta and a women's health clinic in Birmingham, Alabama that he and members of the AOG labeled as an "abortion clinic." Rudolph evaded capture for more than five years, hiding primarily in heavily-forested areas in western North Carolina. He was captured, convicted, and sentenced to life in prison. In his memoir, *Between the Lines of Drift: The Memoirs of a Militant*, Rudolph writes that he detonated a bomb at an abortion clinic in Birmingham in January 1998 in order to stop abortions.

He indicates that he had "nothing personal against" the security guards who were killed and injured in the bombing:

> I did not target them for who they were—but for what they did. What they did was participate in the murder and dismemberment of upwards of 50 children a week.... My actions that day were motivated by my recognition that abortion is murder. Because it is murder, I believe that deadly force is indeed justified in an attempt to stop it.

His memoir recounts his upbringing and his experiences with various religions and Biblical passages:

> Our parents baptized us Catholic, but a few years after moving to Florida, my mother converted to Protestantism. While attending a Pentecostal prayer meeting, she found the Holy Ghost. Dad was skeptical at first. But he soon came around to her point of view. Thus, began out ten-year odyssey across the Pentecostal universe....
>
> In 1972, my father transferred to Miami International Airport. The family moved just north of there to Ft. Lauderdale. In those years, we practically lived in churches and prayer meetings. Twice, sometimes thrice a week, we attended church services. After that brief encounter with the Holy Ghost in New Smyrna Beach, mother could never quite pin him down again. He kept moving around, and she kept looking. She followed the Holy Ghost into Baptist churches, charismatic tent revivals, and Christian retreats.... Mostly we attended informal prayer meetings. Ten to twenty people would gather in someone's living room. They would read Scripture and prophecy, sing, dance, testify, and speak in tongues.

Rudolph's memoir rarely quotes Biblical passages to indicate justifications for his thinking and his actions. However, he ends his memoir with this passage from the Bible:

"Trust in the Lord with all your heart. For He is with you always, even unto the end."

The Case of Robert Lewis Dear

Robert Lewis Dear was convicted and is incarcerated for killing three people and injuring nine others in 2015 in a shooting at a Planned Parenthood clinic in Colorado Springs. Governor John Hickenlooper called Dear's act "a form of terrorism." Dear was described as a "delusional man who had written on a cannabis Internet forum that 'sinners would burn in hell.'" He praised The Army of God, claiming that attacks on abortion clinics "are God's work." In court documents, Dear's ex-wife claimed that:

> He claims to be a Christian and is extremely evangelistic, but he does not follow the Bible in his actions. He says that he will be saved as long as he believes.... He is obsessed with the world coming to an end.[10]

SOME TERRORISTS, GROUPS, AND ORGANIZATIONS ASSOCIATED WITH ISLAM

News media in the U.S., Great Britain, and Europe frequently report on terrorist activities by a rather extensive number of groups and organizations that are alleged to be closely affiliated with Islam, or with specific factions or sects within Islam, particularly those said to be "radical," "far right," "revolutionary," or "fundamentalist." The organizations include al-Qaeda (various spellings), al-Shabaab, Hamas, Hezbollah, Islamic State of Iraq and Levant (ISIS and ISUL), Lashkar-e-Taiba, Taliban, Muslim Brotherhood, Boko Haram, and many more.[11] ISIS has been particularly active in claiming responsibility for some of the ghastliest terrorist attacks in England and France in 2017, including the killings at London Bridge and the bombing of a popular music concert at Manchester.

Al-Qaeda as a Prominent Islamic Terrorist Organization

Al-Qaeda is one of the most frequently mentioned terrorist organizations that is said to be closely affiliated with Islam.[12] There is considerable debate and disagreement regarding the size, strength, and centralization of al-Qaeda. Since the killing of Osama bin Laden in Pakistan in 2010, al-Qaeda has become rather decentralized, complex, and innovative in its ways of recruiting members and promoting violence. Now it has more than two dozen affiliates in more than a dozen countries and is considered to be strongest in northwest Pakistan. As best as I can tell, the U.S. is not one of the countries in which al-Qaeda is currently operating as an organization. The 9-11-2001 terrorist attacks in the U.S. are widely considered to have been planned by al-Qaeda's founder and leader at the time, the late Osama bin Laden, and conducted by persons who identified with al-Qaeda.

In December 1998, the Director of the CIA Counterterrorism Center reported to the president that al-Qaeda was preparing for attacks in the USA, including the training of personnel to hijack aircraft. On September 11, 2001, al-Qaeda attacked the United States, hijacking four airliners within the country and deliberately crashing two into the twin towers of the World Trade Center in New York City, and the third into the western side of the Pentagon in Arlington County, Virginia. The fourth, however, failed to reach its intended target – either the United States Capitol or the White House, both located in Washington, D.C. – due to the rebellion by the passengers to retake the airliner, and instead crashed into the field in Shanksville, Pennsylvania. In total, the attackers killed 2,977 victims and injured more than 6,000 others.

U.S. officials called Anwar al-Awlaki an "example of al-Qaeda reach into" the U.S. in 2008 after probes into his ties to the September 11 attacks hijackers. A former FBI agent identifies Awlaki as a known "senior recruiter for al-Qaeda", and a spiritual motivator. Awlaki's sermons in the U.S. were attended by three of the 9/11 hijackers, as well as accused Fort Hood shooter Nidal Malik Hasan. U.S. intelligence intercepted emails from Hasan to Awlaki between

Profiles of Some Terrorists and Groups

December 2008 and early 2009. On his website, Awlaki has praised Hasan's actions in the Fort Hood shooting.

An unnamed official claimed there was good reason to believe Awlaki "has been involved in very serious terrorist activities since leaving the U.S. [after 9/11], including plotting attacks against America and our allies."

U.S. President Barack Obama approved the targeted killing of al-Awlaki by April 2010, making al-Awlaki the first U.S. citizen ever placed on the CIA target list. That required the consent of the U.S. National Security Council, and officials said it was appropriate for an individual who posed an imminent danger to national security. In May 2010, Faisal Shahzad, who pleaded guilty to the 2010 Times Square car bombing attempt, told interrogators he was "inspired by" al-Awlaki, and sources said Shahzad had made contact with al-Awlaki over the internet. In October 2010, U.S. and U.K. officials linked al-Awlaki to the 2010 cargo plane bomb plot. In September 2011, he was killed in a targeted killing drone attack in Yemen.[13]

Al-Qaeda's belief system is closely related to some of the most radical sects in Islam: Salafism, Salafist jihadism, Qutbism, and Pan-Islamism. Many al-Qaeda leaders demand a complete break from all foreign governments and cultural features in Muslim countries. They want to create a new caliphate that rules over the entire Muslim world. Many leaders claim that a Christian-Jewish alliance is trying to destroy Islam. They claim that the killing of non-combatants is religiously sanctioned, but they ignore religious scripture that they interpret as forbidding the murder of non-combatants and on internecine fighting. They oppose what they consider to be secular laws in favor of strict Sharia law.

Al-Qaeda's many affiliates and factions often instigate sectarian violence among Muslims. Many leaders regard liberal Muslims, Shias, Sufis, and other sects as heretics. They attack their mosques and gatherings. Al-Qaeda sectarian attacks include the bombing and attempted genocide of Yazidi communities in northern Iraq and Kurdistan, the bombing of Sadr City, the massacre at Ashoura, and the April 2007 bombings in Baghdad. Egyptian Ayman al-Zawahiri succeeded Osama bin Laden at his death as nominal leader of al-Qaeda until al-Zawahiri was himself killed by a U.S. drone strike in Yemen in 2011. The group now tries to cultivate small cells of terrorists and so-called "lone wolf terrorists" throughout the world with Internet-transmitted propaganda and guidance for bomb-making, vehicle-ramming, stabbing, and other violent techniques that are intended to cause mayhem and destabilize secular governments.

Terrorist propaganda, guidance, and support by al-Qaeda, Hezbollah, ISIS, and many other organizations are transmitted through the Internet and through many other means to prospective and active terrorists throughout the world. Here are just a few of the people purportedly inspired and influenced by these organizations and their directives.

Some People Associated with Islam and Terrorism [14]

Abdul Razak Ali Artan
In November 2016, Artan, a Somali-born student at the Ohio State University, drove a vehicle into a group of pedestrians on campus. Then he stabbed people with a butcher knife before he was shot to death by a police officer. Months earlier, Artan had identified himself as a Muslim and indicated that he was disturbed by how Muslims were being portrayed in the mass media.

Omar Mateen
In June 2016, Mateen shot and killed fifty people inside Pulse, an LGBTQ nightclub in Orlando, Florida. The FBI found evidence that Mateen "claimed to have family connections to al-Qaeda and to be a member of Hezbollah."

Profiles of Some Terrorists and Groups

Zachary Adam Chesser
Chesser was born in Charlottesville, Virginia. He converted to Islam in his late teens and married a Muslim woman. He was convicted in 2010 for aiding al-Shababb, a branch of al-Qaeda.

Former U.S. Army Major Nidal Malik Hasan
Born in Arlington, Virginia in 1970, Hasan was convicted in 2011 for killing thirteen people and wounding thirty-two other people at Fort Hood, Texas, where he was serving as a staff psychiatrist. Allegedly, Hasan was inspired by al-Qaeda and shouted "Allah Akbar" as he shot his victims. Prior to his attack, Hasan had tried repeatedly to communicate with Anwar al-Awlaki, a famous, controversial spiritual leader of al-Qaeda. He asked for al-Awlaki's interpretation of a number of passages in the Qur'an about jihad and the killing of innocents as well as idolaters.

Mohammed Taheri-Azar
Taheri-Azar is serving a sentence of twenty-six to thirty-three years in prison for intentionally driving a vehicle into a crowd of people on the campus of the University of North Carolina in Chapel Hill in March 2006, injuring nine. After his arrest and while awaiting trial, Taheri-Azar made many claims about the influence of Islam and the Qur'an on his thinking and his behaviors. Here are just a few examples:

Before his attack on campus, Taheri-Azar left a letter in his apartment for the police. It included this statement:

> I am writing this letter to inform you of my reasons for premeditating and attempting to murder citizens and residents of the United States of America on Friday, March 3, 2006 in the city of Chapel Hill, North Carolina by running them over with my automobile and stabbing them with a knife if the opportunities are presented to me by Allah....[15]

Taheri-Azar also made many other statements that relate his behavior to Islam and the Qur'an, including these statements to News Anchor Amber Rupinta of the local ABC network affiliate:

> I live with the holy Koran as my constitution for right and wrong and definition of injustice.... Allah in the Koran gives permission for those who follow Allah to attack those who have waged war against them, with the expectation of eternal paradise in case of martyrdom and/or the living of one's life in obedience of all of Allah's commandments found throughout the Koran's 114 chapters.... I've read all 114 chapters about 20 times since June of 2003 when I started reading the Koran.... I live only to serve Allah by obeying all of his commandments of which I am aware by reading and learning the contents of the Koran.[16]

In a letter to the campus newspaper, the *Daily Tarheel*, Taheri-Azar provided dozens of references to specific chapters and verses of the Qur'an that he felt provided "instructions and guidelines for fighting and killing in the cause of Allah." For example, Taheri wrote that the "cutting of limbs and crucifixion" are allowed by Surah 5 Verse 33 of the Qur'an. He also wrote that "beheading and removing fingers" was allowed by Surah 8 Verse 12 of the Qur'an. He wrote that a major reason for "fighting in the Cause of Allah" was "to stop persecution and oppression of Allah's Followers," as allowed by Surah 2 Verse 193 of the Qur'an.[17]

AHIMSA: NON-VIOLENCE AS A KEY PRINCIPLE OF THREE MAJOR ORIENTAL RELIGIONS

The holy books of Judaism, Christianity, and Islam certainly contain passages that prohibit violence, as well as passages that do *not* prohibit violence. One of the best-known prohibitions, found in several places in the Bible, is the Commandment "Do Not Kill." Yet it is worth considering whether prohibitions against violence are much stronger and more fundamental in other religions. Consider, for example, the principle of "*Ahimsa*" in Buddhism, Hinduism, and Jainism.[18]

> *Ahimsa*... is a term meaning "not to injure" and "compassion...."
> *Ahimsa* is also referred to as nonviolence, and it applies to all living things—including all animals—according to many Indian religions. Ahimsa is one of the cardinal virtues and an important tenet of three major religions (Jainism, Hinduism, and Buddhism). *Ahimsa* is a multidimensional concept, inspired by the premise that all living beings have the spark of the divine spiritual energy; therefore, to hurt another being is to hurt oneself. *Ahimsa* has also been related to the notion that any violence has karmic consequences.... Most popularly, Mahatma Gandhi strongly believed in the principle of *Ahimsa*. *Ahimsa*'s precept of "cause no injury" includes one's deeds, words, and thoughts.... Scholars debate principles of *Ahimsa* when one is faced with war and situations requiring self-defence. The historic literature from India and modern discussions have contributed to theories of Just War, and theories of appropriate self-defence.

DOES READING VIOLENT WORDS AND PASSAGES ACTIVATE CERTAIN PARTS OF THE BRAIN AND ELICIT HOSTILE EMOTIONS?

It is worth considering emerging scientific insights about how the reading of religious texts relates to brain activity and subsequent human emotions. There is mounting evidence that repeated exposure to compassionate words such as "love," "caring," "kindness," and "forgiveness" in religious texts activates parts of the human brain that generate emotions that are congruent with these words. Over time, neural pathways within the brain change so that these linkages become habitual. Contemplating a loving God strengthens portions of our brain—particularly the frontal lobes and the anterior cingulate—places where empathy and reason reside. Unfortunately, a parallel process occurs when we have repeated exposure to hostile and violent words such as "hate," "torture," "destroy," "slay," and "kill." These words activate a different part of the brain—a part that generates emotions that are congruent with these words. Furthermore, reading about and contemplating a wrathful God activates the limbic part of the brain and generates emotions of fear and aggression.[19]

DOES READING VIOLENT WORDS AND PASSAGES CONTRIBUTE TO "DISINHIBITION" AND "DESENSITIZATION"?

Also worth considering is a growing body of empirical psychological research on "disinhibition" and "desensitization."[20] In general, and for many people, the more often we are exposed to violent words, images and stories in media, the less likely we are to be inhibited against behaving aggressively in real life situations. Additionally, the more often we are exposed to violent words, images, and stories in media, the less likely we are to react negatively to violent situations in real life.

Applied to the experience of reading passages in religious books, including the Qur'an and the Bible, or listening to others recite these passages to us, the more often we read or hear violent words, images, and stories, the less likely we are to react negatively to violent situations in real life. Desensitization such as this is reported to be relatively common among police and fire department personnel, combat veterans, emergency medical technicians, ambulance drivers, and others, as they witness violent events and the consequences, including severely injured people, dying people, and dead bodies.

Some psychological research also indicates that disinhibition and desensitization regarding violence is even more likely to occur when the violence is depicted as being justified, when the consequences are positive and rewarding to the violent persons, and when the violence is encountered in social situations in which other people respond affirmatively to the depictions.

Aren't these the kinds of outcomes we can expect when members of terrorist recruitment and training teams often recite violent words and passages of the Qur'an—or any other text—to prospective terrorists, combatants, and trouble-makers?

The findings presented in the chapters that follow can also help us address more fundamental questions:

- How much violence, and what kinds of violence, are portrayed in the passages of the three books considered to be most holy by so many Jews, Christians, and Muslims?
- According to these passages, do the supreme beings of these religions engage in violence, demand violence, excuse violence, and threaten lethal violence by their followers? If so: who, what, when, where, and why?
- What are the most important similarities and differences among the three holy books regarding portrayals of violence and war?
- How do these findings relate to claims made by contemporary political leaders and leading scholars about religious violence and war?
- What can be done by us, as "ordinary citizens," and by political and religious leaders, to reduce the likelihood that passages of the holy books will be used and misused to promote violence in the years ahead?

RELATION TO A PREVIOUS BOOK

This book is an extension of the research I published in my previous book, *War, Terror & Peace in the Qur'an and in Islam: Insights for Military and Political Leaders*. As indicated by its title, that book focuses on portrayals of war, terror, and peace in the Qur'an and in Islam historically, from 610-2004 C.E. It was written primarily for military and government leaders. The focus of *this* book is broader and more encompassing, as well as current and future-oriented. It is about physical violence against humans in any situation—past, present, and future. Often the violence portrayed in holy books does not involve warfare and battles between or among military forces. Much of the violence is within and between families, clans, tribes, religions, and nations. It is inter-personal, intra-group, inter-group, and even international. Sometimes the violence is by human beings. At other times the violence is by natural, supernatural, spiritual, deistic, or demonic forces against human beings on earth. Surely, we can gain a more robust understanding of a considerable amount of supposed "religious" violence as it is committed by "lone wolf" terrorists, terrorist cells, ISIS, ISUL, the Taliban, al-Qaeda and other networks, organizations, and agencies if we recognize how often and in what ways violence is portrayed in the "holy books."

The intended audience for this book also is much broader and more general than was the audience for my earlier book. This book is written especially for open-minded people who are curious about how these three holy books portray physical violence and how these portrayals can influence violence, globally, in the decades ahead. At the same time, however, this book is also written to have value for members of the clergy, religious scholars, professors and students, and government leaders who have extensive familiarity with one or more of these books. Also, as suggested by the subtitle of this book, I focus on psychological and sociological aspects of violence and portrayals of violence, rather than on moral, ethical, political, philosophical, legal, criminological, and other aspects of violence.

As in my earlier book, my research uses the social science research method called "content analysis" in order to increase the clarity, objectivity, accuracy, and replicability of my findings.

A Caveat

As with my earlier book, this book does not have a thesis. It is not intended to prove or disprove anything. It is not based on any religious or political ideology. I do *not* assume or assert that religious beliefs or familiarity with passages in the holy books are necessary or sufficient to motivate, inspire, or elicit violent behavior from human beings in general, although this might be the case with some kinds of people such as some of the so-called "lone wolf" mass murderers. There is no question that many other factors and forces are involved in eliciting violent behavior by most human beings, if not all of them. As asserted by so many behavioral and social scientists for so long now, physical violence by humans usually results from a complex combination of forces that include the biological and psychological conditions of individuals, their socialization experiences and social relationships, and any number of elements in the social situations faced by the individuals before and at the time of the violence.

CONCERNING THE POWER OF VIOLENT WORDS IN RELIGIOUS TEXTS

As you read through the pages ahead, it can be helpful to consider how various kinds of people are likely to respond to written and spoken statements that describe, threaten, predict, advocate, or demand physically violent actions by "God," "Allah," or other forces; or by persons, groups, or organizations against one or more human beings, groups, or organizations.

What kinds of written and spoken words, phrases, and statements seem violent? Which ones are likely to provoke physical violence in people who are "just curious," who are obsessed with violence, who are "mischief-makers"? How about the influences on people who are extremely alienated, agitated, desperate, delusional, or irrational? And how about the influences on people who are extreme literalists, opportunists, propagandists, recruiters, and committed practitioners of violence? How do these kinds of people respond to words such as "burn," "torture," "destroy," "slay," and "kill," particularly when they encounter them, again and again, in printed, spoken, or electronic material and images that attract them?

Consider how these words might have motivated and directed the behaviors of the late Osama bin Laden and the men who hijacked the passenger jet planes and flew them into the World Trade Center, the

Pentagon, and a field in western Pennsylvania on September 11, 2001. Noted historian of religion Philip Jenkins contends that:

> Parts of the Qur'an can shock. One verse warns, "Those who make war against God and his apostle—-shall be put to death or crucified." Another begins, "When you meet the unbelievers on the battlefield, strike off their heads." When Osama bin Laden issued his declaration of war against the West in 1996, he quoted this verse, together with others from al-Anfal and al-Tawba.

Jenkins goes on to associate the Qur'an with the hijackers of 9-11-2001:

> We have a good idea what was passing through the minds of the September 11 hijackers as they made their way to the airports. Their al-Qaeda handlers had instructed them to meditate on al-Anfal (the Spoils) and al-Tawba (Repentance), two lengthy surahs, or chapters, from the Qur'an. These passages make for harrowing reading. God promises to "cast terror into the hearts of those who are bent on denying the truth; strike, then, their necks!" God instructs his Muslim followers to kill unbelievers, to capture them, to ambush them:
>
> "Then, when the sacred months have passed, slay the idolaters wherever ye find them, and take them captive, and besiege them, and prepare for them each ambush."

In his well-regarded book *Laying Down the Sword*,[21] Philip Jenkins contends that the Bible has far more violent passages than many people realize, and that the Qur'an has considerably fewer violent passages than many people think to be the case. Both of the books abound in violence, more or less. Jenkins also asserts that the Bible is no less violent than the Qur'an and that all scriptures are about equal in violent content. Jenkins also wisely encourages us to realize that violent passages alone probably are not sufficient enough to motivate, elicit, and justify violent actions by most people, although they can be very influential in contributing to violent actions in certain kinds of situations.[22]

Here are some of Jenkins' important and provocative assertions in his own words:

> The Qur'an is no bloodier or more warlike than either the Hebrew Bible or the larger text beloved by Christians. Indeed that Islamic text has far fewer passages demanding to be confronted or accommodated.[23]
>
> While the Bible reports violence in the distant past, some argue the Qur'an commands violence here and now. (However) It is not obvious that the Qur'an was commanding violence without end against unbelievers.[24]
>
> The Bible overflows with "texts of terror," to borrow a phrase coined by American theologian Phyllis Trible, and biblical violence is often marked by indiscriminate savagery.[25]
>
> But in terms of the violent and unacceptable faces of their fundamental scriptures, differences between the faiths are minimal.[26]

The chapters ahead can help us determine the validity of Jenkins' assertions and the often more-polemic assertions of many other authors of books on these topics. More importantly, the chapters ahead can help us determine how, and how often, violence and war are portrayed in the three fundamental holy books of Judaism, Christianity, and Islam. Even more importantly, the chapters ahead can help us prepare for how these books might be used and misused to promote and justify violence, terror, and war throughout the world in the decades ahead. And by the way, I start with an analysis of violence and war in the Qur'an because Islam and the Qur'an are so controversial in contemporary news media stories in the U.S., Britain, and in Europe, even though the Old Testament and the New Testament were compiled and disseminated many years before the Qur'an.

Notes

1. Paul Fregosi. *Jihad in the West: Muslim Conquests from the 7th to the 21st Centuries.* Amherst, New York. Prometheus Books. 1998. P. 221. See also Schwartz-Barcott, 2004: 169.
2. https://en.wikipedia.org/wiki/list_of_designated_terrorist_groups.
3. "United States/State/Department/List." Wikipedia. https://en.wikipedia.org/wiki/United States/State/Department/list.
4. "Domestic Terrorism in the United States." Wikipedia. Accessed March 29, 2017. https://en.wikipedia.org/wiki/Domestic_terrorism_in_the_United States.
5. *Jewish Terrorism in Israel.* Columbia University Press. 2009. Pp. 33
6. Sources: Ami Pedhazur and Arie Perlinger. *Jewish Terrorism in Israel.* NY: Columbia University Press. 2009. Pp. 47-61.; "Jewish Religious Terrorism." Wikipedia. https://en.wikipedia.org/wiki/Jewish_religious_terrorism.
7. "Christian Terrorism." Wikipedia. https://en.wikipedia.org/wiki/Christian_terrorism.
8. Mark Juergensmeyer. "Christian Violence in America." Annals of the American Academy of Political and Social Science. 1998.
9. "Army of God." Wikipedia. https://en/Wikipedia.org/wiki/Army_of_God.; "Terrorist Organization Profile, Army of God." National Consortium for the Study of Terrorism and Responses to Terrorism. October 5, 2011.
10. "Christian Terrorism." Wikipedia. https://en.wikipedia.org/wiki/Christian_ terrorism.; "Psychologists Call Suspect in Colorado Clinic Shooting Delusional." NBCNews.com. April 28, 2016. http://www.nbcnews.com/news/us/news/Colorado-clinic-shooting-psychologists-call-suspect-robert-dear-delusional.
11. Google search. http://www.google.com/?govs_rd_terrorist+organizations.
12. "Al-Qaeda." Wikipedia. Accessed on March 31, 2017. https://en.wikipedia.org/wiki/Al-Qaeda.
13. Ibid.
14. https://en.wikipedia.org/wiki/Rizwan_Farook_and_Tashfee_Malik; https://en.wikipedia.org/wiki/Zachary_Adam_Chesser; https://en.wikipedia.org/wiki/Naser_Jason_Abdo; https://en.wikipedia.org/wiki/Faisal_Shahzad; https://en.wikipedia.org/wiki/Najibullah_Zazi.

15. "Mohammed Taheri-Azar's letter to police." http://www.herald-sun.com/orange10-716750 html. Herald-Sun. 2006-03-24.
16. "Taheri-azar Writes to Eyewitness News." American Broadcasting Company. Raleigh-Durham. http://abclocal.go.com/wtvd/story?Section=local&id=3992674.; "More on the North Carolina Jihadi, Mohammed Taheri-Azar." Daniel Pipes. March 14, 2006. (http://www.danielpipes.org/blog/576).
17. *The Daily Tarheel-* Mohammed Reza Taheri-azar letter Meditation II and III http://www.dailytarheel.com/media/paper885/documents/jzjo063s.pdf.
18. "Ahimsa." Wikipedia. https://en.wikipedia.org/wiki/Ahimsa.
19. Andrew Newberg and Mark Robert Waldman, *How God Changes Your Brain: Breakthrough Findings from a Leading Neuroscientist.* NY: Ballantine Books. 2010. Also see the review by Michael Gerson concerning Newberg's research. www.washingtonpost.com/wp-dyn/content/article/2009/04/14/AR200904.
20. Feldman, Robert S. *Social Psychology.* 1995: Pp. 282-284
21. Jenkins, Philip. *Laying Down the Sword: Why We Can't Ignore the Bible's Violent Verses.* NY: HarperOne. Harper Collins Publishers. 201: Pp. 1-2.
22. Op. cit., 251.
23. Op. cit., 74.
24. Op. cit., 10.
25. Op. cit., 12.
26. Op. cit., 6.

Chapter 2

Violence, Terror, and War as Portrayed in the Qur'an

Epigraphs

> For Muslims the Qur'an is the book of God. It is the eternal, uncreated, literal word of God sent down from heaven, revealed one final time to the Prophet Muhammad as a guide for humankind.
> —John Esposito. *Islam: The Straight Path*

> The movement adopted the slogan: "The Qur'an is our constitution. The Prophet is our Guide: Death for the glory of Allah is our greatest ambition."
> —Peter Marsden. *The Taliban: War, Religion and the New Order in Afghanistan*

> You lose compassion for people when you keep reading or hearing that Allah or God is going to punish them, hurt them, burn them. You become desensitized. You come to think that they aren't really humans like you. You don't care very much if others hurt them if Allah or God is going to hurt them anyway—eventually. Maybe you even become more likely to go ahead and hurt them if you

think they are oppressing people and places you care about—to pull the trigger or blow up the bomb.
—Mohammed Taheri-Azar. A devout Muslim convicted and imprisoned for attempted vehicular homicide in the U.S., 2006.[1]

INTRODUCTION

According to the Qur'an, the most sacred book of Islam, is it Allah's will that believers engage in violence, terror, and war? If so, when, where, how, and why is this Allah's will?

To answer these questions, and many related questions, this chapter examines some of the most important but often neglected quantitative and qualitative aspects of physical violence, terror, and warfare as portrayed in two of the most widely distributed English language editions of the Qur'an.

As indicated in the previous chapter, historian of religion Philip Jenkins contends that:

> Parts of the Qur'an can shock. One verse warns, "Those who make war against God and his apostle—shall be put to death or crucified." Another begins, "When you meet the unbelievers on the battlefield, strike off their heads." When Osama bin Laden issued his declaration of war against the West in 1996, he quoted this verse, together with others from al-Anfal and al-Tawba (prominent surahs in the Qur'an).

Jenkins goes on to associate the Qur'an with the hijackers of 9-11-2001:

> We have a good idea what was passing through the minds of the September 11 hijackers as they made their way to the airports. Their al-Qaeda handlers had instructed them to meditate on al-Anfal (the Spoils) and al-Tawba (Repentance), two lengthy surahs, or chapters, from the Qur'an. These passages make for harrowing reading. God promises to "cast terror into the hearts of those who are bent on denying the truth; strike, then, their necks!"

Violence, Terror, and War as Portrayed in the Qur'an

God instructs his Muslim followers to kill unbelievers, to capture them, to ambush them:

"Then, when the sacred months have passed, slay the idolaters wherever ye find them, and take them captive, and besiege them, and prepare for them each ambush."

By way of comment, isn't it possible—even likely—that words and passages like these in the Qur'an have prompted violent behaviors by the people in the following profiles? Isn't this kind of influence likely to continue or perhaps even intensify in the decades ahead?

PROFILES OF SOME MUSLIMS ASSOCIATED WITH RELIGIOUS TERRORISM

Abdul Razak Ali Artan, November 29, 2016: "Terror Suspected in Campus Attack."

Columbus, Ohio: A Somali-born Ohio State University student plowed his car into a group of pedestrians on campus and then got out and began stabbing people with a butcher knife Monday before he was shot to death by a police officer.

Police said that they were investigating whether it was a terrorist attack.... The attacker was identified as Abdul Razak Ali Artan.... Ohio State University Police Chief Craig Stone said the assailant deliberately drove his small Honda over a curb outside an engineering classroom building and then began knifing people.... In an article in the campus newspaper in August, Artan identified himself as a Muslim and a third-year logistics management student who transferred from Columbus State University in the Fall. He said he was looking for a place to pray openly and worried how he would be received. He wrote, "I was kind of scared with everything going on in the media. I'm a Muslim, it's not what media portrays me to be...." The Islamic State group has urged sympathizers online to carry out lone-wolf attacks in their home countries with whatever weapons are available to them. [2]

Omar Mateen, June 12, 2016: "Worst Mass Shooting in U.S. History"

On Monday, June 13th, like so many newspapers across the U.S., the *Providence Journal's* front page announced the shocking news of yet another mass shooting that might have been inspired by Islamic terrorists:

- "Hate & Terror"
- "50 Killed in Massacre at an Orlando Gay Nightclub"
- "In a 911 Call, Gunman Pledged Allegiance to ISIS"

The front page included a 96-square-inch color photo of survivors carrying a badly wounded victim from out of the nightclub. It featured a lead story by three reporters of the *Washington Post*:

> ORLANDO: The gunman who opened fire inside a crowded nightclub here early Sunday morning, launching a rampage that killed 50 people and injured 53 others in the deadliest shooting spree in the country's history, had pledged allegiance to the Islamic State before the attack, according to U.S. law enforcement officials.

On Tuesday, June 14, the same newspaper carried an article by the *Associated Press*. The headline of the article is: "FBI: Gunman 'Homegrown Terrorist.'" Among the many other revelations that might relate to portrayals of violence in books and mass media:

> The FBI became aware of Mateen in 2013 when co-workers reported that the private security guard claimed to have family connections to al-Qaida and to be a member of Hezbollah.... He was also quoted as saying he hoped that law enforcement would raid his apartment and assault his wife and child so that he could martyr himself....

In a ten-month investigation by the FBI in 2013:

Mateen claimed he made the remarks in anger because co-workers were teasing him and discriminating against him as a Muslim.... His name surfaced again as part of another investigation into the Nusra Front bomber. The FBI found Mateen and the man had attended the same mosque and knew each other casually, but the investigation turned up "no ties of any consequence."

Mohammed Taheri-Azar
Mohammed Taheri-Azar is serving a sentence of twenty-six to thirty-three years in prison for intentionally driving a rented SUV into a crowd of people on the campus of the University of North Carolina in March 2006. He graduated from there the previous year with a double major in psychology and philosophy. He voluntarily turned himself in to the local police within an hour of the incident. He pled guilty to attempted murder for the incident, which injured nine people, all of whom survived.

Born in Tehran, Iran, in 1983, Taheri immigrated to the U.S. at two years of age with his parents and older sister. He attended high school in Charlotte, North Carolina.

Before the incident, Taheri left a letter in his apartment for the police. It included these statements:

> I am writing this letter to inform you of my reasons for premeditating and attempting to murder citizens and residents of the United States of America on Friday, March 3, 2006 in the city of Chapel Hill, North Carolina by running them over with my automobile and stabbing them with a knife if the opportunities are presented to me by Allah. I did intend to use a handgun to murder the citizens... but the process of receiving a permit for a handgun in this city is highly restricted and out of my reach at the present, most likely due to my foreign nationality. [3]

Taheri also made many other statements that relate his behavior to Islam and the Qur'an, including these statements to News Anchor Amber Rupinta of the local ABC network affiliate:

I live with the holy Koran as my constitution for right and wrong and definition of injustice...Allah in the Koran gives permission for those who follow Allah to attack those who have waged war against them, with the expectation of eternal paradise in case of martyrdom and/or the living of one's life in obedience of all of Allah's commandments found throughout the Koran's 114 chapters.... I've read all 114 chapters about 20 times since June of 2003 when I started reading the Koran. The U.S. government is responsible for the deaths and torture of countless followers of Allah, my brothers and sisters. My attack on Americans at UNC-CH March 3 was in retaliation for similar attacks orchestrated by the U.S. government on my fellow followers of Allah in Iraq, Afghanistan, Palestine, Saudi Arabia and other Islamic territories. I did not act out of hatred for America but out of love for Allah instead. I live only to serve Allah by obeying all of his commandments of which I am aware by reading and learning the contents of the Koran." [4]

In a letter to the campus newspaper, the *Daily Tarheel*, Taheri provided dozens of references to specific chapters and verses of the Qur'an that he felt provided "instructions and guidelines for fighting and killing in the cause of Allah." For example, Taheri wrote that the "cutting of limbs and crucifixion" are allowed by Surah 5 Verse 33 of the Qur'an. He also wrote that "beheading and removing fingers" was allowed by Surah 8 Verse 12 of the Qur'an. He wrote that a major reason for "fighting in the Cause of Allah" was "to stop persecution and oppression of Allah's Followers," as allowed by Surah 2 Verse 193 of the Qur'an.[5]

With this testimony by Taheri, is there any doubt that a number of the Qur'an's passages had great influence on him before and after the incident in question? And, as mentioned in Chapter 1 of this book, in 2016 I had more than twenty-five lengthy phone conversations with Taheri-Azar while he was incarcerated. I also visited him in prison for two hours in March 2016. Those conversations confirmed that Taheri-Azar is a very devout Muslim who regrets his attack in 2006. In those conversations

Violence, Terror, and War as Portrayed in the Qur'an

with me, Taheri-Azar repeatedly explained how more than forty passages in the Qur'an convinced him to commit violence in the name of Allah.[6]

SOME OTHER ALLEGED MUSLIM TERRORISTS

Syed Farook and Tashfeen Malik were the now-deceased husband and wife couple who attacked a center for disabled children in San Bernardino, California in December 2015, killing fourteen people and wounding seventeen people before they were killed by police.

Zachary Adam Chesser is an American Muslim convert who was convicted as a terrorist in 2010 for aiding al-Shababb, a branch of al-Qaeda. Chesser pled guilty to conspiracy in 2011 and was sentenced to twenty-five years in federal prison. He was born in Charlottesville, Virginia in 1989 to upper middle-class parents. After his parents divorced, he moved with his mother, who is a lawyer and prosecutor, to Fairfax County, Virginia. He did well in school and in school sports. He worked as a caretaker at an Islamic Center in Fairfax. In 2009, he dropped out of George Mason University, married a Ugandan Muslim woman, and had a son.

U.S. Army Pfc. Naser Jason Abdo received a life sentence for plotting to kill fellow Army soldiers at Fort Hood, Texas, in July 2011. He was born in Garland, Texas, in 1990. A Muslim, he planned a religious mission to attack fellow soldiers.

U.S. Army Major Nidal Malik Hasan is an Army psychiatrist who was born in Arlington County, Virginia, in 1970 and educated at Virginia Tech. He was convicted and sentenced to death for killing 13 people and wounding 32 others at Fort Hood, Texas, in November 2009. He reportedly shouted "Allah Akbar" as he shot his victims. Hasan's relations with al-Qaeda and his religious beliefs are very relevant regarding violence related to Islam and the Qur'an. For months before Hasan's attack, he sent as many as twenty e-mails to Anwar al-Awlaki, the imam who was widely considered to be a spiritual leader of al-Qaeda, before he was killed in 2011. In one of the e-mails, Hasan asked al-Awlaki's interpretation of a number of the Qur'an's verses about killing innocent people while conducting suicide attacks. Hasan also asked al-Awlaki how he could transfer personal funds abroad without being detected by U.S. authorities.[7]

Faisal Shahzad is a Pakistani-U.S. citizen educated at the University of Bridgeport, Connecticut. He was sentenced to life in prison for an attempted car-bombing in Times Square, New York City, in 2010.

Najibullah Zazi is an Afghan-U.S. citizen educated at a high school in Flushing New York. He pleaded guilty to being a member of an al-Qaeda group that planned suicide bombings of the New York City subway system in 2009.

EASY ACCESS TO ENGLISH LANGUAGE TRANSLATIONS OF THE QUR'AN—AND WITHOUT REGARD TO "CONTEXT"

Many of the English language versions of the Qur'an are readily available to anyone, anywhere in the world, who has access to the Internet, Google, and other search engines. For example, the Internet site "http://Quran.com, The Noble Quran" provides all surahs and verses of the Quran both in Arabic and in English. Generally speaking, unless people are being closely observed or prohibited from doing so, most people throughout the world are free to read, interpret, and react to any word, phrase, verse, and chapter of the Qur'an, in almost any language, without knowing anything about Islam and without taking any "context" into account. Their purpose can be to *use* the Qur'an for their own ends—*not* to understand it correctly or within context. Valid interpretation, understanding, and "context" are the obsessions of many scholars, clerics, and sundry intellectuals. They produce countless books, articles, and arguments about these matters. For a readily available example, see how one of the most popular contemporary translations of the Qur'an, by Abdel Haleem, goes on for page after page trying to convince readers that it has the most informed

Violence, Terror, and War as Portrayed in the Qur'an 35

insights about "context" and the most valid interpretation of the Qur'an.[8] While this might be true of Haleem's interpretation, this can be totally irrelevant to people who read or listen to passages of the Qur'an *not* to understand them, but to be able to *use* them to motivate, plan, and justify violence committed by themselves and by others. Because of this new reality, it is worth contemplating how different kinds of people—not just committed terrorists—interpret and react to any one word, to several words, or to any number of words, phrases, and passages in the Qur'an. This book attempts to accomplish this.

REGARDING THE HISTORICAL CONTEXT OF THE ORIGINS OF ISLAM AND THE QUR'AN

Here is a concise rendering of the historical context of the origins of Islam and the Qur'an. This is based primarily on the accounts in Maxime Rodinson's esteemed book, *Mohammed,* and Joseph L. Esposito's book, *Islam.*[9]

This rendering is intended for readers who do not feel that they are very familiar with this subject, but they are interested in it and believe that knowing more about historical context will help them understand the many passages from the Qur'an that are presented in this book.

CONFLICT, WAR, AND PEACE IN AND AROUND ARABIA IN THE LIFE OF MUHAMMAD

There is considerable variation among many scholars regarding the frequency and lethality of conflict and warfare among human societies in and around the Arabian Peninsula at the time of Muhammad. It seems fair to say that peace often was tenuous and fleeting, at best. Conflict was common, and yet actual warfare was rather infrequent, brief, sometimes violent, and often inconclusive. This was particularly true of the nomadic Bedouin tribes that roamed the Arabian Peninsula in the years preceding

Muhammad's birth in Mecca in 570 or 571 CE. Often the "real" wars (i.e.: social conflict between military organizations that possess trained and disciplined combat forces equipped with deadly weapons) occurred on the periphery of Arabia and in other parts of the Middle East where armies of the Persian, Byzantine, and Abyssinian empires clashed in efforts to preserve or extend their empires.

Nomadic pastoralists, principally Bedouin tribes, constituted a considerable portion of the Arab population of the peninsula. They were pantheistic, worshipping a variety of places, animals, and forces of nature. Some of the more powerful and stationary clans dominated the relatively few small villages and cities on the peninsula: Mecca, Medina, and Tabuk among them. Sacred icons of some of these clans were housed in and around the Ka'ba in Mecca. Often, various clans and tribes quarreled with each other over access to sacred shrines, oases, grazing lands, palm and date trees, and livestock. They raided each other's camps and settlements at the oases and along the caravan routes to Gaza, Damascus, and Baghdad. Sometimes powerful merchants in the settlements bribed Bedouin tribes to protect their own caravans or to raid caravans of competing tribes and settlements, sharing the booty.

Weapons were rather primitive, in contrast to the weapons of the Roman Empire, which had fallen centuries ago. The desolate, arid desert environment of the peninsula constrained food production, access to fresh water, and limited the size, density, and growth of human populations and settlements. Violent encounters usually lasted only a few minutes or a few hours, at most, although the confrontations could drag on for weeks, even months. Casualties usually were limited, especially immediate fatalities due to wounds suffered in battle. Most combatants lived to quarrel, feud, and fight another day, for days upon days.

This is the world that Muhammad experienced: first as a poor, illiterate orphan and shepherd boy, then as a hostler in his uncle's caravans, next as a prosperous merchant who was married to a wealthy widow, and

Violence, Terror, and War as Portrayed in the Qur'an

eventually as a charismatic, dynamic, and celebrated religious, military, and political leader—the first prophet of Islam.

Table 1 provides a summary of key events in Muhammad's life and in the founding of Islam.

Table 1. Some Key Events in the Life of Muhammad and Islam.

570-571	Muhammad is born in Mecca as a member of the Quraysh clan. Father deceased.
576-577	Mother dies. Muhammad is cared-for by relatives and a Bedouin nurse.
577-587	Muhammad occasionally works as a shepherd boy and as a hostler on caravans.
595	Muhammad marries Khadija, a wealthy widow. Becomes a successful merchant.
610	Experiences his first revelation while meditating in a cave at Mount Hira. Occasionally recites his revelations to close confidants in his Quraysh clan.
619	Revelations and recitations continue. Wife Khadija dies.
622	*Hegira*. Muhammad escapes from Mecca to Medina under pressure from hostile Meccans.
624	Nakhla: Muhammad orders a raid on a caravan at Nakhla, which succeeds. Battle at Badr: Muhammad organizes and leads a small army in an ambush that becomes a stunning victory.
625	Battle at Uhud: Muhammad is wounded and almost defeated while leading his army in defense of Medina.
627	Battle of "The Trench": Leads an army that withstands an attack by Meccan forces outside Medina. Directs the slaughter and enslaving of Banu Quraysh forces at Medina.
628	Battle of Hudaybiya: Negotiates a truce with Quraysh while trying to return to Mecca. Khaybar: Poisoned by Zanab after the siege and sacking of Khaybar.
629	*Hajj*: Leads a peaceful first pilgrimage into Mecca. Mu'ta: Orders a Muslim army into Palestine against the Byzantines. This foray is repulsed.
630	Al-Fat'h: Leads 10,000 troops towards Mecca. Negotiates terms of surrender for Mecca. Occupies Mecca and establishes Islamic rule. Leads 20,000 troops to Tabuk, Palestine, to collect tribute.
632	Muhammad makes his "Pilgrimage of Farewell" to Mecca. Dies in Medina.

A Note Regarding Research Methods

As indicated in the previous chapter, the research I have conducted primarily is intended to deepen our understanding of how physical violence against human beings is portrayed in the Qur'an, the Old Testament, and the New Testament. I readily admit that my research has its limitations, as is the case with all research in sociology and psychology. In the Appendix, I describe in considerable detail the methods I've used so that you can make your own decisions about the validity, objectivity, and value of this work.

Two English Translations of the Qur'an

I use two widely-distributed and highly-regarded English language versions of the Qur'an: a very traditional one by Pickthall, and a very modern one by Haleem.

The principal version is Mohammed Marmaduke Pickthall's version, *The Meaning of the Glorious Koran*. It has been and remains highly regarded and widely distributed through many printings and editions since it was first published in 1930. It is readily available throughout the world. Pickthall converted to Islam. He lived much of his life in the Middle East as a Muslim. He was fluent in Arabic and several other languages of the Middle East. In fact, M.A.S. Abdel Haleem, the well-regarded author of the current bestselling English translation, *The Qur'an*,[10] commends Pickthall's translation this way: "Although his language may now seem almost artificially archaic, his translation keeps close to the original Arabic, and is still very popular among Arabs and Muslims." Many esteemed scholars also rely on Pickthall's translation of the Qur'an as their primary source. Among these people is the religious scholar, Philip Jenkins, previously mentioned, in his book *Laying Down the Sword*.

Violence, Terror, and War as Portrayed in the Qur'an

DEPICTIONS OF PHYSICAL VIOLENCE, AND A DEFINITION

In this book, the word "violence" is based on *The New Webster's Encyclopedic Dictionary:* [11] "severe or injurious treatment or action... characterized by extremely rough, harsh, destructive physical force." Our focus is on depictions, portrayals, descriptions, and references to physical force that injures or destroys human beings or their creations, or that is intended to destroy them or their creations. These creations include families, clans, nations, and other animate and inanimate materials and possessions such as icons, weapons, shelters, villages, and cities. We are especially interested in portrayals of physical force directed at human beings by other human beings and by the deities, gods, and the spirits that they worship or fear.

Please consider that, *if the Qur'an is totally violent*, each of its 114 surahs (chapters), each of its 6,220 verses (in the Pickthall version), and each of its passages within each verse would contain words and phrases that describe, advocate, demand, threaten, or predict physical violence by one or more forces, spirits, people, groups, or organizations against one or more forces, spirits, people, groups, or organizations. On the other hand, *if none of this is true of the Qur'an, then a strong case can be made that it is totally non-violent.*

So then, just how violent is the Qur'an, quantitatively speaking? Let us first consider the title of the Qur'an and the titles of its surahs.

HOW VIOLENT IS THE QUR'AN, QUANTITATIVELY AND REGARDED OBJECTIVELY?

Violent Titles in the Qur'an
The word "Qur'an" in Arabic usually is translated into English as "recitation." As such, it is not likely to convey violence or a sense of violence to most readers. This is also probably true for most of the titles of the surahs (chapters). The surahs have titles, but the verses do not have

titles. How violent are the titles of the surahs likely to be to the kinds of people identified above?

We found that at least 85 (75%) of the Qur'an's 114 surahs (S) have titles in English that are *not* likely to be regarded as violent or to convey violence to the vast majority of readers or listeners. The exception might be for violence-prone propagandists, recruiters, and perpetrators of violence who are inclined to interpret almost any title, or anything else, as advocating violence. In general, the titles are very simple, short (one, two, or three words), topical, non-accusatory, intriguing, evocative, and perhaps even poetic. For example, consider this sample of titles: "The Opening" (S1), "The Cow" (S2), "Jonah" (S10), "The Romans" (S30), "The Believer" (S40), "The Ascending Stairway" (S70), "The City" (S90), "The Coursers" (S100), "Succour" (S110), and "Mankind" (S114). To most kinds of readers these titles are not likely to be obviously or explicitly violent, or to advocate physical violence against human beings, as would be the case if a title was something like "Kill All Foreigners" or "Destroy Your Enemies and Their Children." However, about 16 (14%) of the 114 surah titles might suggest or convey opposition, conflict, danger, defeat, conquest, or possibly even physical violence to some readers and listeners, especially if the titles are taken literally rather than metaphorically, symbolically, or without regard to historical context. These Surah titles and numbers include: "Spoils of War" (S8), "Those Who Set the Ranks" (S37), "The Troops" (S39), "Victory" (S48), "The Hypocrites" (S63), "Divorce" (S65), "Banning" (S66), "Those Who Drag Forth" (S79), "The Overthrowing" (S81), "The Cleaving" (S82), "Defrauding" (S83), "The Sundering" (S84), "The Overwhelming" (S88), "The Earthquake" (S99), "The Calamity" (S101), and "Rivalry in Worldly Increase" (S102).

Of these titles, "The Earthquake" might be the title most likely to convey an image of physical violence to some readers and listeners, although, taken literally, many readers probably assume that the "violence" of earthquakes is by geological forces of nature, rather than by human beings, organizations, or other forces. As titles, "The Overthrowing" and

"The Overwhelming" also might suggest physical violence to some users of the Qur'an even though these titles do not explicitly or necessarily convey that the "overthrowing" or the "overwhelming" necessarily are or must be physically violent. Consider that a leader and a regime can be overthrown without violence, as is the case with a bloodless *coup d'état*. Many things can be "overwhelming" without being physically violent, such as a dream, a love affair, a new job, or an utterly spiritual experience. Admittedly, any particular reader may or may not regard these titles this way.

Violent Words and Phrases in the Qur'an
What words and phrases in the Qur'an's passages are likely to convey *physical violence* as they are presented in the English language translations by Pickthall and by Haleem? As mentioned previously, the definition of physical violence that we use is "severe or injurious treatment or action characterized by extremely rough, harsh, destructive physical force." Additionally, particular attention is given to depictions of physical violence by humans and their deities against other humans and their creations including their families, dwellings, towns, lands, other possessions, and deities they worship or fear.

We found that words including "doom," "fire," "flame," "torture," "slay," and "kill" are conveyed as physical violence with some regularity in many surahs and quite a few verses of the Qur'an. Note that the number of verses in the surahs vary greatly, from only three verses in Surah 108 to 286 verses in Surah 2. Table 2 presents our findings on this matter.

Table 2. Estimates of the Number (Percentages) of Words and Phrases Presented as Physical Violence in the 114 Surahs and 6,220 Verses.

		Surahs	Verses
		# (%) of 114	# (%) of 6,220
1	Word "doom" conveyed as violence	62 (54%)	198 (3.2%)
2	Words "fire" or "flame" conveyed as violence	65 (57%)	132 (2.1%)
3	Other words and phrases conveyed as violence	82 (72%)	409 (6.5%)
4	Verses with two or more types of words and phrases conveyed as violence	32 (28%)	70 (1.1%)

"Doom" as Physical Violence

Row 1 of Table 2 shows that the word "doom" as physical violence occurs at least once (but usually more often than just once) in 62 (54%) of the 114 surahs. "Doom" is presented in such a way that it is likely to convey violence as a description of a past event, as a threat, or as an imperative. For example, some verses in Surah 2 ("The Cow") focus on "disbelievers" (non-Muslims) and on people who say they believe in Allah but who are deceiving themselves. Surah 2 Verse 10 then states, "In their hearts is a disease, and Allah increaseth their disease. A painful doom is theirs because they lie."

"Doom" occurs as physical violence like this in at least 198 of the 6,220 verses. This constitutes only about 3.2% of the Qur'an's verses. However, it is important to note that many, but not all, of these verses convey that "doom" will occur in the future, especially on the "Day of Judgement." These passages usually do *not* compel believers themselves to impose "doom" on other people. Then again, these passages also do *not* prohibit believers from doing so. Is it possible that some people who read or hear verses such as this might assume that it is permissible for them to go ahead and "doom" disbelievers and miscreants because Allah is doing so or intends to do so?

Violence, Terror, and War as Portrayed in the Qur'an

"Fire" and "Flame" as Physical Violence

Are the words "fire" and "flame" as destructive physical forces likely to convey violence to readers and listeners of statements such as these?

> *Lo! Those who disbelieve Our revelations, We shall expose them to the Fire. As often as their skins are consumed We shall exchange them for fresh skins that they may taste the torment. Lo! Allah is ever Mighty, Wise. (Surah 4: 56)
>
> *Their wealth and their children will avail them naught against Allah. Such are rightful owners of the Fire; they will abide therein. (Surah 58: 16-17)

If so, then, as shown in Table 2, we found these kinds of statements in 57% of the 114 surahs and in 132 (2.1%) of the Qur'an's verses.

Violence Conveyed with Other Words and Phrases

Of course, violence can be conveyed to readers and listeners of the Qur'an through other words, phrases, and statements besides the words "doom," "fire," and "flame." Consider these examples:

> *How many a township have We destroyed! As a raid by night or while they slept at noon. Our terror came unto them.
>
> No plea had they, when Our terror came unto them, save that they said: Lo! We were wrong-doers. (Surah 7: 4-5)

We found examples such as this in 82 (72%) of the surahs, as shown in Row 3 of Table 2. About 6.5% (409) of the Qur'an's verses might convey violence through words and phrases such as these. Also notice the presence of the word "terror" conveyed as physical violence in the verses cited from Surah 7. While the word "terror" is not common in the Qur'an, it certainly is present—and it is conveyed as physical violence. We found twelve instances of the word "terror" conveyed as physical violence in Pickthall's translation of the Qur'an. The most immediate and unconditional occurrence is this one: *"We shall cast terror into the hearts... of those who disbelieve." (Surah 3: 151)

Surah 7 presents the word "terror" seven times: twice in Verse 4, twice in Verse 134, and once each in Verses 71, 135, and 152. Most of these depictions of terror are past tense and they portray Allah as claiming that he casts "terror" upon the Pharaoh and Egyptians because they were persecuting Moses and the Israelites. Other instances of the word "terror" as violence occur in Surah 14: 42, Surah 20: 102, and Surah 21: 97. In these three verses, disbelievers are portrayed as "staring wide eyed in terror" on Judgment Day because of various misdeeds or because of their failure to believe in Islam.

By way of comment, consider the possibility that passages such as these can encourage some kinds of readers to engage in terror rather than wait for Judgment Day or for Allah to do so. Philip Jenkins discusses this possibility at some length in the first chapter of his book. He seems doubtful that passages like these actually encourage contemporary believers to take violence into their own hands.

Verses that Convey Several Kinds of Violence

Row 4 of Table 2 shows that about 28% of the surahs contain verses that convey more than just one kind of violence. This is also the case with little more than one percent (70/6,220) of the verses in the Qur'an, as is the case with this example:

> *If thou couldst see how the angels receive those who disbelieve, smiting their faces and their backs and (saying): Taste the punishment of burning! (Surah 7: 49)

In this verse we find two distinct kinds of violence: "smiting" and "burning." By the way, it is worth pondering whether verses such as this are likely to encourage potential and actual terrorists to smite and burn people they consider to be disbelievers, rather than wait for "angels" to do so. Or perhaps, some people might consider themselves to be the "angels."

Violence, Terror, and War as Portrayed in the Qur'an

Quantitatively then, it seems reasonable to conclude that many kinds of readers, including casual readers, could rather easily encounter a surah that contains words and phrases that might convey violence to that reader, since over one-half of the surahs contain words and phrases likely to be considered violent—without regard to context. This is less likely to be the case with the titles of the surahs, however, since only a small percentage (14%) have titles that *might* convey some sense of violence, although even that is debatable. As to the Qur'an's 6,220 verses, only a very small percentage (less than 12%) of the verses have words and phrases that are likely to convey violence to most readers, without regard to context.

How are Portrayals of Violence and Warfare Distributed in the Qur'an?

Another way of analyzing the quantity of portrayals of violence in the Qur'an is to consider how these portrayals are distributed through the Qur'an, from the first Surah (S1) to the final Surah (S114). Are violent passages concentrated in only a few surahs? If so, are they at the front of the Qur'an where they might be easily encountered by anyone and where they might tempt people to assume that the entire Qur'an is loaded with violent passages? Or, conversely, are the violent passages concentrated in a relatively remote and easily overlooked section of the Qur'an, making it more likely that some people can conclude that the Qur'an has few, if any, violent passages? Table 3 can help us answer these questions.

46   Violence, Terror, Genocide, and War

Table 3. Portrayals of Violence, Battles, or War in Parts of the Qur'an.

	Row #	A Total # of verses	B # (%) of verses that portray or refer to violence	C # (%) of verses that portray battles or war	D # (%) of verses that portray violence in battles or war
1	Surahs # 1-9	1,366	202 (14.7%)	119 (8.7%)	33 (2.4%)
2	Surahs # 10-50	3,293	379 (11.5%)	34 (1%)	10 (0.3%)
3	Surahs # 51-91	1,382	144 (10.4%)	10 (0.7%)	3 (0.2%)
4	Surahs # 92-114	179	16 (8.9%)	3 (1.7%)*	3 (1.7%)*
5	TOTALS	6,220	741 (11.9%)	166 (2.66%)	49 (0.7%)

Note. These three verses are all in just one surah— Surah 105 ("The Elephant").

Explanations of the Findings in Table 3

Table 3 presents a summary of the statistics on the frequency and percentages of the Qur'an's verses that portray or refer to violence (Column B), that portray or refer to military battles or war (Column C), and that portray or refer to violence in the verses that portray or refer to battles or war (Column D).

General Findings

The most general and important findings are on the bottom row (Row 5). Cell A5 shows that there are a total of 6,220 verses in the Pickthall edition and the Haleem edition of the Qur'an. Cell B5 shows that I found that 741 (11.9%) of those verses portrayed or referred to violence. Cell C5 shows that 166 (2.66%) of the Qur'an's verses portray or refer to battles or to war. Cell D5 shows that only 49 (0.7%) of the Qur'an's 6,220 verses portray violence in battles or war. Also worth considering is that only 49 (30%) of the 166 verses that portray battles or war also portray or refer to violence in those battles or war.

Of course, you as a reader are free to make your own interpretation of these data. My interpretation is that only a small percentage (11.9%)

Violence, Terror, and War as Portrayed in the Qur'an

of the Qur'an's verses portray or refer to violence. This finding does *not* support anyone's claim that the Qur'an is "a violent book" or that it is "filled with violence." But this finding also does *not* support claims that the Qur'an is a totally non-violent or peaceful book. Neither assertion is valid when considering the Qur'an as a whole.

The datum in cell C5 demonstrates that only a very small percentage (2.66%) of the Qur'an's 6,220 verses portray battles or war. Cell D5 shows that an even smaller percentage (0.7%) of the verses depict violence in battles or war. Therefore, people are mistaken if and when they assert that the Qur'an fundamentally or essentially is a manual, manifesto, or history of battle or war. They also are mistaken if and when they assert that portrayals of battles or war in the Qur'an always are violent or that they are overwhelmingly violent.

Here are a few implications derived from these findings regarding how readily the Qur'an lends itself to use or misuse by opportunists and literalists who are oriented towards violence. All things considered, people such as this:

1. must search to find the 11.9% of verses that portray or refer to violence,
2. must search even harder to find the 2.66% of verses that portray battles or war,
3. and they must search even harder to find the 0.7% of the verses that portray violence in battles or in war.

FINDINGS RELATED TO THE FOUR SECTIONS OF THE QUR'AN SHOWN IN TABLE 3

Rows 1-4 of Table 3 show that there are some important variations within the four different, sequential sections of the Qur'an as to the frequencies and percentages of verses that portray violence (Column B), that portray battles or war (Column C), and that portray violence in battles or war (Column D).

48 VIOLENCE, TERROR, GENOCIDE, AND WAR

As shown in Row 1 of Table 3, Surahs 1-9 of the Qur'an have the highest percentages of verses that portray violence (14.7%, as shown in Cell B1), that portray battles or war (8.7% in Cell C1), and that portray violence in battles or in war (2.4% in Cell D1). Of course, this finding might be expected in part because these first nine Surahs in the Qur'an include three of the Surahs that are frequently referred to as the "Qur'an's war Surahs." These are Surahs 3 ("The Family of Imran"), 8 ("The Spoils of War"), and 9 ("Repentance"). The historical context of these three Surahs includes the famous battles of Muhammad and his Muslim forces against the military forces of the Quraysh at the battles of Badr and Uhud.

Rows 2, 3, and 4 of Table 3 show that all of these comparable percentages decrease somewhat as we move from Surahs 10-50, to Surahs 51-91, and then to Surahs 92-114 at the end of the Qur'an. This decrease in percentages is less pronounced regarding the percentage of verses that portray violence (Column B), where the decrease is only from 14.7% (Cell B1) to 11.5% (Cell B2) to 10.4% (Cell B3) to 8.9% (Cell B4). It seems fair to say that one implication of this pattern is that most people who scan through the Qur'an or who read through it carefully will find some violent verses through all sections of the Qur'an, but they will find proportionately less violence as they move from the surahs and verses at the front of the Qur'an to those at the rear of the Qur'an.

This same pattern also pertains to verses that portray battles or war (Column C) and violence in battles or war (Column D). In fact, as explained in the asterisked note at the bottom of Table 3 regarding cells C4 (1.7%) and C5 (1.7%), the only portrayal of war and of violence in war in the final Surahs (92-114) are in just one Surah (105) "The Elephant." These verses refer to an armed confrontation between two military forces in the year of Muhammad's birth, generally considered to be 570 CE. In other words, it is likely that most people will have to do a considerable amount of searching in order to find verses that portray battles or war as well as verses that portray violence in battles or war in most of the Surahs (10-114) and verses of the Qur'an. This is less likely to be the case

Violence, Terror, and War as Portrayed in the Qur'an

when reading Surahs 2-9 (Row 1 in Table 3). For anyone who tries to read the Qur'an sequentially, after reading Surah 1 ("The Opening"), with its seven simple non-violent verses, they are rather abruptly confronted by some of the more concentrated violent images in the Qur'an. This could easily discourage these readers and lead them to conclude, quite erroneously, that the Qur'an is indeed a book of violence. As evidence, here are Verses 7 and 10 of Surah 2 ("The Cow") regarding "disbelievers." These are the 14th and 17th Verses among the 6,220 verses of the Qur'an. Often, they appear on just the second page of the Qur'an's more than one-hundred pages, in many of its editions and languages:

> *Allah hath sealed their hearing and their hearts, and on their eyes there is a covering. Theirs will be an awful doom. (Surah 2: 7)
>
> *In their hearts is a disease, and Allah increaseth their disease. A painful doom is theirs because they lie. (Surah 2: 10)

Readers who stop reading the Qur'an at this point, because of verses such as these, are likely to conclude that the remainder of the Qur'an is just as violent. If so, they would be badly mistaken. As shown in Table 3, once again, the "front" surahs and verses of the Qur'an are not very representative of the remainder of the Qur'an in terms of violence, battles, and war.

Therefore, based on the findings presented in Table 3, my conclusion is that, speaking quantitatively, the Qur'an as a whole is *not* predominantly or highly violent. It is *not* predominantly or highly oriented towards battles or war. And it does *not* focus heavily on violence when it does portray battles or war. Going a bit further then, *extreme, categorical, and polarized assertions are mistaken about the amount of violence, terror, battles, and war in the Qur'an*. It is neither violent nor non-violent as a whole. It is occasionally violent. Then again, as we shall see when we consider the qualities of violence, when the Qur'an is violent, sometimes it is extremely violent. *Occasionally* it advocates violence in shockingly brutal ways.

Does Violence Dominate Any of the Surahs?

There are no surahs in the Qur'an in which each and every verse conveys violence. In fact, there are only three surahs in which more than one-half of the verses convey violence. These are Surah 101 "Calamity" (seven of the eleven verses convey violence), Surah 105 "The Elephant" (three of its five verses convey violence), and Surah 111 "Palm Fibre" (three of its five verses convey violence). These are three of the shortest surahs in the Qur'an. Relatively speaking, it is easier for them to be dominated by just a small number of verses that convey violence. It is also worth noting that the violence in Surah 101 is about the violence that will occur on Judgment Day in the form of natural forces. In Surah 105, "The Elephant" (analyzed more fully later in this chapter), the violence relates to an actual historical event in the year of Muhammad's birth. The three violent verses of the five verses in this surah portray Allah as the source of flying objects that destroy a military force from Abyssinia that was advancing upon Mecca in order to destroy the Ka'bah. By the way, Surah 111 is the only surah in the Qur'an that names two of Muhammad's enemies and conveys violence against them for harassing Muhammad.[12]

As shown in Table 4, these three Surahs (101, 105, and 111) are among the fifteen surahs in the Qur'an in which at least 25% of the verses convey violence.

Violence, Terror, and War as Portrayed in the Qur'an

Table 4. Surahs in which 25% or More of the Verses Convey Violence.

Surah #	Title	Fraction (%) of violent verses to total verses
101	Calamity	7/11 (64%)
105	The Elephant	3/5 (60%)
111	Palm Fibre	3/5 (60%)
104	The Traducer	3/9 (33%)
67	The Sovereignty	9/30 (30%)
22	The Pilgrimage	22/78 (28%)
54	The Moon	15/55 (27%)
55	The Beneficient	15/55 (27%)
58	She That Disputeth	6/22 (27%)
59	Exile	6/24 (25%)
46	The Wind-Carved Sandhills	9/35 (26%)
66	The Banning	3/12 (25%)

Of course, you can decide for yourself whether the data in Table 4 indicate that the Qur'an is dominated by violence. Only three of the surahs have 50% or more verses with violence. Only thirteen of the 114 surahs (11.4%) convey violence in 25% or more of their verses. By the way, another twenty surahs (not shown in Table 4) convey violence in 10-24% of their verses. Therefore, it seems to me that, regarded generally and quantitatively, the Qur'an is not dominated by violence—nor are 111 of its 114 surahs.

THE NATURE AND QUALITIES OF VIOLENCE IN THE QUR'AN

Now let us consider the *qualities* of violence portrayed or conveyed in the Qur'an. Who commits violent actions or demands violent actions by others? What kinds of violent actions? Against whom? When? Where? Why? With what consequences? Are Muslims—the "believers" in Islam—portrayed as the victims of violence far more frequently than as the perpetrators of violence? Is Muhammad portrayed as a victim more frequently than as a perpetrator of violence? What kinds of violence are portrayed most frequently in the Qur'an? Injuring? Torturing? Amputating? Killing? Burning? Destroying? Is the violence absolute and unconditional? Or is the violence usually conditional? Does the violence depend on how the perpetrators or the victims behave, or on other factors such as their religious orientations, the size of their respective armies, or elements of nature, such as the weather, the seasons, or the phases of the moon? This next section provides answers to all of these questions—and more. We start by considering who is portrayed in the Qur'an as performing, threatening, predicting, advocating, or demanding violence.

Table 5 shows the frequencies of various aspects of qualitative violence portrayed in the Qur'an in terms of who performs violence (Part A), who threatens or predicts violence (Part B), and who advocates or demands violence (Part C).

Violence, Terror, and War as Portrayed in the Qur'an

Table 5. Who Performs, Threatens, or Demands Violence in the Qur'an?

		Surahs # (%) of 114	Verses # (%) of 6,220
A. Violence *performed* by:			
1	Muslims	3 (2.6%)	9 (< 0.1%)
2	Muhammad	2 (1.75%)	4 (< 0.1%)
3	Allah*	63 (57%)	250 (4%)
4	Others (e.g. "disbelievers")	33 (29%)	79 (1.2%)
B. Violence *threatened* or *predicted* by:			
1	Muslims	0 (0%)	0 (0%)
2	Muhammad	0 (0%)	0 (0%)
3	Allah*	85 (74%)	340 (5.4%)
4	Others/all people	4 (3.5%)	9 (< 0.1%)
C. Allah *advocates* or *demands* violence by:			
1	Muslims	15 (13%)	40 (0.6%)
2	Muhammad	10 (8.7%)	10 (< 0.1%)
3	Others	0 (0%)	0 (0%)

Note. There are quite a few verses in which Allah is portrayed as being violent in more than one way: describing, performing, threatening, predicting violence, as well as demanding violence by/and/or against others.

Performers of Violence

As for performers of violence (Part A of Table 5), notice that Allah is decidedly the most frequently portrayed performer. This is the case in sixty-three (57%) of the 114 surahs and in 250 of 6,220 (4.0%) of the verses. So, it is relatively easy for readers to find a surah which portrays Allah as performing violence, but it is much less likely that readers will find a verse in which this is the case unless they have direct references to these verses or they do quite a bit of searching. Usually Allah is portrayed as the performer of violence against various places, people, and clans because they do not accept Islam or Allah's authority—not because they have committed physical violence against Muslims, although there certainly are instances of this, as well. It is also important to know that Allah usually is presented as asserting that he performed the violence in the past or that he will perform it in the future, usually on Judgment Day, rather than at the present time. Verse 4 of Surah 7 is one of the most-often quoted examples of this:

> *How many a township have We destroyed! As a raid by night or while they slept at noon, Our terror came unto them. No plea had they, when Our terror came unto them, save that they said: "Oh! We were wrong-doers. (Surah 7:4)

Here are some other examples of verses in which Allah claims to be the performer of violence:

> *And verily messengers (of Allah) were mocked before thee, but long I bore with those who disbelieved. At length I seized them, and how (awful) was My punishment! (Surah 13: 32)

> *He said: I have been given it only on account of knowledge I possess. Knew he not that Allah had destroyed already of the generations before him men who were mightier than him in strength and greater in respect of following? The guilty are not questioned of their sins. (Surah 28: 78)

> *So We caused the earth to swallow him and his dwelling place. Then he had no host to help him against Allah, nor was he of those who can save themselves. (Surah 28: 81)

> *So We sent them the flood and the locusts and the vermin and the frogs and the blood—a succession of clear signs. But they were arrogant and became guilty. (Surah 7: 133)

> *Therefore We took retribution from them; therefore We drowned them in the sea: because they denied Our revelations and were heedless of them. (Surah 7: 136)

By the way, quite a few verses in the Qur'an portray Allah as both a performer and as a promiser of violence in the future. For example:

> *Have they not travelled in the land to see the nature of the consequence for those who were before them? Allah wiped the out. And for the disbelievers there will be the like thereof. (Surah 47: 10)

Row 1 of Part A shows that Muslims are portrayed as performers of violence, or as co-performers of violence with Allah, in only 2.6% of the surahs and in less than 0.1% of the verses. Row 2 shows that Muhammad is portrayed as the perpetrator of violence even less frequently—in less than 2% of the surahs and in less than 0.1% of the verses. Here are two of the very few examples, one of which is repeated from above:

> *How many a township have We destroyed! As a raid by night or while they slept at noon. Our terror came unto them. (Surah 7: 4)

> *And He brought those of the People of the Scripture who supported them down from their strongholds, and cast panic into their hearts. Some ye slew, and ye made captive some. (Surah 33: 26)

Occasionally the Qur'an portrays others, besides Allah, Muslims, or Muhammad, as performing violent acts, as is the case with enemies of Islam such as the Pharaoh, Satan, the Jinn, "disbelievers," and "hypocrites." This occurs in 33 of 114 (29%) of the surahs and in a much smaller percentage of the verses 1.2% (79 of 6,220) as shown in Row 4 of Part A. Here are some examples:

> *Then because of their breaking of their covenant, and their disbelieving in the revelations of Allah, and their slaying of the Prophets wrongfully, and their saying: Our hearts are hardened—

> Nay, but Allah hath set a seal upon them for their disbelief, so that they believe not save a few. (Surah 4: 155)
>
> *And (remember) when We did deliver you from Pharaoh's folk, who were afflicting you with dreadful torment, slaying your sons and sparing your women: That was a tremendous trial for your Lord. (Surah 2: 49)
>
> *Lo! Pharaoh exalted himself in the earth and made its people castes. A tribe among them he oppressed, killing their sons and sparing their women. Lo! He was of those who work corruption. (Surah 28: 4)
>
> *And Allah repulsed the disbelievers in their wrath; they gained no good. Allah averted their attack from the believers. Allah is Strong. Mighty. (Surah 33: 25)

By the way, the verse that immediately follows this verse in Surah 33 portrays both Allah and Muhammad as performers of violence against "People of the Scripture" (i.e.: Jews at Mecca, in this case) and implies that this violence is justified:

> *And He brought those of the People of the Scripture who supported them down from their strongholds, and cast panic into their hearts. Some ye slew, and ye made captive some. (Surah 33: 25)

In sum, while a slight majority of the surahs in the Qur'an portray performers of violent acts, relatively few of the verses do so. Additionally, Allah is portrayed as a performer far more frequently than are Muslims, Muhammad, or others, including disbelievers, Satan, the Jinn, Jews, and Christians.

Predictors and Threateners of Violence
Part B shows that the Qur'an portrays Allah as being the most frequent predictor or threatener of violence. This occurs in 74% of the surahs and

Violence, Terror, and War as Portrayed in the Qur'an

5.4% of the verses. Here are two examples of these kinds of verses that occur occasionally in the Qur'an:

> *But they who deny Our revelations and scorn them—such are rightful owners of the Fire; they will abide therein. (Surah 7: 36)

> *Lo! They who persecute believing men and believing women and repent not, theirs verily will be the doom of hell, and theirs the doom of burning. (Surah 85: 10)

It is worth knowing that there are relatively few verses that portray anyone, any agency, or any force other than Allah as a predictor or threatener of violence. In the following case it is the Pharaoh:

> *(Pharaoh) said: Ye put your faith in him before I give you leave. Lo! He doubtless is your chief who taught you magic! But verily ye shall come to know. Verily I will cut off your hands and your feet alternately, and verily I will crucify you every one. (Surah 26: 49)

Who Advocates or Demands Violence in the Qur'an?

How often does Allah advocate or demand violence, and by whom? Part C shows that violence is advocated or demanded in a relatively small percentage of surahs and in an even smaller percentage of the verses. Allah demands violence by Muslims in general in 13% (15 of 114) of the surahs and in only 0.6% (40 of 6,220) of the verses. Here are some examples, the first of which is the famous "retaliation" verse that often is equated with a passage in Hammurabi's Code and with passages in the Old Testament and New Testament:

> *O ye who believe! Retaliation is prescribed for you in the matter of the murdered; the freeman for the freeman, and the slave for the slave, and the female for the female. And for him who is forgiven somewhat by his (injured) brother, prosecution according to usage and payment unto him in kindness. This is an alleviation and a mercy from your Lord. He who transgresseth after this will have a painful doom. (Surah 2: 178)

*Fight in the way of Allah against those who fight against you, but begin not hostilities. Lo! Allah loveth not aggressors.

> And slay them wherever ye find them, and drive them out of the places whence they drove you out, for persecution is worse than slaughter. And fight not with them at the Inviolable Place of Worship until they first attack you there, but if they attack you (there) then slay them. Such is the reward of disbelievers. (Surah 2: 190-191)

By the way, Verses 193 and 194 of Surah 2 continue these demands from Allah, by Muslims, under specific conditions. These are some of the most frequently quoted verses that demand violence.

Row 2 of Part C shows that Allah demands or advocates that Muhammad perform acts that might be violent in 8.7% (10 of 114) of the surahs and a very small percentage (< 0.1%) of the verses. Here are two of these Verses:

> *Nay, but if ye persevere, and keep from evil, and (the enemy) attack you suddenly, your Lord will help you with five thousand angels sweeping on. (Surah 3: 125)

> *O Prophet! Strive against the disbelievers and the hypocrites, and be stern with them. Hell will be their home, a hapless journey's end. (Surah 66: 9)

Who are the Sources and Targets of Violence?

Of the 741 verses in the Qur'an that depict physical violence along with the sources and targets of that violence, 612 (83%) portray Allah as the source, describer, threatener, promiser, or demander of violence by and/or against others. As shown in Table 6 the most frequent targets of that violence are people referred to with terms that often seem to be interchangeable: non-believers, un-believers, deniers, idolaters, hypocrites, and evil persons. Column 3 shows that these are the targets of Allah's violence in 47% (289 of 612 verses). The second most frequent target of Allah's violence

Violence, Terror, and War as Portrayed in the Qur'an

are other people —such as the Egyptian Pharaoh —and tribes and clans, most frequently the Quraysh clan into which Muhammad was born. These are indicated in Column 5. They constitute 45% (275 of 612) of Allah's targets. By way of comment, it is worth knowing that the Qur'an often portrays these other people and clans as also being non-believers, deniers, idolaters, hypocrites, and evil.

The Qur'an also occasionally identifies one, several, or all Jews and Christians (often referred to as "people of the Scripture") as being the targets of Allah's violence, even though they are monotheists. Column 4 shows that this is relatively infrequent, however (1.4%, 9 of 612), even though there are hundreds of references in the Qur'an to Jews, Christians, and "people of the Scripture." The vast majority of these references do not portray Allah as a source of violence against them. These facts are well worth noting and disseminating in contemporary world affairs because they indicate that the Qur'an does *not* portray violence by or against Jews and Christians very frequently.

Column 7 indicates that 5% (31 of 612) of these passages portray Allah as the source of violence against any and all human beings who commit specific acts of deviance, such as hoarding gold or silver or misusing the wealth of orphans, apparently without regard to their religious orientations. Some of these verses are examined later in this chapter.

Table 6 also shows that a small percentage (1.3%, 8 of 612) of these verses portray Allah's violence towards some Muslims, if and when they deviate from his rules. Failure to pay the poor tax when they are able to do so, and failure to adequately support Islamic forces in battles are among these infractions.

As might be expected, Allah never directs his violence towards the Prophet Muhammad (Column 1). More surprising, perhaps, is that while Allah frequently is portrayed as despising Satan, the Jinn, and other evil spirits as the enemies of Islam, Allah is not portrayed as a source of physical violence against them. Perhaps this is because they are assumed to be "spirits" without any of the physical properties of human beings.

60   Violence, Terror, Genocide, and War

Table 6. The Targets of Allah's Violence in 612 Verses of the Qur'an.

Muhammad	Some Muslims	Non-believers, deniers, idolaters	Jews, Christians	Clans, other people	Satan, Jinn	All deviant people
0	8 (1.3%)	289 (47%)	9 (1.4%)	275 (45%)	0	31 (5%)

Is Any of the Violence Absolute, Unconditional, or Timeless?
Consider that violence would be totally absolute, unconditional, and timeless if there were passages in the Qur'an such as this *hypothetical* example: "I, Allah, command all believers of Islam to immediately and forever torture and slay any and all non-believers of Islam wherever they are encountered in this World."

In this *hypothetical* example, Allah is commanding that all Muslims always and forever commit physical violence in the form of "torture" and "slaying" against anyone who does not believe in Islam. This is an absolute and timeless demand for violence. Its only condition is that the violence is directed at only one category of people—all people who do not believe in Islam. Needless to say, this is a very broad category!

I have not found any verses in any versions of the Qur'an that are as absolute, timeless, imperative, and lethal regarding physical violence as this hypothetical example. There are several reasons for this. First, the statements of violence that occur in the Qur'an usually are in a sentence or a small passage within a specific verse. Often these violent statements are mitigated or qualified in other passages in the verse or by passages in adjacent verses. Second, most of the violence in passages of the Qur'an are past tense or future tense, rather than present tense or without regard to tense or temporality. Often these passages refer to violence that occurred long before Muhammad was born (e.g. the Egyptian Pharaoh's persecution of the Israelites) or violence that will occur on Judgment Day when, as Allah often promises, all disbelievers, hypocrites, evil persons, and other kinds of violators of the Qur'an's tenets will burn in hell. Third, much of the violence in the Qur'an is also conditional and contingent on a variety of forces, factors, or events, such as the disbelievers explicitly insulting Islam, breaking a treaty, or initiating violence against Muslims.

And yet, occasionally we find passages and verses in the Qur'an that are nearly absolute, unconditional, and timeless in their portrayals of violence. Usually the violence is directed at *non*-believers—not against believers—who disturb Allah in any number of ways.

For example, Surah 48 ("Victory") has a verse couplet in which Allah categorizes all people as to whether they are believers or unbelievers. He promises Paradise to the believers. He promises Hell to hypocrites and idolaters who do little more than "think an evil thought" about him.

> *That He may bring the believing men and the believing women into Gardens underneath which rivers flow, wherein they will abide, and may remit from them their evil deeds— That, in the sight of Allah, is the supreme triumph— And may punish the hypocritical men and the hypocritical women, and the idolatrous men and the idolatrous women, who think an evil thought concerning Allah. For them is the evil turn of fortune, and Allah is wroth against them and hath cursed them, and hath made ready for them hell, a hapless journey's end. (Surah 48: 5-6)

Another example of the verses that are nearly timeless in portraying violence is this one:

> *Lo! Those who disbelieve Our revelations. We shall expose them to the Fire. As often as their skins are consumed We shall exchange them for fresh skins that they may taste the torment. Lo! Allah is ever Mighty, Wise. (Surah 4: 56)

Comment: To me this passage conveys a threat of violence that is timeless and is nearly absolute. Allah threatens or promises extreme physical violence against anyone who disbelieves any of his revelations. The only condition is that they disbelieve. There are no other conditions. Passages such as this are relatively frequent in the Qur'an. Some scholars refer to these passages as examples of what they call "divine retribution"[13] in that Allah, as a divine deity, is promising to "get even" with anyone who does not believe his revelations in the Qur'an, simply because they do not believe these revelations and, as such, they insult him.

Is it possible that contemporary opportunists use this passage and other passages like it to somehow justify efforts to burn anyone who disbelieves any of the revelations of the Qur'an? Is it possible that some leaders and rank-and-file members of terrorist groups such as al-Qaeda, ISIS, and ISUL are doing this or that they will do so in the years ahead?

An Example of a Famous Violent Passage that is Rather Conditional

Critics of Islam often mention Verse 5 in Surah 9 as being utterly violent. Actually, it contains several major conditions. It requires that the "the sacred months have passed." It targets only "idolaters" who do not "repent and establish worship and pay the poor-due." It even goes on to state that "Allah is Forgiving, Merciful" for the idolaters who comply with these conditions. It also is worth knowing that the two verses that immediately precede this verse in Surah 9 seem to indicate that the violence in Verse 5 pertains only, or primarily, to idolaters who break treaties with believers.

> *Then, when the sacred months have passed, slay the idolaters wherever ye find them, and take them (captive), and besiege them, and prepare for them each ambush. But if they repent and establish worship and pay the poor-due, then leave their way free. Lo! Allah is Forgiving, Merciful. (Surah 9: 5)

Adjacent Verses Often Provide Restrictions on Absolute Violence

Often in the Qur'an, one particular verse may portray violence absolutely —or nearly so— without conditions or restrictions as to temporality. But then, adjacent verses provide more restrictions on the violence in that one verse—if they are taken together. Examples of this are found in the often-quoted "violent" Verses 190-193 of Surah 2 ("The Cow").

*(190) Fight in the way of Allah against those who fight against you, but begin no hostilities. Lo! Allah loveth not aggressors.

(191) And slay them wherever ye find them, and drive them out of the places whence they drove you out, for persecution is worse than slaughter. And fight not with them at the Inviolable Place of Worship until they first attack you there, but if they attack you (there) then slay them. Such is the reward of disbelievers.

(192) But if they desist, then lo! Allah is Forgiving. Merciful.

(193) And fight them until persecution is no more, and religion is for Allah. But if they desist, then let there be no hostility except against wrongdoers.

Taken as a whole, Verses 190-193 specify quite a few conditions and restrictions on violence. For example, two conditions are required before believers are allowed to stop fighting their enemies. Persecution must end, but religion also must be for Allah. Isn't this an eternal ambiguity? Also, somewhat ambiguous in these passages of the Qur'an (and in the Qur'an in general) is what constitutes aggression by non-Muslims. Does name-calling, discrimination, slapping, torture, or accidental slaying constitute aggression?

Does "Fighting" Necessarily Involve Physical Violence?

There also are verses that are nearly absolute, unconditional, and timeless in demanding that believers *fight* disbelievers—but without explicitly stating that the fighting must include or constitute physical violence. While "fighting" can occur without damage and destruction resulting from it, as would be the case if the fighting is inept, feigned, or only verbal —as with taunts, insults, and threats—I have found that it usually *does* convey physical violence between or among adversaries in the Qur'an. One of the most famous of these verses about "fighting" is Verse 39 in Surah 8—the famous "Spoils of War" Surah:

> *And fight them until persecution is no more, and religion is all for Allah. But if they cease, then lo! Allah is Seer of what they do. (Surah 8: 39)

Another verse that demands *fighting* by believers is timeless and almost unconditional, except for the fact that its target is limited to "nonbelievers" "who are near you." Here is the verse, first from Pickthall's translation, and then from the more contemporary translation by Haleem:

> *O ye who believe! Fight those of the disbelievers who are near to you, and let them find harshness in you, and know that Allah is with those who keep their duty (unto Him). (Surah 9: 123)[14]

> *You who believe, fight the disbelievers near you and let them find you standing firm: be aware that God is with those who are mindful of Him. (Surah 9: 123)[15]

Surah 22 "The Pilgrimage" as a Remarkably Violent Surah

Surah 22 is a remarkably violent surah in many respects even though only 22 of its 78 verses (28%) refer to or portray physical violence. For example, Verse 15 (discussed more fully in the section on "peculiar" verses) seems to portray Allah as suggesting suicide to anyone who doubts that Muhammad will not be victorious.

> *Whoso is wont to think (through envy) that Allah will not give him (Muhammad) victory in the world and in the Hereafter (and is) enraged at the thought of his victory), let him stretch a rope up to the roof (of his dwelling), and let him hang himself. Then let him see whether his strategy dispelleth that whereat he rageth. (Surah 22:15)

Verse 39 of Surah 22 allows people who have been wronged to "fight," and it promises that Allah will give them victory. It does not specify that the "fight" must entail physical violence, although many other verses in this Surah certainly contain explicit physical violence. Verses 19-21 are examples of this. Taken as a whole, these verses explicitly st ate that "believers" and "disbelievers" are "two opponents." Then the verses specify the kinds of physical violence that will be administered to disbelievers.

> *(19) These twain (the believers and the disbelievers) are two opponents who contend concerning their Lord. But as for those who disbelieve, garments of fire will be cut out for them; boiling fluid will be poured down on their heads.
>
> (20) Whereby that which is in their bellies, and their skins. Lo! Will be melted.
>
> (21) And for them are hooked rods of iron.

Surah 47, "Muhammad"
Rather ironically, some of the most violence-laden surahs are *not* the so called "war and battle" surahs. Examples of this is Surah 47 ("Muhammad"). It is one of the most famous and often-recited surahs because it is the only surah that is named for the Prophet Muhammad. It has only thirty-eight verses. All of them are relatively short, but seven of those thirty-eight verses explicitly convey physical violence. One of these seven verses, Verse 4, is the longest verse of the thirty-eight. It is among the most explicitly violent verses in the entire Qur'an. Here is Pickthall's translation of Verse 4:

> *Now when ye meet in battle those who disbelieve, then it is smiting of the necks until, when ye have routed them, then making fast of bonds, and afterward wither grace or ransom till the war lay down its burdens. That (is the ordinance). And if Allah willed He could have punished them (without you) but (thus it is ordained) that He may try some of you by means of others. And those who are slain in the way of Allah, He rendereth not their actions vain. (Surah 47: 4)

By way of comment, notice the phrase "smiting of the necks" in this verse. It is a phrase that occurs several times in Pickthall's version of the Qur'an. Could this phrase be interpreted by some people, including some terrorists in ISIS, as a synonym for or a command for "beheading"? Could this phrase have been interpreted by the 9-11-2001 hijackers as a command to smite the necks and throats of the airline pilots with box cutters?

The verses that follow Verse 4 of Surah 47 make even more explicit the motivations and rewards for martyrdom: "He will guide them and improve their state, And bring them in unto the Garden which He hath made known to them." (Surah 47: 5-6)

Five other verses (Verses 8, 10, 12, 15, 27) among the thirty-eight verses in Surah 47 also convey physical violence by Allah and Muslims against disbelievers. Two of the other verses also demand violence by Muslims against *other Muslims* who refuse to fight against disbelievers. Several other verses (Verses 35 and 36) go on to extol how Muslim martyrs will be justly rewarded with Paradise in the afterlife. Verse 35 also commands believers to *not* call out for peace when they are winning against disbelievers: "So do not falter and cry out for peace when ye (will be) the uppermost, and Allah is with you, and He will not grudge (the reward of) your actions." (Surah 47: 35)

A Note About the Context of Surah 47, "Muhammad"
Here is what Pickthall conveys regarding the context of this famous surah:

> Muhammad. This Surah takes its name for the mention of the Prophet by name in v. 2. Most commentators agree that v. 18 was revealed when the Prophet, forced to flee from Mecca, looked back, weeping, for the last sight of his native city. Some have considered the whole Surah to be a Meccan revelation, but with no good reason. It belongs to the first and second years after the Hijrah, with the exception of v. 18, which was revealed during the Hijrah.[16]

Let me suggest, as I have done several times in this book, that context and interpretations about context such as this can be utterly irrelevant to people whose purpose is *not* to understand the Qur'an but to *use* verses

Violence, Terror, and War as Portrayed in the Qur'an

of the Qur'an for other reasons. Ignoring context can make it easier to recruit and motivate others, to justify their own violent actions, and to find reasons to believe that, if they commit violent actions against any actual or suspected "disbelievers" of Islam, they will become martyrs and will be rewarded with eternal Paradise.

"Terror" in the Qur'an

As mentioned earlier in this chapter, the English word "terror" appears at least twelve times in Pickthall's version of the Qur'an, and it does so in such ways that convey physical violence against opponents of Islam. The most immediate and unconditional occurrence is this one:

> *We shall cast terror into the hearts of those who disbelieve because they ascribe unto Allah partners, for which no warrant hath been revealed. Their habitation is the Fire, and hapless the abode of the wrong-doers. (Surah 3: 151)

Surah 7 presents the word "terror" seven times: twice in Verse 4, twice in Verse 134, and once each time in Verse 71, Verse 135, and Verse 152. Most of these occurrences are in the past tense. They portray Allah claiming that he cast "terror" upon the Pharaoh and Egyptians as they were persecuting Moses and the Israelites.

Three other instances of the word "terror" occur in Surah 14: 42, Surah 20: 102, and Surah 21: 97. In these three verses, disbelievers are portrayed as "staring wide-eyed in terror" on Judgment Day because of various misdeeds or because of their failure to believe in Islam.

Another occurrence of the word "terror" as physical violence portrays Allah as using terror to force Jews to "ruin their homes" and flee into exile. Could contemporary literalists and opportunists use this passage to justify their efforts to force Jews to abandon their homes and flee into exile—perhaps from the West Bank of Israel, or elsewhere in the world?

> *He it is Who hath caused those of the People of the Scripture who disbelieved to go forth from their homes unto the first exile. Ye

deemed not that they would go forth, while they deemed that their strongholds would protect them from Allah. But Allah reached them from a place whereof they recked not, and cast terror in their hearts so that they ruined their houses with their own hands and the hands of the believers. So learn a lesson, O ye who have eyes.

And if Allah had not decreed migration for them, He verily would have punished them in this world, and theirs in the Hereafter is the punishment of Fire. (Surah 59: 2-3)

Violence Directed at All Miscreants, Regardless of Religious Orientation

Occasionally there are passages and verses in which religious orientation is irrelevant. Religion is not a condition. This aspect of the Qur'an often is unrecognized or ignored by its critics, many of whom contend that the Qur'an only portrays violence against non-Muslims. And yet, believers as well as non-believers are subject to Allah's violence if they incur his wrath because of a number of specific misbehaviors. These misbehaviors include adultery, "traduction," accusing honorable women, wrongfully using the wealth of orphans, usury, and hoarding of gold and silver.

Adulterers

Notice that in this first example the violence (scourging) is demanded as punishment against anyone who is an adulterer or an adulteress, without regard for social context, their religion, or any other factor.

> *The adulterer and the adulteress, scourge ye each one of them (with) a hundred stripes. And let not pity for the twain withhold you from obedience to Allah, if you believe in Allah and the Last Day. And let a party of believers witness their punishments. (Surah 24: 2)

Traducers of Virtuous Women

*Lo! As for those who traduce virtuous, believing women (who are) careless, cursed are they in the world and the Hereafter. Theirs will be an awful doom. (Surah 24: 23)

Accusers of Honorable Women

This next example apparently is directed at any one, not just Muslims or non-Muslims, who "accuse honourable women," unless they have at least four witnesses.

> *And those who accuse honourable women but not with four witnesses, scourge them (with) eighty stripes and never (afterward) accept their testimony—They indeed are evil-doers—-Save those who afterward repent and make amends. (For such) lo! Allah is Forgiving, Merciful. (Surah 24: 4-5)

Those Who Wrongly Use the Wealth of Orphans

Here is another verse that is not restricted to believers or disbelievers. It also is nearly absolute and timeless, although it is slightly conditional (note the phrase "wrongfully"). It also does not demand punishment by other people so much as it promises that the miscreants will be "exposed to burning flame" without indicating how or when this will occur.

> *Lo! Those who devour the wealth of orphans wrongfully, they do but swallow fire into their bellies, and they will be exposed to burning flame. (Surah 4: 10)

Usurers

*...As for him who returneth (to usury)—Such are rightful owners of the Fire. They will abide therein. (Surah 2: 275)

Braggers
"Think not that those who exult in what they have given, and love to be praised for what they have not done— Think not, they are in safety from the doom. A painful doom is theirs. (Surah 3: 188)

Also subject to Allah's doom on the Day of Resurrection are hoarders (Surah 3: 180) and those who refuse to contribute to support Allah's wars (Surah 3: 181)[17].

Surahs and Verses Without Violence

Certainly there are surahs in the Qur'an that do *not* portray or refer to physical violence. I found nineteen of them. This constitutes 16.6% of the 114 surahs. These violence-free surahs are Surahs 1, 49, 60, 62, 63, 86, 93, 94, 95, 97, 103, 106, 107, 108, 109, 110, 112, 113, and 114. This set includes the first and final surahs in the Qur'an (Surahs 1 and 114). They contain no words, phrases, or images in the English language that are likely to be considered violent by most people and by authors of books on this topic. These are two of the most frequently recited surahs in the Qur'an. According to Pickthall, some sects require that both of these surahs are recited daily, or even five times a day. Surah 1 is usually recited at the beginning of each of the five daily Muslim prayer services.

One of these violence-free surahs, Surah 97 ("Power"), often is regarded as one of the first surahs revealed to Muhammad by Allah through the angel Gabriel.[18] This occurred on Mount Hira, years before Muhammad's first battle, at Badr. There also are at least another four Surahs which are nearly violence-free: Surahs 15, 30, 55, and 61. Less than 5% of their verses contain violent words, and none of their verses advocate or demand violence in the future.

"Peace" in the Qur'an

References to peace, images of peace, and the word "peace" are *not* very frequent in the English versions of the Qur'an by Pickthall and Haleem. Their indexes do not even include the word "peace." I have found about

Violence, Terror, and War as Portrayed in the Qur'an

sixty occurrences of the word. About 25% (N = 15) of these occurrences refer to peace as a state of mind or as grace. Allah promises peace of mind, or he bestows peace upon believers in Islam, as a reward for submission or appropriate behavior, often on Judgment Day in Paradise (e.g. Surah 56: 26). Allah also instructs believers to greet each other in Paradise by saying "Peace" (Surah 56: 91).

Here are other examples:

> *Whereby Allah guideth him to seeketh His good pleasure unto paths of peace. He bringeth them out of darkness unto light by His decree, and guideth them unto a straight path. (Surah 5: 16)
>
> *The (faithful) slaves of the Beneficent are they who walk upon the earth modestly, and when the foolish ones address them answer: Peace. (Surah 25: 63)

Somewhat more frequent, but still rather rare in the Qur'an, are references to "peace" as a quality of interpersonal behavior and intergroup relations that is the opposite of physical violence. These passages occur in about 13 of 114 (11.4%) of the surahs and in about 0.7% (45 of 6,220) of the verses, sometimes more than once in a particular surah or verse. It is important to note that 65% (33 of 45) of these instances refer to peace as the opposite of violence *within* Islam; whereas a smaller percentage (35%) refer to peace between Muslims and non-Muslims of one sort or another, such as Arabs of the Quraysh (Qureshi) clan, Jews, Christians, idolaters, and others. Here is an example of a verse calling for peace between two factions of Muslims:

> *And if two parties of believers fall to fighting, then make peace between them. And if one party of them doeth wrong to the other, fight ye that which doeth wrong till it return unto the ordinance of Allah; then, if it return, make peace between them justly, and act equitably. Lo! Allah loveth the equitable. (Surah 49: 9)

Now, as to passages about peace between Muslims and non-Muslims, usually peace is allowed only under specific conditions, such as when the enemy offers peace first and Muslims are winning in battle. Here is a well-known set of verses (already presented in this chapter) in the famous Surah 8 ("Spoils of War"). It refers to Muslims facing enemies who have broken a treaty or who are "treacherous." [19]

> *Make ready for them all thou canst of (armed) force and of horses tethered, that thereby ye may dismay the enemy of Allah and your enemy, and others beside them whom ye know not. Allah knoweth them. Whatsoever ye spend in the way of Allah it will be repaid to you in full, and ye will not be wronged.
>
> And if they incline to peace, incline thou also to it, and trust in Allah. Lo! He is the Hearer, the Knower. (Surah 8: 60-61)

And yet, on other hand, there also are verses that explicitly command believers to *not* cry out for peace in specific circumstances such as when they are winning in battle. Verse couplet 34-35 of Surah 47 is an example of this.

> *Lo! Those who disbelieve and turn from the way of Allah and then die disbelievers, Allah surely will not pardon them
>
> So do not falter and cry out for peace when ye (will be) the uppermost, and Allah is with you, and He will not grudge (the reward of) your actions. (Surah 47: 34-35)

How Violent Are the So-Called "War and Battle" Surahs?

Quite surprisingly, I found that none of the so-called "war and battle surahs" are dominated by war or battles and, furthermore, none of them were dominated by physical violence. In none of the 114 surahs do verses about war or battles begin the surah, end the surah, or dominate the surah either quantitatively or qualitatively. There are at least nine surahs that frequently are considered by experts, such as Pickthall and Haleem, to be "war" or "battle" surahs. Often this is because of the surah titles, the historical context of when the surah was assumed to have been written, or because of specific references within the surah. Table 7 presents

Violence, Terror, and War as Portrayed in the Qur'an

information about these surahs. All of these surahs contain some verses that include the word "battle" or "war." They also include some verses that explicitly describe, refer to, advocate, command, predict, or threaten physical violence in warfare or battles by some deities, entities, or forces against other ones.

However, as indicated in Table 7:

- Physical violence does not dominate a large percentage of the verses in any of these surahs. Verses conveying physical violence never comprise more than 25% of the verses in any of these surahs. Usually the percentage is considerably smaller—about 15%.
- Warfare and battles do not dominate a large percentage of the verses in any of these surahs (as indicated in Column B1 of Table 7). Usually the percentage of verses explicitly about war or battle only comprise less than 15% of the verses in the surahs, although the percentages certainly are higher in Surah 8 (28%) and in Surah 48 (21%).
- Even more remarkably, and perhaps counter-intuitively, a considerable percentage of the verses about wars or battles do *not* convey physical violence (as indicated in Column B2 of Table 7). Verses about war and battle often convey rules about when believers may and may not engage in war or in a battle. Other verses simply mention that a particular battle took place, without portraying any violence. For example, here is Verse 123 in Surah 3: *"Allah had already given you (Muhammad) the victory at Badr, when ye were contemptible. So observe your duty to Allah in order that ye may be thankful."

Table 7. Physical Violence in the "War and Battle" Surahs.

Surah # and name	A # of violent verses/ Total # of verses (%)	B1 # (%) of verses about military war or battles: Total # of verses	B2 # (%) of verses about military war or battles: That also portray violence in war or battles
2: The Cow	42/286 (14.7%)	11 (3.8%)	7 (2.4%)
3: Family of Imran	40/200 (20%)	19 (9.5%)	9 (4.%)
4: Women	30/177 (17%)	13 (7.3%)	8 (4.5%)
7: The Heights	38/206 (18.4%)	1	1
8: Spoils of War (al-Anfal) The Battle of Badr	18/75 (24%)	21 (28%)	10 (13.3%)
9: Repentance	24/129 (19.4%)	17 (13.1%)	7 (5.4%)
33: The Clans	11/73 (15%)	10 (13.6%)	6 (8.2%)
47: Muhammad	7/38 (18.4%)	4 (10.5%)	2 (5.2%)
48: Victory	4/29 (13.8%)	6 (21%)	0

However, it also is true that most of the so-called war and battle surahs have a number of verses that portray physical violence in wars and battles very explicitly and in shocking ways. Consider the case of the often-quoted and controversial Surah 8. Pickthall translates its title from Arabic as "Spoils of War." Haleem translates it from Arabic as "Battle Gains." Here are several of the ten verses in Surah 8 that mention war or battle and also convey physical violence in that war or battle:

> *O ye who believe! When ye meet those who disbelieve in battle, turn not your backs to them. Whoso on that day turneth his back to them, unless maneuvering for battle or intent to join a company,

he truly hath incurred wrath from Allah, and his habitation will be hell, hapless journey's end. (Surah 8: 15-16)

*If thou comest on them in the war, deal with them so as to strike fear in those who are behind them, that haply they may remember. (Surah 8: 57)

Regarding Surah 8 and Its Context

Surah 8 is often regarded as the most prominent of the war and battle surahs in the Qur'an. This reputation is reinforced by the findings presented in Table 7. Compared to the other surahs listed in Table 7, Surah 8 has the highest percentage of violent verses (24%). It also has the highest percentage of verses about military war or battles (28%). Additionally, it has the highest percentage (13.3%) of verses that portray physical violence in verse about war or battles.

Commonly titled "al-Anfal" in Arabic, Pickthall translates it into English as "Spoils of War." Haleem translates it as "Battle Gains." It is the only surah of the 114 in the Qur'an that has the word "war" or "battle" in its title when translated into English. This surah has seventy-five verses of varying length and varying content, some of which are not obviously related to war or battles. As with so many other scholars, both Pickthall and Haleem assert that the verses in this surah also vary considerably as to subject matter, the years and places where they were first revealed to Muhammad, as well as to when, where, and by whom they were recorded and assembled. Recall that Muhammad could not read or write in Arabic or in any other language.

As indicated in Chapter 1 of this book, the "Terrorist Manual" that was used by some of the 9-11 terrorist hijackers instructed the terrorists to refer to and meditate on this surah, *al-Anfal*, as well as *al-Tabby*, on the evening before they conducted the 9-11 attacks. It seems reasonable to assume that this surah was, has been, and remains one of the most influential surahs in the Qur'an regarding how Muslims should behave in battle. But there are other reasons, as well. Regarding context, both

Pickthall and Haleem state that some of the verses in this surah were revealed to Muhammad either before, during, or after his famous first battle—his surprising victory at Badr. They also indicate that the Battle of Badr is the most important historical event and context for understanding this surah. However, none of the seventy-five verses in this surah mention Badr by name—nor do they restrict their assertions or images to any specific battle, including Badr. Of course, many people are free to ignore or dismiss historical context. They also are free to select any one verse at random or to select only a verse or several verses that suit their predispositions, biases, or purposes at the time. And, of course, anyone is also free to try to comprehend all seventy-five verses in this surah, with or without regard for historical context. Is it possible that this is exactly what has been happening in many of the cases of terrorist attacks and military battles instigated by some people and some military forces in the name of Allah, Islam, or both?

SOME RATHER UNUSUAL AND OFTEN-OVERLOOKED PASSAGES IN THE QUR'AN REGARDING VIOLENCE AND WAR

Now let us consider some of the rather unusual passages in the Qur'an that are often overlooked even though they portray physical violence and could easily influence physical violence against individuals, groups, and governments in future decades.

Some Unusual Passages About Violence Among Jews, Christians, and Muslims

Do the Torah, the Gospel, and the Qur'an require believers to "Fight in the Way of Allah" and for the same reasons? Verse 111 of Surah 9 seems to require this—and even more.

> *Lo! Allah hath bought from the believers their lives and their wealth because the Garden will be theirs; they shall fight in the way of Allah and shall slay and be slain. It is a promise which is binding on Him in the Torah and the Gospel and the Qur'an.

Who fulfilleth His covenant better than Allah? Rejoice then in your bargain that ye have made, for that is the supreme triumph. (Surah 9:111)

Does Allah command Muhammad to inform Jewish rabbis and Christian monks who hoard gold and silver that they will suffer "grievous punishment and branding"? Yes, this seems to be what Surah 9: 34-35 commands.

> *O ye who believe! Lo! Many of the (Jewish) rabbis and the (Christian) monks devour the wealth of mankind wantonly and debar (men) from the way of Allah. They who hoard up gold and silver and spend it not in the way of Allah, unto them give tidings (O Muhammad) of a painful doom.
>
> On the day when it will (all) be heated in the fire of hell, on their foreheads and their flanks and their backs will be branded therewith (and it will be said unto them): Here is that which ye hoarded for yourselves. Now taste of what ye used to hoard. (Surah 9: 34-35)

Comment: Notice how the types of violence are very explicit in these passages. The foreheads, sides, and backs of the miscreants will be branded by fire. The miscreants are limited to rabbis and monks who "hoard gold and silver." Is it possible that some contemporary people will use this passage to attack Jewish rabbis and Christian monks?

Can Surah 59 ("Exile") be a major enduring provocation for hatred and violence between Jews and Muslims? Can it also be misused by some people to try to exile Jewish people?

> *In the name of Allah, the beneficent, the Merciful.
>
> All that is in the heavens and all that is in the earth glorifieth Allah, and He is the Mighty, the Wise.
>
> He it is Who hath caused those of the People of the Scripture who disbelieved to go forth from their homes unto the first exile. Ye

deemed not that they would go forth, while they deemed that their strongholds would protect them from Allah. But Allah reached them from a place whereof they wrecked not and cast terror in their hearts so that they ruined their houses with their own hands and the hands of the believers. So learn a lesson. O ye who have eyes!

And if Allah had not decreed migration for them, He verily would have punished them in this world, and theirs in the Hereafter is the punishment of the Fire. (Surah 59: 1-3)

Comment: Consider how these verses might influence you if you are a highly agitated, deranged, confused, naïve, or disingenuous young adult male or female Muslim or Jew who is proud of your religious heritage. Isn't it possible, even highly likely, that some highly agitated or deranged people would focus on the following aspects of these verses?

- These verses portray Allah as claiming to be the source of violence against the People of the Scripture *who disbelieved* in Allah.
- The violence Allah created was that he "cast terror in their hearts" so that they "ruined their own houses with their own hands and the hands of the believers." Note the presence of the word "terror." Allah claims to be the source of the terror. Could this word and this claim serve to provoke some Muslims to commit acts of terror against Jews?
- Doing this "caused those People of the Scripture who disbelieved to go forth from their homes unto the first exile."
- As such, "Allah decreed migration for them."
- Had Allah not done this (caused their migration) Allah "would have punished them in this world."
- "...and theirs in the Hereafter is the punishment of the Fire."

Comment: Isn't it likely that some people will be shocked and dismayed to read that Allah is claiming to be the source—the primary cause— of forced exiling of Jewish people? If so, could some Jewish readers feel resentment, anger, even hostility towards Allah and perhaps towards all Muslims because of verses such as these? Furthermore, could some Jewish

Violence, Terror, and War as Portrayed in the Qur'an 79

readers interpret these verses as saying that Allah caused the Jews to ruin their own home and migrate simply because they "disbelieved" in Allah?

Now, as to how some Muslim readers might react to these verses, isn't it possible, even likely, that some Muslim readers could conclude that Allah forced Jews to migrate simply because they did not believe in Allah? Might some contemporary Muslims also be expected to force Jews to migrate simply because they do not believe in Allah?

If so, then, is it possible to understand how this surah (Surah 59, named "Exile" rather appropriately), can be understood as an enduring basis for suspicion, hostility, and violence between some Jews and some Muslims?

Now as to context. If some readers are concerned about context, they can read dozens of published claims by exegetics, clerics, self-proclaimed experts, and antagonists regarding the historical context of Surah 59. Here is what Pickthall provides for us before he presents this surah: [20]

> Surah LIX *Al-Hashr*, "Exile," takes its name from vv.2-17, which refer to the exile of the Bani Nadir, a Jewish tribe of Al Madinah (for treason and projected murder of the Prophet) and for confiscation of their property. The "Hypocrites," as the lukewarm Muslims were called, had secretly sympathized with these Jews, whose opposition had grown strong since the Muslim reverse at Mt. Uhud, and had promised to side with them if it came to a collision with Muslims; and to emigrate with them if they were forced to emigrate. But when the Muslims marched against the Bani Nadir, and the latter took refuge in their strong towers, the Hypocrites did nothing. And when at length they were reduced and exiled, the Hypocrites did not go with them into exile. The date of revelation is the fourth year of the Hijrah.

It should be noted that only five of the twenty-four verses in Surah 59 contain words or phrases of violence. Some of the verses, including Verse 23, even claim that Allah is the source of "peace." This surah also contains verses that are about domestic relations. Some other verses are highly spiritual and encouraging, while other verses convey suspicion, fear, and violence. Nonetheless, it is worth noting how Surah 59 also presents Allah as admitting that He is the source of "terror" against some Jewish people simply because they did not accept Allah.

Allah's Use of Natural Forces to Destroy Unbelievers

Occasionally in the Qur'an there are passages in which Allah claims to use natural forces of lightning, winds, floods, and earthquakes to destroy tribes that disturb him. Here are examples from Surah 69: 4-7:

> *(The tribes of) Thamud and A'ad disbelieved in the judgment to come. As for Thamud, they were destroyed by the lighting. And as for A'ad, they were destroyed by a fierce roaring wind, Which He imposed on them for seven long nights and eight long days so that thou mightiest have seen men lying overthrown, as they were hollow trunks of palm-trees.

Surah 105 as a Possible Inspiration for Airborne Attacks and for "Pre-Emptive" Attacks

Surah 105 ("The Elephant") has only five verses. Not only are they very short verses, but three of the five verses (60%) portray physical violence. As such, quantitatively speaking, Surah 105 is the most violent of all 114 surahs in the Qur'an:

> *THE ELEPHANT
>
> In the name of Allah, the Beneficent, the Merciful. Hast thou not seen how thy Lord dealt with the owners of the Elephant? Did He not bring their stratagem to naught? And sent against them swarms of flying creatures, Which pelted them with stones of baked clay, And made them like green crops devoured (by cattle)?

Surah 105 might be especially important in several ways that have contemporary relevance. In this surah, Allah asserts that he is the perpetrator of violence, albeit what might be called "defensive" or "pre-emptive violence" against a hostile force that is approaching Mecca in order to destroy it. Allah also claims that he uses natural forces that

Violence, Terror, and War as Portrayed in the Qur'an   81

are airborne ("flying creatures" that release "stones of baked clay")—not Meccans or any other humans—to convey this violence and destroy the adversary. Notice how it is Allah ("thy Lord") who claims that he is the one who negated "their stratagem."

Regarding Context
Pickthall[21] writes that this attack was a well-known historical event given special relevance by Muslims because it occurred the same year as Muhammad's birth in 570 or 571 CE. Pickthall explains the context of Surah 105 this way:

> The allusion is to the campaign of Abraha, the Abyssinian ruler of Al-Yaman, against Mecca, with the purpose of destroying the Ka'bah in the year of the Prophet's birth. He had with him an elephant which much impressed the Arabs. Tradition says that the elephant refused to advance on the last stage of the march, and that swarms of flying creatures pelted the Abyssinians with stones. Another tradition says that they retired in disorder owning to an outbreak of smallpox in the camp. At the time when this surah was revealed, many men in Mecca must have known what happened. Dr. Krenkow, a sound Arabic scholar, is of opinion that the flying creatures may well have been swarms of insects carrying infection. In any case the Ka'bah was saved from destruction after its defenders had despaired.

Comment: Considering that contemporary people throughout the world are free to read this surah without any regard whatsoever for context, or that it is written in past tense, is it possible that this surah can inspire some people to engage in pre-emptive strikes using airborne objects or biological agents? Isn't it possible that this surah inspired Osama Bin Laden and some of the assailants who were involved in the deadly airborne attacks of the jet passenger planes against the World Trade Center and the Pentagon on 9-11-2001? Could this surah be used to inspire future attacks by assailants to use drones and other aircraft to disperse airborne toxic biological and chemical agents, and to justify those attacks afterwards by the assailants? While I have no evidence that this has happened or will happen, it seems to me that the prospect is worth considering.

While this prospect might seem preposterous to some readers, please keep in mind that true believers in Islam are supposed to regard every verse in the Qur'an as holy, divine, complete, unchanging, and eternally relevant.[22] The verses are not considered to be anachronistic or irrelevant even if they refer to a real or imagined object, situation, or event in ancient history.

A Surah in Which Allah Suggests Suicide for Those Who Doubt that He Will Give Muhammad Victory in the World and in the Hereafter

> *Whoso is wont to think (through envy) that Allah will not give him (Muhammad) victory in the world and the Hereafter (and is enraged at the thought of his victory), let him stretch a rope up to the roof (of his dwelling), and let him hang himself. Then let him see whether his strategy dispelleth that whereat he ragest! (Surah 12: 15)

Comment: This is the only verse I found in the Qur'an that mentions suicide. It also mentions a method for committing suicide (hanging oneself from the roof of one's dwelling) and the reason for it (for any person who doubts that Muhammad will be victorious "in the world and the Hereafter.") Might some people who are agitated, deranged or delusional interpret this verse in such a way as to commit suicide or to suggest suicide to other people who doubt the supremacy of Allah, Muhammad, and Islam?

SUMMARY OF MAIN FINDINGS OF THIS CHAPTER

- Most (75%) of the Qur'an's 114 surahs do not have titles in English that are likely to be regarded as violent by most people. Of

Violence, Terror, and War as Portrayed in the Qur'an

the relatively small number of surahs whose titles might suggest conflict to some people, only one of the surahs (Surah 8) has a title that includes the word "war," but its primary topic is the "spoils" of war rather than war itself.

- Words such as "doom," "slay," and "burn" as physical violence are found in more than one-half (54%) of the surahs, but in less than 12% of the Qur'an's 6,220 verses. The word "terror" as physical violence occurs about twelve times in the entire Qur'an.
- Relatively few of the verses with violent words and phrases *require* Muhammad or followers of Allah to engage in physical violence, although quite a few of the verses *allow* Muslims to engage in violence under certain conditions, against unbelievers, as well as against other Muslims.
- It is also true, however, that very few of the verses with violent words and phrases *prohibit* Muslims from engaging in physical violence, particularly against unbelievers.

Thus, it can be said that it is not difficult to find a surah in the Qur'an that has at least one verse that contains violent words and phrases, but it is considerably more difficult to find a verse in the Qur'an that contains violent words and phrases, particularly in many of the surahs after surahs # 2-9.

- Only a relatively small percentage (11.9%) of the Qur'an's verses portray or refer to physical violence against human beings.
- Only a small percentage of verses (2.66%) portray or refer to battles or warfare, and less than one percent (0.7%) of the Qur'an's verses portray actual physical violence in battles or war.
- Surahs 2-9 have the highest concentrations/percentages of verses (14.7%) that portray or refer to violence, battles or war (8.7%), and violence in war (2.4%). These percentages decrease appreciably in subsequent sections of the Qur'an.

Thus, it can be said that the surahs at the front of the Qur'an are not representative of the frequency and quantity of portrayals of violence throughout the Qur'an.

- Only in thirteen of the surahs do 25% or more of the verses portray or refer to violence, and in only three very short surahs do more than 50% of the verses portray violence.

Therefore, it is fair to say that *the Qur'an is not filled with violence.* Taken as a whole, *the Qur'an is not a very violent, bellicose, belligerent, or militaristic book.* This is worth appreciating for a number of reasons. Muhammad and his followers were subjected to extreme ridicule and persecution for about twenty years (610-630 CE). They engaged in a number of violent raids and in both offensive and defensive battles for about seven years. Rather suddenly and unexpectedly, Muhammad's forces became stunningly triumphant.

- In the Qur'an, Allah is decidedly the most frequently-portrayed performer, threatener, warner, predictor, and demander of violence by his followers. He is portrayed as the performer of violence in 57% of the surahs and in 4% of the verses. Allah is portrayed as committing violence because people do not accept Islam, they do not accept his authority, or they anger him in various ways. This includes Muslims as well as non-Muslims.
- Often Allah's violence is in the past, as when he claims to have destroyed the Egyptian military forces that were pursuing Moses and the Israelites across the Red Sea. Also frequent are promises by Allah that he will commit violence in the future, particularly on Judgment Day, often by subjecting miscreants to painful torture and death by hellfire.
- Muhammad and Muslims are only infrequently portrayed as performers or co-performers of violence, often in conjunction with Allah.
- Only occasionally are non-Muslims portrayed as performers of violence.

Thus, it can be said that, contrary to widespread contemporary beliefs, *non-Muslims are not often portrayed as the performers of violence against Muslims.*

Violence, Terror, and War as Portrayed in the Qur'an

- Allah also is the most frequently portrayed predictor and threatener of violence. This occurs in 74% of the surahs and 5.4% of the verses. Relatively few verses portray anyone but Allah as a predictor or threatener of violence.
- Allah also is most frequently portrayed as the demander of violence by others. This occurs in 13% of the surahs and only 0.6% of the verses.
- Allah demands that Muhammad and his followers perform violence in 8.7% of the surahs and in less than 0.1% of the verses.
- There are about 741 verses in the Qur'an that depict both the sources and the targets of violence. Allah is the source of violence in 612 (83%) of these verses. 47% of Allah's targets are non-believers in general. 45% of his targets are the Quraysh clan and other Arabic clans. Only 1.4% of Allah's targets are "Children of the Scripture" (Jews and Christians). 1.3% of Allah's targets are some Muslims who commit specific offenses that anger Allah. 5% of Allah's targets are any and all people who deviate from Allah's rules, regardless of their religious orientation.
- Occasionally there are verses in which Allah demands or threatens violence against any and all people, regardless of religious orientation, for offenses including adultery, traduction, accusing honorable women of offenses, and wrongfully using the wealth of orphans, usury, hoarding gold and silver, and bragging.
- Allah is not portrayed as being violent towards Muhammad, Satan, or the Jinn, although Allah often is portrayed as despising Satan and the Jinn and other spirits.
- It is worth noting that, contrary to widespread contemporary assumptions, the Qur'an does not often portray violence by or against Jews or Christians.
- Few if any verses in the Qur'an portray violence or terror that is totally absolute, all-encompassing, timeless, imperative, and lethal. Rather, violence is portrayed as being contingent on a variety of forces, factors, and events that Allah considers to be insults against him or violations of his rules by one or more people or groups. Very

often in the Qur'an, verses that are adjacent to a violent verse place restriction on said violence.
- The word "fight" is fairly frequent in the Qur'an, but it is not always obvious that the word conveys physical violence.
- Some of the surahs with the most violent verses are not the so-called "war and battle surahs." Surah 22 ("The Pilgrimage") and Surah 47 ("Muhammad") are examples of this.
- "Smiting the necks" of opponents is a violent phrase that occurs about a dozen times in the Qur'an.
- At least 16.6% of the surahs (19 of 114) do *not* portray or refer to physical violence against human beings.
- "Peace" in the Qur'an is relatively infrequent. It occurs about sixty times. Twenty-five percent of these occurrences portray "peace" as a state of mind, rather than the opposite of violence or military warfare. "Peace" as the opposite of violence or war is portrayed in thirteen of the Qur'ans 114 surahs (11.4%) and in only 45 of its 6,220 verses (0.7%).
- Thirty-three of these forty-five occurrences refer to peace as the opposite of violence within Islam. "Peace" as a desirable non-violent condition between Muslims and non-Muslims only occurs in twelve verses. Peace between Muslims and non-Muslims is allowed only under specific conditions, as when Muslims are winning in battle and the enemy offers peace first. Some verses prohibit Muslims from calling out for peace when they are winning in battle.

Verses about peace as an alternative to military battles and war could be very important in the years ahead if battles occur between Muslim and non-Muslim forces. Possibly verses like these should be called to the attention of leaders of ISIS, al-Qaeda, and other terrorist groups to indicate that "peace" is not generally prohibited, but that the Qur'an places some restrictions on Muslims calling out for peace.

- None of the so-called "war and battle" surahs are dominated by verses that portray or refer to war or battles; nor does physical violence pervade portrayals or references to wars and battles. Physical violence never comprises more than 25% of the verses in

Violence, Terror, and War as Portrayed in the Qur'an

these surahs, and usually physical violence is only in about 15% of the verses. Wars and battles comprise less than 15% of the verses in these surahs, except for Surahs 8 and 48.

- Of the so-called "war and battle surahs," Surah 8 ("The Spoils of War") has 28% of its verses about war and battle, but only 13.3% of its verses portray physical violence in battles or war.
- There are a number of often-overlooked, but unusual passages in the Qur'an that portray violence or war. One of these verses claims that the Torah, the Gospel, and the Qur'an each require believers to "fight in the way of Allah."

Another unusual but troubling verse portrays Allah commanding Muhammad to inform Jewish rabbis and Christian monks who hoard gold and silver that they will suffer "grievous punishment and branding." This is one of the few verses in the Qur'an that specifically targets Jews and Christians.

- Allah often is portrayed as using natural forces including lightning, winds, floods, and droughts —not Muslims— to destroy unbelievers and others who anger him.
- Surah 105 portrays pre-emptive strikes in the form of airborne objects and possible biological agents against opponents of Allah.

In this chapter, we asked whether this surah has been used or could be used in the future to suggest or incite airborne attacks with drones, missiles, and chemical or biological warfare.

- One Surah suggests suicide by hanging for anyone who doubts that Allah will provide victory to Muhammad and his followers.
- One surah (Surah 59, "Exile") portrays Allah casting terror into the hearts of the members of a Jewish tribe (the Bani Nadir) in order to expel them from a city and force them to migrate elsewhere.

Could this surah be a major source of enduring provocation and hatred between Muslims and Jews? However, this verse does not seem to demand or threaten the extermination of this ethnic-religious group. In fact, I did not find any verses in the Qur'an that call for, portray, or refer to the complete extermination of a racial, ethnic, or religious group or entity. There are many forms of violence depicted in the Qur'an, but genocide does not seem to be one of them. Furthermore, I did not find any verses that portray war or battles as a means to exterminate an entire ethnic or religious group. The main purposes of war in the Qur'an are to end persecution of Muslims, to allow Muslims to practice Islam without interference, and to restore Muslim lands to Muslims.

SOME SUGGESTIONS BASED ON THE FINDINGS IN CHAPTER 2

The final chapter in this book provides a large number of suggestions for reducing the risks of what we might refer to as "holy book influenced violence" in the decades ahead. I will just make three suggestions here, based on the findings presented in this chapter regarding the Qur'an:

1. Let us try our best to encourage skeptics, doubters, and religious and political leaders to at least scan all or most of the 114 surahs in the Qur'an, including the first and last surahs (Surahs 1 and 14), not just Surah 8 (the "Spoils of War"), or a few of the other surahs at the front of the Qur'an that have the highest concentrations of verses that portray violence and war.

2. Let us try our best to emphasize in our conversations and exchanges with other people that it is not accurate or fair to make extreme, categorical, and polarized assertions about the quantities and qualities of violence, terror, battles, and warfare portrayed in the Qur'an. The surahs and verses of the Qur'an are only occasionally violent. The violence usually is by Allah. Reasons usually are given for the violence. The targets of the violence often include Muslims as well as non-Muslims who anger Allah or deviate from his rules.

3. Let us acknowledge that there are no verses in the Qur'an which explicitly demand, prescribe, or describe genocide. Nor are there verses in the Qur'an that describe or encourage contemporary forms of violence, including violence against "soft targets," such as

Violence, Terror, and War as Portrayed in the Qur'an

crowds of people at marketplaces, cafes, concerts, athletic events, schools, churches, and places of mass transportation including bridges, rail stations, and airports.

Now let us determine how the Old Testament and the New Testament compare with and contrast to the Qur'an in their portrayals of violence, terror, genocide, and war. Having predated the Qur'an by many centuries, are they far more violent than the Qur'an? Less so? Is there any reason to believe that they influenced the content of the Qur'an on these topics in ways that have not yet been discovered, realized, or fully appreciated? Are their portrayals of violence, terror, and war much less applicable to contemporary world affairs and to interpersonal and inter-group conflicts? These are some of the questions to be pondered in the next few chapters.

Notes

1. In a personal phone conversation with the author, June 30, 2016.
2. Andrew Welsh-Huggins and Julie Carr Smyth. The Associated Press. As published in *The Providence Journal.* Page A1. "Terror Suspected in Campus Attack." Page A1. Monday, November 29, 2017.
3. "Mohammed Taheri-Azar's letter to police" http://www.herald-sun.com/orange10-716750 html. *Herald-Sun.* 2006-03-24.
4. "Taheri-azar Writes to Eyewitness News" http://abclocal.go.com/wtvd/story? Section=local&id=3992674. American Broadcasting Company. 2006-03-14. "More on the North Carolina Jihadist, Mohammed Taheri-azar" http://www.danielpipes.org/blog/576. DanielPipes.org.2006-03-14.
5. "Mohammed Reza Taheri-azar Letter Meditation II and III." *The Daily Tarheel.* http://www.dailytarheel.com/media/paper885/documents/jzjo063s.pdf.
6. Schwartz-Barcott, "Conversations with Ali." Unpublished essay. March 31, 2017.
7. Google search: https://google.com/?gws_major+nidal+malik+hasan.
8. Haleem, M. A. S. Abdel, *The Qur'an.* NY: Oxford University Press. 2010, xxi-xxvi.
9. *The Straight Path* (Third Edition). NY: Oxford University Press. 1998.
10. Oxford University Press, 2004, xxviii.
11. New York and London, 1975, 1107.
12. Pickthall, Mohammed Marmaduke. *The Meaning of the Glorious Koran.* Eleventh Edition. NY: Mentor Books. The New American Library. 1955, 453.
13. Jenkins, *Laying Down the Sword*, 36.
14. Pickthall, *The Meaning of the Glorious Koran*, 156.
15. Haleem, *The Qur'an*, 127.
16. Pickthall, *The Meaning of the Glorious Koran*, 361.
17. Op. cit., 76.
18. Op. cit., 445
19. Op. cit., 361.
20. Op. cit., 392.
21. Op. cit., 450.
22. Op. cit., 3.

Chapter 3

Portrayals of Violence in the Old Testament

Epigraphs

*And I will make void the counsel of Judah and Jerusalem in this place; and I will cause them to fall by the sword before their enemies, and by the hands of them that seek their lives: and their carcasses will I give to the meat for the fowls of the heaven, and for the beasts of the earth. (Jer. 19: 7)

*Thou are my battle axe and weapons of war: for with thee will I break in pieces the nations, and with thee will I destroy kingdoms. (Jer. 51: 20)

*And the Lord said unto Joshua, See, I have given into thine hand Jericho, and the king thereof, and the mighty men of valor.

And they utterly destroyed all that was in the city, both man and woman, young and old, and ox, and sheep, and ass, with the edge of the sword. (Josh. 6: 2, 21)

*Woe unto the inhabitants of the sea coast, the nation of the Cherethites! The word of the Lord is against you; O Canaan, the land of the Philistines, I will even destroy thee, that there shall be no inhabitant. (Zeph. 2: 5)

*(11) The Lord will be terrible unto them: for he will famish all the gods of the earth; and men shall worship him, every one from its place, even all the isles of the heathen.

(12) Ye Ethiopians also, ye shall be slain by my sword.

(13) And he will stretch out his hand against the north, and destroy Assyria; and will make Nineveh a desolation, and dry like a wilderness. (Zeph. 2: 11-13)

*(18) If a man have a stubborn and rebellious son, which will not obey the voice of his father, or the voice of his mother, and that when they have chastened him, will not hearken unto them:

(19) Then shall his father and his mother lay hold on him, and bring him out unto the elders of his city, and unto the gate of his place;

(20) And they shall say unto the elders of his city, This our son is stubborn and rebellious, he will not obey our voice; he is a glutton, and a drunkard.

(21) And all the men of his city shall stone him with stones, that he die: so shalt thou put evil away from among you; and all Israel shall hear, and fear. (Deut. 21: 18-21)

INTRODUCTION TO THE OLD TESTAMENT

These epigraphs provide a sense of the kinds of violence and war that are portrayed in verses in the Old Testament (OT). They portray God as threatening violence, committing violence, and demanding violence, sometimes by and against his own chosen people—the Israelites. There are many other aspects of violence in the OT, although I do not mean to

Portrayals of Violence in the Old Testament

suggest or claim that it is thoroughly or primarily violent. This chapter presents my findings about the quantities and qualities of physical violence, terror, genocide, and war, using the same analytic and coding procedures that I used for the same purpose with the Qur'an and with the New Testament (NT), as presented in other chapters of this book.

Once again let me readily admit that I am not an expert on any of the holy books, including the OT. In this case, even though I have spent countless hours reading every word and coding relevant passages as objectively as possible, I am simply trying to present my best effort to report on the topic as objectively as possible from the perspectives of sociology and psychology. Similar to the focus in the preceding chapters, the primary questions addressed here are:

1. How often and in what ways are physical violence, terror, genocide, and war against human beings portrayed in the OT; particularly in the first book and the final book attributed to Moses: Genesis and Deuteronomy, but also, in its thirty-seven other books?

2. In what ways might these portrayals of violence and war be used, misused, and abused by some people now and in the future to promote, commit, and try to justify violence against other human beings?

OVERVIEW AND CONTEXT

By way of background, and as indicated in an earlier chapter, the Old Testament (OT) is extremely long and quite complex in many ways when compared to the New Testament and the Qur'an. It consists of more than three times as many chapters (929), verses (23,145*), and words (645,117) as the (NT) (260 chapters, 7,956 verses, and 138,020 words). Of course, the OT has a rather widespread reputation, particularly among detractors, for portraying a lot of anger, conflict, warfare, and violence. Other detractors simply dismiss it as being utterly anachronistic, obsolete, and irrelevant. Some of them claim that its books were written more than 2,300 years ago by dozens of different prophets who were trying to justify many acts of genocide by Israelite people against the Philistines and dozens of other clans and tribes that were occupying the lands in and around Judea. The analysis that follows in this chapter can help us determine the validity of these claims.

According to the "Introduction" in the King James Version (KJV) of the Bible, [1] the thirty-nine books of the OT are arranged more or less chronologically in four parts: The Pentateuch, The Historical Books, The Poetical Books, and the Prophetic Books. The Pentateuch consists of the first five books in the OT: Genesis, Exodus, Leviticus, Numbers, and Deuteronomy. They are attributed to the first prophet, Moses, and are assumed to have been written by him between 1445-1405 B.C. (B.C.E.) in the last years of his life. The Historical Books interpret about "one thousand years of Israelite history, from the fifteenth to the fifth century B.C." They generally divide this history into four "periods": "The Pre-Monarchic Period," "The Era of the United Monarchy," "The Era of the Divided Monarchy," and the "Era of the Exile and the Return to Canaan." The Poetical Books include Psalms (songs) and Proverbs, and provide guidelines for daily life, worship, and relations with other people. The Prophetic Books often convey warnings and guidelines about "the increasingly complex and changing world of international affairs from the eighth through the fifth centuries B.C."

Note: The dates, names, verse numbers, and other details presented here are the ones in the KJV of the "Protestant" Bible that is fully identified in the Bibliography. Some of these dates, names, verse numbers, and other details are slightly different in other versions of the "Protestant" Bible, the "Catholic" Bible, and in various versions of the Jewish holy books. I have not found these differences to be significant regarding how often and in what ways violence, terror, genocide, and warfare are portrayed in these books of the OT.

I have read all of these books in the process of doing this study. I would need to write an entire book in order to analyze each and every passage in the OT that portrays or refers to threats and acts of physical

Portrayals of Violence in the Old Testament 95

violence against humans, including violence in battles and wars. That is not practical or necessary here. Many of the thirty-nine books are very similar in the quantities (proportionate to their length) and qualities of violence and war that are portrayed in them. This is particularly true of most of the books in the Pentateuch and the Historical Books. Furthermore, many of the books recount the same historical events of violence and warfare. These events include portrayals of violence and persecution when Moses and his Israelites first inhabited Judah, their persecution during exile in Egypt, their escape from Egypt, and their battles against various tribes that resided in the lands between Egypt and Canaan. Additional major events include Israelite battles against the tribes that occupied Canaan once the Israelites arrived there, their battles against nations that invaded the land of Israel once it had been established by the Israelites, their conflicts among themselves, and threats of violence and retribution against them as sinners by their God and by dozens of their leaders and prophets.

With this in mind, let us first consider violence and war in two of the most famous books of the OT— Genesis and Deuteronomy. These are the first and last of the five books of Moses that not only begin the OT, but also begin and constitute the core of many versions of the Jewish *Torah*. Regarding the *Torah*, in their book, *The Great Religions by Which Men Live*,[2] Ross and Hills write:

> Often Jews have known God as the Lawgiver for their people. The Law he gave is called the *Torah*, which means "Teaching." The *Torah* consists of five books, sometimes called the Pentateuch. The books are Genesis, Exodus, Leviticus, Numbers, and Deuteronomy. All Jews are encouraged to study them. The complete *Torah* is regularly read each year in the synagogues, a portion on each Sabbath. The *Torah* contains the legends of its own origin. According to these legends, God gave the Law to Moses on Mount Sinai, while the Hebrews were camping in the wilderness after escaping from Egypt.

After reporting on my analysis of Genesis and Deuteronomy, I present a concise analysis of the other books of the OT. Along the way, I provide comparisons with and contrasts to the Qur'an and the NT. I also raise questions about how various passages about violence and war might be used and misused by contemporary people and groups who are inclined towards violence now and in the decades ahead. No claim is made that Genesis and Deuteronomy are representative of the entire OT regarding violence or war. Then again, these two books often are identified as being among the most influential, famous, and violent books in the OT.

Note: Hundreds of claims are made on Internet search engines, including Google, about which holy books are most violent and which books in the OT are most violent. Genesis and Deuteronomy are cited frequently in this regard.[3]

By the way, please recall that our focus is on portrayals of physical violence against human beings—not on conflict, anger, wrathfulness, revenge, curses, or other topics that may or may not involve physical violence—unless they do so explicitly. We say this because various authors of the thirty-nine books in the OT portray "God," the "Lord," and "the Lord God" as being angry, wrathful, and vengeful. We also do not count violence towards animals other than human beings, or the sacrificing of animals other than human beings. Ritual sacrificing of animals was quite common during the times and places depicted in the OT. References to that practice are quite frequent in it.

GENESIS: THE FIRST BOOK OF MOSES

Some Context
According to the King James Version (KJV)[4] that was also used in analyzing the New Testament (NT):

> Genesis is the foundational book to the rest of the Bible. Its important theological themes include the doctrines of God, Creation,

man, sin, and salvation.... Genesis covers more time than any other book in the Bible.... It records the beginning of time, life, sin, salvation, the human race, and the Hebrew nation. It begins with primeval history centered in four major events: The Creation, the Fall, the Flood, and the dispersion of the nations. Genesis then narrates the history of four great patriarchs: Abraham, Isaac, Jacob, and Joseph.... Moses very likely wrote all of the books of the Pentateuch after his call to lead the people out of Egypt.... in the final forty years of his life (1445-1405 B.C.).

Therefore, it is worth considering that, if Moses indeed is the author of Genesis, he witnessed very few of the events that he describes in Genesis. Also, in contrast to the origins of the Qur'an, there are differences among Biblical scholars as to whether Moses received the verses of Genesis directly from God, from an archangel, or in other ways. Apparently, some members of some Christian denominations believe that all verses in the entire Bible essentially are "the word of God."

Verses in Genesis that Portray or Refer to Physical Violence or War

Here are the verses in Genesis (Gen.) that portray or refer to physical violence against human beings. It is worth keeping in mind that Genesis has fifty chapters that present 1,533 verses in the KJV identified previously. Genesis describes and interprets major events over a period of many thousands of years in the emergence of the cosmos, the heavens, the Earth, oceans, plants animals, human beings, and tribes, clans, and nations in the Middle East, with a special focus on the Hebrews.

1. Cain slew his brother Abel.

> *And Cain talked with Abel his brother: and it came to pass, when they were in the field, that Cain rose up against Abel his brother, and slew him. (Gen. 4: 8)

This is the first verse in Genesis that refers to an act of physical violence against a human being—and a ghastly one at that. The following verse seems to convey that God had no foreknowledge of this fratricide and that he disapproved of it.

> *And the Lord said unto Cain, "Where is Abel thy brother?" And he said, "I know not: am I my brother's keeper?" (Gen. 4: 9)

2. Verses in which God threatens a worldwide flood, then creates it, destroying everything but Noah, his immediate family, the ark, and the mated pairs of animals on the ark.

There are a series of verses that convey that God decided to flood the earth and destroy everything except for Noah, his family, the ark, and the mated pairs of animals of each species that Noah will load on to the ark. Genesis 6: 11 suggests the reason for this:

> *The earth also was corrupt before God, and the earth was filled with violence. (Gen. 6: 11)

> *And God said unto Noah, The end of all flesh is come before me; for the earth is filled with violence through them; and, behold, I will destroy them with the earth. (Gen. 6: 13)

> God then orders Noah to *"Make thee an ark of gopher wood." (Gen. 6: 14)

God also is portrayed as repeating this threat to Noah about the flood:

> *And behold, I, even I, do bring a flood of waters upon the earth, to destroy all flesh, wherein is the breath of life, from under heaven; and everything that is in the earth shall die. (Gen. 6: 17)

God repeats this threat a third time:

> *For yet seven days, and I will cause it to rain upon the earth forty days and forty nights; and every living substance that I have made will I destroy from off the face of the earth. (Gen. 7: 4)

Portrayals of Violence in the Old Testament

These threats become acts of violence by God in Genesis 7: 21, 22, and 23.

> *And all flesh died that moved upon the earth, both of fowl, and of cattle, and of beast, and of every creeping thing that creepeth upon the earth, and every man
>
> All in whose nostrils was the breath of life, of all that was in the dry land, died.
>
> And every living substance was destroyed which was upon the face of the ground, both man, and cattle, and the creeping things, and the fowl of the heaven; and they were destroyed from the earth: and Noah only remained alive, and they that were with him in the ark. (Gen. 7: 21-23)

By the way, after the flood, God promises Noah that he will not again commit destruction like this.

3. The Lord sends devastating plagues against Pharaoh.

> *And the Lord plagued Pharaoh and his house with great plagues because of Sarai Abram's wife. (Gen. 12: 17)

4. The Battle of Kings.

> *And there went out the king of Sodom, and the king of Gomorrah, and the King of Admah, and the king of Zeboii, and the king of Bela (the same is Zoar;) and they joined battle with them in the vale of Siddim. (Gen. 14: 8)
>
> *And the vale of Siddim was full of slime pits; and the kings of Sodom and Gomorrah fled, and fell there; and they that remained fled to the mountain. (Gen. 14: 10)

Comment: Adjacent verses seem to convey that "fell there" means that they were slain there, but this is not perfectly clear, so it is not registered as physical violence against them.

5. Abram leads his force to rescue his brother Lot.

> *And when Abram heard that his brother was taken captive, he armed his trained servants, born in his own house, three hundred and eighteen, and pursued them unto Dan.... And he divided himself against them, he and his servants by night, and smote them, and pursued them unto Hobah, which is on the left hand of Damascus. (Gen. 14: 14-15)

6. Reference to "the slaughter of Chedorlaomer."

> *And the king of Sodom went out to meet him after his return from the slaughter of Chedorlaomer, and of the kings that were with him, at the valley of Shaveh, which is the king's dale. (Gen. 14: 17)

Note: Chapter 15 and other chapters in Genesis have plenty of verses that refer to the ritual killing and sacrificing of pigeons, rams, and other animals by Abram in accordance with covenants with God. There also are quite a few verses about ritual circumcision. However, these verses were not counted as "physical violence" in Table 8 according to our definition of "violence" in this book.

7. A violent act related to the "wickedness of the men of Sodom." [5]

> *But the men put forth their hand, and pulled Lot into the house to them, and shut to the door.... And they smote the men that were at the door of the house with blindness, both small and great: so that they wearied themselves to find the door. (Gen. 19: 10-11)

8. A claim that "the Lord" destroyed the cities of the plain.

> *Then the Lord rained upon Sodom and upon Gomorrah brimstone and fire from the Lord out of heaven; and he overthrew those cities, and all the plain, and all the inhabitants of the cities, and that which grew upon the ground. (Gen. 19: 24-25)

Comment: The next verse, Genesis 19: 26, is a famous verse about Lot's wife looking back and becoming a "pillar of salt." To register this as physical violence is debatable. It might be metaphorical. It does not convey who did this and it does not necessarily convey that this was physical violence. Therefore, this verse was not registered in Table 8 as portraying physical violence.

> *But his wife looked back from behind him, and she became a pillar of salt. (Gen. 19: 26)

9. Another reference to God having destroyed Sodom and Gomorrah.

> *And it came to pass, when God destroyed the cities of the plain, that God remembered Abraham, and sent Lot out of the midst of the overthrow, when he overthrew the cities in which Lot dwelt. (Gen. 19: 29)

10. Simeon and Levi commit violence to avenge the rape of their sister Dinah.

> *(25) And it came to pass on the third day, when they were sore, that two of the sons of Jacob, Simeon and Levi, Dinah's brethren, took each man his sword, and came upon the city boldly, and slew all the males.
>
> (26) And they slew Hamor and Shechem his son with the edge of the sword, and took Dinah out of Shechem's house, and went out.
>
> (27) The sons of Jacob came upon the slain, and spoiled the city, because they had defiled their sister.
>
> (29) And all their wealth, and all their little ones, and their wives took they captive, and spoiled even all that was in the house. (Gen. 34: 25-27, 29)

11. A reference to Midian having been slain.

> *And Husham died, and Hadad the son of Beddad, who smote Midian in the field of Moab, reigned in his stead: and the name of his city was Avith. (Gen. 36: 35)

Some Exclusions: There are several other rather famous passages in Genesis about actual or alleged events which some people might consider as portrayals of violence. However, they are not registered as such in Table 8 because they fall short of our working definition of physical violence as it is used throughout this book: "Severe or injurious treatment or action... characterized by extremely rough, harsh, destructive physical force."

Excluded events include: two of Lot's daughters getting Lot drunk in order to copulate with him and conceive and bear his children; God's demand (eventually retracted by God) that Abraham sacrifice his son Isaac in submission to God's will; Abraham sacrificing a ram provided by God, rather than his son Isaac; and many other events of ritual, religious sacrificing of pigeons, goats, rams, and other animals in obeisance to God. Also excluded are a wide range of conflicts and plots within and between various families, groups, tribes, and clans unless they entail obvious physical violence against human beings.

There is also a verse in which the phrase "the terror of God" seems to mean the "fear of God." It does not indicate that physical violence occurred to any human being. For this reason, it was not registered in Table 8 as portraying physical violence:

> *And they journeyed; and the terror of God was upon the cities that were round about them, and they did not pursue after the sons of Jacob. (Gen. 35: 5)

Another set of verses that might convey physical violence to some readers refer to the famous accounts of the famous Jewish leader Joseph and his "coat of many colors." There is a plot to slay Joseph, but he is thrown into a pit instead (Gen. 37: 24), then ransomed for twenty pieces of silver (Gen. 37: 28). The plotters put the blood of a kid goat on Joseph's coat to trick his father Jacob into thinking that his beloved son Joseph is dead. But Joseph is not dead. He not only survives, but he goes on to lead the Jewish people in Egypt for many years. There is no indication that Joseph was injured when he was thrown into the pit, or that the plotters intended to injure him by doing that. For these reasons, I did not register these verses as conveying physical violence.

Table 8 summarizes physical violence portrayed in Genesis as described above.

Table 8. Violence and War as Portrayed in Genesis.

1	Number of verses that portray violence against humans	22 (for 9 events)
2	Violence by non-Jews (when apparent)	2
3	Violence by Jews (when apparent)	6 (for 3 events)
4	God portrayed as:	
	a. Committing violence	7 (for 3 events)
	b. Predicting, threatening, or warning about violence	3 (for 1 event)
	c. Demanding violence by others	0
	d. Rejecting or repudiating violence	0
5	Repudiations of violence by others	0
6	Portrayals and references to doom, fire, and hellfire as violence	1
7	Portrayals of military wars or battles	1
	a. Portrayals of violence in wars or battles	1

Explanation and Analysis of Table 8

Row 1 in Table 8 indicates that I found twenty-two verses in Genesis (as explained in the previous section of this chapter) that clearly refer to or portray acts of physical violence against humans. However, we should note that thirteen of these twenty-two verses are part of sets of verses that refer to a particular event such as the Lord creating the flood that destroyed everything except Noah, the ark, and the pairs of animals of various species that he protected in the ark (Gen. 7: 21-23). The twenty-two verses actually refer to only nine violent events. For example, there is only one verse (Gen. 4: 8) that portrays Cain actually slaying his brother Abel.

Rows 2, 3, and 4a indicate the sources of violence in these twenty-two verses, but only when the sources are identified in the verses or in adjacent verses. This is not always the case. As best as I could tell from the words in the verses, people other than Jews are portrayed as committing violence in only two verses (Gen. 4: 8 and Gen. 14: 8). This is registered as the number "2" in Row 2.

Row 3 indicates that I found six verses in which Jewish people, including Abram (Gen. 14: 15) were identified as committing violent acts. However, these six verses only refer to three violent events: Cain killing Abel (Gen. 14: 15), Jewish forces battling non-Jewish forces in what is referred to as "the slaughter at Chedorlaomer (Gen. 14: 8), and Simeon and Levi avenging the sexual assault of their sister Dinah (Gen. 34: 25-27, 29).

Row 4a indicates that seven verses were found in Genesis which portray God as committing violence. This is according to Moses—the assumed author of Genesis. Only three violent events are covered in these seven verses, however: "The Flood" (three verses), God destroying Sodom and Gomorrah (three verses), and God sending a plague against Pharaoh and his followers in Egypt (Gen. 12: 17).

Comment: In contrast to some verses in the Qur'an, some verses in Genesis portray an author (presumably Moses) who is conveying to us what God supposedly conveyed to him about events that Moses did not experience and would not experience. In some cases, such as the flood that involved Noah, these events occurred long before Moses' birth. By contrast, the Qur'an sometimes provides verses in which Allah is the direct source—the speaker, if you will, speaking for himself and asserting that he intentionally commits, will commit, or has committed violence against human beings. Let me suggest that this is an extremely important difference between the Qur'an and the Bible. The Qur'an occasionally portrays Allah making his own claims of violence. By contrast, these verses in Genesis occasionally tell us what Moses recorded about what God purportedly said and did.

Portrayals of Violence in the Old Testament

I offer this observation analytically, not critically nor as a moral judgment. And I offer it to encourage us to consider how some people in the contemporary world might read these passages and give their own meanings to them. If some readers believe that Allah is directly commanding them to slay other human beings, is this more compelling than if they believe that Moses is telling them that God once sent a flood that destroyed everything on Earth except for Noah, his animals, and the ark?

Returning now to Table 8, Row 4b indicates that I found only three verses in Genesis (Gen. 6: 13, 17 and Gen. 7: 4) which portray God as threatening or promising violence. All three of these verses pertain to the same event: God's warning to Noah about the flood that he was about to send to destroy the earth and all inhabitants except Noah and the animals he selected. Row 4c shows that I did not find any verses in Genesis which portray God as demanding violence by anyone against any human beings. Rows 4d and 5 show that I did not find any verses in which God or any person explicitly repudiated or rejected violence.

Row 6 indicates that I found one verse (Gen. 19: 24) which portrayed the Lord using brimstone and fire "out of heaven" to destroy Sodom and Gomorrah. Row 7 registers one verse (Gen. 14: 8) that refers to a military battle in which Jewish and non-Jewish military forces battled against each other. Apparently, violence occurred during the battle. It included the killing of the kings of Sodom and Gomorrah (Gen. 14: 10).

An Interpretation: Let me suggest that the findings summarized in Table 8 do *not* support the conclusion that Genesis is a violent book—at least not in terms of having very many verses that portray physical violence against human beings. Only twenty-two (1.4%) of its 1,533 verses portray this kind of violence. These twenty-two verses refer to only nine events in which the violent act occurred or was predicted to occur. Genesis refers to and describes hundreds of events that involve dozens of different tribes and countless people over a period of thousands of years. It seems rather remarkable, to me at least, that only nine events were explicitly violent. Furthermore, only one military battle is portrayed in Genesis—the "Battle of the Kings." It involved a number of kings, including the King of Chedorlaomer. Genesis 4: 17 refers to it as the "slaughter of Chedorlaomer." So, in sum, Genesis is not a very violent book, although some of its verses portray violence in some famous Biblical events including God's flooding of the earth, Cain killing his brother Abel, and God's destruction of Sodom and Gomorrah,

In conclusion, it seems to me that Genesis is aptly named. Essentially it is an account—a story—about the beginning and the emergence of the cosmos, the earth, livings things, and some clans, tribes and their interactions in the Middle East until close to the end of Moses' life, about 3,400 years ago.[6] The account certainly describes hundreds of events, many conflicts, problems, births, deaths, and other human encounters. Relatively few of these events entail physical violence or wars.

Of course, other books in the OT can be considerably more violent and bellicose than Genesis. With that in mind, let us now turn to a highly influential book that has a reputation for being quite violent: Moses' fifth and final book—Deuteronomy (Deut.).

DEUTERONOMY: THE FIFTH BOOK OF MOSES

Some Background

According to the KJV, Deuteronomy's importance transcends its 959 verses in its thirty-four chapters.[7]

> Deuteronomy is one of the most significant books in the Old Testament. Judging from the number of quotations or citations of Deuteronomy in the New Testament, its influence has been extremely great.... Deuteronomy is also a treasure chest of theological concepts that have influenced the religious thought and life of ancient Israel, Jews, and Christians down through the ages.

As to its historical setting, the KJV states:

For thirty-eight years after they had refused to enter Canaan, the Israelites remained in the wilderness of Parann and at Kadesh-barnea, until the old generation died off. They resumed their journey by a long detour around Edom. Finally, they were encamped at Moab, awaiting final instructions to go over and possess the land God had promised to their fathers. It was a most exciting and momentous occasion. According to the Book of Deuteronomy, Moses took this occasion to deliver three addresses to the people of Israel, all of them farewell addresses, because he had been told that he could not enter the land with the people. The substance of the addresses is found in Deuteronomy.

While it might be tangential to our study, we should acknowledge that there are different perspectives on the authorship of Deuteronomy, as well as of the other books of the OT and the NT. Fundamentalists generally contend that the authors are the ancient prophets and disciples whose names are attached to the books—Moses, in the case of the five books of the Pentateuch. They contend that the authors were conveying "the words of God" as those words had been conveyed to them, either directly from God or through an intermediary, such as Gabriel the archangel. Scholars who are more liberal, skeptical, and critical generally contend that all or most of the material in the holy books have been reworked over the centuries by so many different religious leaders, editors, translators, and scribes that authorship has been an uncertain, complex, and collective process.

The "Outline of Deuteronomy" in the KJV[8] indicates that the book contains a wide range of topics in addition to many portrayals of violent events and battles that Moses and the Israelites experienced. The battles include Hormah, Moab, Ammon, "the Conquest of Heshbon," and "the Conquest of Bashan." The "Outline" also highlights the Ten Commandments (including "Do not kill"), "Israel's policy of war," "The Conduct of War," and "Laws relating to murder, war, and family affairs," among other topics.

Deuteronomy includes verses that assert that God spoke directly to Moses and commanded Moses to make His (God's) decisions, actions, and commandments known to all Israelites.

> *These are the words of the covenant, which the Lord commanded Moses to make with the children of Israel. (Deut. 29:1)

Deuteronomy starts with Moses saying the Lord God tells him to take the Israelites and, with Joshua as his military aide, conquer various tribes that impede their progress as they pass on their way to the Promised Land of Judea. Many passages in Deuteronomy portray Moses instructing his people on the many rules and commandments that God spoke to him. These include rules about eating, personal sanitation, tithes, sacrificing animals to God, sexual relations and marriage, and dealing with thieves, adulterers, apostates, idolaters, and servants. Deuteronomy ends with the Lord allowing Moses to go up on a mountain and see the promised land of Judea, a land that he will not be allowed to enter before he dies.

Verses and Events that Portray Violence and War
Please keep in mind that our interest is in how a wide variety of people throughout the world—not just scholars, historians, and members of the clergy—might use, misuse, and give meaning to verses that seem to portray or refer to violence and war. For example, how might a variety of contemporary Jews, Palestinians, Muslims, Christians, and other people react if they read or hear verses in the OT which portray God as telling Israelites to occupy Canaan and many other tribal lands and destroy all their inhabitants? And how might a wide variety of people react when they read and hear verses in which God tells Moses and Israelites to kill any and all apostates and idolaters, even if they are their mothers, wives, sons, or friends?

I found that at least ninety-seven (10.1%) of Deuteronomy's 959 verses refer to or portray violence against human beings. Some of these verses refer to the same violent event or to similar violent events, such as Moses

Portrayals of Violence in the Old Testament

and his Israelites having "slain Sihom the King of the Amorites" and "Og the King of Bashan" (Deut. 1: 4). For this reason, in the following exposition, I focus on verses and events that are relatively distinct rather than those that duplicate or repeat other verses. And, as in the chapters on the Qur'an and the NT, I concentrate on the various kinds of violence that are portrayed in Deuteronomy in terms of who did what kinds of violence to whom, for what reasons, and with what consequences. Occasionally I present some additional verses in order to provide some context for understanding the verses that portray or refer to violence.

The Defeat at Hormah

A number of verses in the first chapter of Deuteronomy deal with the defeat of Israelite forces under Moses at Hormah. The verses convey that, as the Israelites prepared to go to war against the Amorites at Mount Hormah, the Lord warned Moses to call-off the attack because the Israelites would be defeated. Essentially, the Lord is portrayed as having rejected violence in this case. But Moses disobeyed this command and went ahead with the attack. It failed. The Amorites confronted the attackers, chased them, and destroyed some of them. It was a defeat for the Israelites. Deuteronomy 1: 41-44 are particularly relevant:

> *(41) Then ye answered and said unto me, We have sinned against the Lord, we will go up and fight, according to all that the Lord our God commanded us. And when ye had girded on every man his weapons of war, ye were ready to go up into the hill.
>
> (42) And the Lord said unto me, Say unto them, Go not up, neither fight; for I am not among you; lest you be smitten before your enemies.
>
> (43) So I spake unto you; and ye would not hear, but rebelled against the commandment of the Lord, and went presumptuously up into the hill.

(44) And the Amorites, which dwelt in that mountain, came out against you, and chased you, as bees do, and destroyed you in Seir, even unto Hormah.

Several other verses also indicate that the Lord instructed Moses and the Israelites to not fight against some of the tribes along the route to Jordan. For example, Deuteronomy 2: 9:

*And the Lord said unto me, Distress not the Moabites, neither contend with them in battle: for I will not give thee of their land for a possession; because I have given it unto the children of Lot for a possession.

By way of comment, notice that in the preceding verses the Lord is portrayed as not only rejecting violence in these circumstances, but he is also portrayed as giving explanations for why he is refusing to give permission to Moses to engage in battle in violence.

By way of explanation, in Table 9, Deuteronomy 1: 42 and 44 count as separate items in Row 1. Deuteronomy 1: 44 counts as an item in both Row 2 and Row 3 because the violence included both non-Jews (the Amorites) and Jews (Row 3). Deuteronomy 1: 44 counts in Row 4a as Moses (in parentheses) committing violence, and in Row 4b as God warning about violence. This verse also counts in Row 4d (rejecting violence) as well as in Row 7 and 7a—portrayals of a battle and of violence in a battle—the battle of Hormah.

Chapter 3 of Deuteronomy portrays the Lord directing Moses to conquer and destroy other tribes and occupy their lands.

*(1) Then we turned, and went up the way to Bashan: and Og the king of Bashan came out against us, he and all his people, to battle at Edrei.

(2) And the Lord said unto me, Fear him not; for I will deliver him, and all his people, and his land, into thy hand; and thou

Portrayals of Violence in the Old Testament

shalt do unto him as thou didst unto Sihom king of the Amorites, which dwelt at Heshbon.

(3) So the Lord our God delivered into our hands Og also, the king of Bashan, and all his people: and we smote him until none was left to him remaining.

(4) And we took all his cities at that time, there was not a city which we took not from them, three score cities, all the region of Argob, the kingdom of Og in Bashan....

(6) And we utterly destroyed them, as we did unto Sihom king of Heshbon, utterly destroying the men, women, and children, of every city. (Deut. 3: 1-4, and 6)

A side note: In stark contrast to verses of violent destruction of entire tribes and their residences, Deuteronomy also has verses that demand that Moses and the Israelites create "three cities of refuge" to protect Israelites who slay their neighbors unintentionally and without malice. These verses are not registered in Table 9, however, because they do not portray actual violence or warfare.

*Then Moses severed three cities on this side of the Jordan toward the sun rising;

That the slayer might flee, thither, which should kill his neighbor unawares, and hated him not in times past; and that, fleeing unto one of these cities he might live. (Deut. 4: 41-42)

Chapter 19 also has a set of verses (Deut. 19: 3-7) that more or less repeat this command from the Lord (as well as from Moses, perhaps) that three cities of refuge should be created for followers who unintentionally slay their neighbors without malice. However, there also are two verses (Deut. 19: 11-12) that very explicitly command some followers to arrange the avenge-killing of anyone who slays a neighbor intentionally.

112 VIOLENCE, TERROR, GENOCIDE, AND WAR

> *But if any man hate his neighbor, and lie in wait for him, and rise up against him, and smite him mortally that he die, and flee into one of these cities:
>
> Then the elders of his city shall send and fetch him thence, and deliver him into the hand of the avenger of blood, that he may die. (Deut. 19: 11-12)

By way of comment, it seems as though these verses are not restricted to Israelites either as the killers or as "neighbors" who become their victims. Are these verses relevant to people living today, particularly to Israelis whose neighbors are not Israelis?

*"Thou shalt not kill." This is Deuteronomy 5: 17. It is the seventeenth of twenty-one (not just ten) commandments in this part of Deuteronomy. It is portrayed as Moses instructing the Israelites according to what God directly told him (Deut. 5: 2): *"The Lord our God made a covenant with us in Horeb." By the way, it is registered in Table 9 as one of God's rejections of physical violence.

Instructions as the Israelites Prepare to Enter "The Promised Land"

Chapter 7 has more than a dozen verses that refer to or portray violence. Some of these portray God as committing violence. Others portray God as threatening violence. Some portray God as demanding violence by Moses and the Israelites. At least one set of verses (Deut. 7: 23-24) actually combines all three of these aspects of violence: God threatens it, commits it, and demands that Moses and his followers commit violence, as well. Please notice that some of these verses are rather timeless and universal in that they are not obviously limited to a particular time or place.

> *But the Lord thy God shall deliver them unto thee, and shall destroy them with a mighty destruction, until they be destroyed.

Portrayals of Violence in the Old Testament

> And he shall deliver their kings into thine hand, and thou shall destroy their name from under heaven: there shall no man be able to stand before thee, until thou have destroyed them. (Deut. 7: 23-24)

By way of comment, Verses 23-24 might be unique in how they portray violence in three ways: God threatens violence, claims he commits violence and also demands violence from his followers. This might be unprecedented in any of the holy books of the other religions, although I cannot assert this with certainty.

> *When the Lord thy God shall bring thee into the land whither thou goest to possess it, and hath cast out many nations before thee, the Kittites, and the Girgashites, and the Amorites, and the Canaanites, and the Perissites, and the Hivites, and the Jebusites, seven nations greater and mightier than thou:
>
> And when the Lord thy God shall deliver them before thee; thou shalt smite them, and utterly destroy them, thou shalt make no covenant with them, nor show mercy unto them. (Deut. 7: 1-2)

By the way, following these verses in which God instructs Moses and the Israelites to destroy many other nations, there is a verse which portrays God as threatening to destroy any Israelites who might be tempted to "turn away" from God towards "other gods."

> *For they will turn away thy son from following me, that they may serve other gods: so will the anger of the Lord be kindled against you, and destroy thee suddenly.
>
> But thus shall ye deal with them; ye shall destroy their altars, and break down their images, and cut down their groves, and burn their graven images with fire. (Deut. 7: 4-5)

Deuteronomy 7: 6 is one of many verses in the OT in which God is portrayed as assuring the Israelites that they are a "chosen people." It also seems to provide a reason for this—namely that they are "holy" and "special":

> *For thou are a holy people unto the Lord thy God: the Lord they God hath chosen thee to be a special people that are upon the face of the earth.

Subsequent verses in Chapter 7 quickly return to more references to violence. Deuteronomy 7: 10 seems to portray God as instructing Israelites to destroy anyone who hates Him and that He will have no mercy towards those who hate Him:

> *And repayeth them that hate him to their face, to destroy them: he will not be slack to him that hateth him, he will repay him to his face.

Could it be that this verse, and others like it, are understood by some people in contemporary times to assert that God is demanding that they kill anyone who they believe hates God and that God is joining them in killing those who supposedly hate Him?

Also worth contemplating is whether verses including this one in the OT are similar to, yet distinct from, verses in the Qur'an in which Allah commands his followers to slay certain kinds of people, such as idolaters. However, as shown in an earlier chapter in this book, in the Qur'an, Allah assures his followers that it actually is him—Allah—who is doing the slaying when his followers slay others according to Allah's commands. If so, then can it be said that the Qur'an's passages absolve the human slayers of their violent actions, whereas the OT only conveys that God is joining with them in the act of violence?

Now here is another very noteworthy verse in Deuteronomy regarding violence. Notice that the writer (presumably Moses) mentions that the Lord has destroyed nations, then the writer warns his readers that they too will perish if they are not obedient to the Lord:

*As the nations which the Lord destroyeth before your face, so shall ye perish; because ye would not be obedient unto the voice of the Lord your God. (Deut. 8: 20)

BOTH THE LORD AND THE ISRAELITES DESTROY SPECIFIC "NATIONS" IN CANAAN

Quite a few verses in Deuteronomy portray violence against the Egyptians who had exploited Moses and the Israelites, the nations along the route to Canaan, and then the nations that occupied Canaan as the Israelites tried to enter there. One of these occupants was the Anakim tribe.

> *(1) Hear, O Israel: Thou art to pass over Jordan this day, to go in to possess nations greater and mightier than thyself, cities great and fenced up to heaven,
>
> (2) A people great and tall, the children of the Anakim, whom thou knowest, and of whom thou hast heard say, Who can stand before the children of Anak!
>
> (3) Understand there for this day, that the Lord thy God is he which goeth over before thee; as a consuming fire he shall destroy them, and he shall bring them down before thy face: so shalt thou drive them out, and destroy them quickly, as the Lord hath said unto thee. (Deut. 9: 1-3)

Comment: In this verse, it seems that the author is asserting that God first threatens to damage the Anakim, but then the Israelites also are commanded to destroy them.

Verses in Chapter 12 also seem to call upon Moses and the Israelites to destroy all the nations and tribe nations in Canaan, perhaps constituting genocide:

> *(2) Ye shall utterly destroy all the places, wherein the nations which ye shall possess served their gods, upon the high mountains, and upon the hills, and under every green tree:
>
> (3) And ye shall overthrow their altars, and break their pillars, and burn their groves with fire; and ye shall hew down the graven images of their gods, and destroy the names of them out of that place. (Deut. 12: 2-3)

Moses Claims He Restrained God from Violence against the Israelites

A number of verses in Deuteronomy seem to portray Moses claiming that, at times, he restrained a wrathful God from violent actions against the Israelites because of sins and disobedience on their part.

> *For I was afraid of the anger and hot displeasure wherewith the Lord was wroth against you to destroy you. But the Lord hearkened unto me at that time also. (Deut. 9: 19)
>
> *I prayed therefore unto the Lord, and said, O Lord God, destroy not thy people and thine inheritance, which thou hast redeemed through thy greatness, which thou hast brought forth out of Egypt with a mighty hand. (Deut. 9: 26)

By the way, I registered these verses as attempted "rejections of violence" by Moses in Row 4d of Table 9.

Some Commands for Violence against Idolaters and Apostates

Deuteronomy includes some very explicit verses in which the Lord (possibly along with Moses in the same verse) commands Israelites to commit lethal violence against anyone—including their own mothers, close kin, and friends— who tempts them to worship other gods. Some of

Portrayals of Violence in the Old Testament

these verses actually specify procedures that should be used in order to determine if entire cities of idolaters and apostates should be destroyed.

> *(6) If thy brother, the son of thy mother, or thy son, or thy daughter, or the wife of thy bosom, or thy friend, which is as thine own soul, entice thee secretly, saying Let us go and serve other gods, which thou hast not known, thou, nor thy fathers;
>
> (7) Namely, of the gods of the people which are round about you, nigh unto thee, or far off from thee, from the one end of the earth even unto the other end of the earth;
>
> (8) Thou shalt not consent unto him, nor hear unto him; neither shall thine eye pity him, neither shalt thou spare, neither shalt thou conceal him:
>
> (9) But thou shalt surely kill him; thine hand shall be first upon him to put him to death, and afterward the hand of all the people.
>
> (10) And thou shall stone him with stones that he die; because he hath sought to thrust thee away from the Lord thy God, which brought thee out of the land of Egypt, from the house of bondage.
>
> (11) And all Israel shall hear, and fear, and shall do no more any such wickedness as this is among you. (Deut. 13: 6-11)

By the way, Deuteronomy 13: 12-16, which immediately follows these verses, provide explicit instructions on how Israelites are to determine whether inhabitants of certain cities are idolatrous and, if so, how they should be destroyed. Deuteronomy 13: 15-16 are the two verses that demand violence and destruction.

> *(15) Thou shalt surely smite the inhabitants of that city with the edge of the sword, destroying it utterly, and all that is therein, and the cattle thereof, with the edge of the sword.
>
> (16) And thou shalt gather all the spoil of it into the midst of the street thereof, and shalt burn with fire the city, and all the spoil

thereof every whit, for the Lord thy God: and it shall be a heap for ever; it shall not be built again.

By way of comment, these verses, and other verses like these in Deuteronomy and in other books of the OT, often are quoted directly by religious scholars, including Philip Jenkins,[9] as evidence of commands to commit what essentially constitutes genocide. Notice also that these verses command followers to kill not just the human inhabitants of the cities but also the cattle. Verse 16 even specifies that the destruction should be so thorough that the city *"shall not be built again."

By the way, near the end of this chapter, we present definitions of genocide and we consider how genocide is portrayed in the OT.

"Laws Concerning War"

Chapter 20 of Deuteronomy is titled "Laws Concerning War" in the KJV. The title is very appropriate in that most of the twenty short verses in this very short chapter do exactly that. The words "war" and "battle" are mentioned at least six times in this chapter. Six of the twenty verses are very explicit in how Israelites should commit violence against their enemies in battle. I will only present the most distinctive verses about these matters. It is worth noting that this chapter repeats some of the themes of earlier chapters, but it also adds some nuances regarding violence. Also noteworthy is that quite a few of the verses are similar to verses in the Qur'an regarding preparations for war, exemptions from battle for certain kinds of men, and how to engage the enemy.

As an aside, I can't help but wonder whether these OT verses somehow diffused across many different cultures to the Quraysh and other tribes in Arabia over a period of hundreds of years in such a way that they inspired similar verses in the Qur'an.

The first eight verses tell Israelites how to prepare for battle. Deuteronomy 20: 4 assures the Israelites that God will go with them into

Portrayals of Violence in the Old Testament

battle, and save them: *"For the Lord your God is he that goeth with you, to fight for you against your enemies, to save you." (Deut. 20: 4)

Other verses exempt from battle any men who are recently "betrothed" but have not consummated their marriage, so to speak, as well as men who have just planted new vineyards, and men who are "fearful and fainthearted" (as in Verse 8, for example).

Several verses instruct followers to offer a peace of sorts to their enemies before they are attacked, so long as the enemy will also submit to the Israelites and allow their lands to be inhabited. This is another verse about war that is similar to verses in the Qur'an, as indicated in earlier chapters.

> *(10) When thou comest nigh unto a city to fight against it, then proclaim peace unto it.
>
> (11) And it shall be, if it make thee answer of peace, and open unto thee, then it shall be, that all the people that is found therein shall be tributaries unto thee, and they shall serve thee.
>
> (12) And if it will make no peace with thee, but will make war against thee, then thou shalt besiege it:
>
> (13) And when the Lord thy God hath delivered it into thine hands, thou shalt smite every male thereof with the edge of the sword:
>
> (14) But the women, and the little ones, and the cattle, and all that is in the city, even all the spoil thereof, shalt thou take unto thyself; and thou shall eat the spoil of thine enemies, which the Lord thy God hath given thee. (Deut. 20: 10-14)

By way of another comment, it seems to me that the preceding verses are rather timeless and universal in that they do not explicitly restrict the commands to a particular time, place, religion, or political context. It also seems to me that these verses are quite similar to verses in the Qur'an that are presented in an earlier chapter of this book.

The verses that immediately follow Deuteronomy 20: 10-14 provide an exception as well as a commandment to destroy everything, with specific reference to a number of specific tribes. Verse 18 also provides a reason for destruction to be so total—perhaps even constituting genocide. The reason given is that these other tribes supposedly commit "abominations."

*(15) Thus shalt thou do unto all the cities which are very far off from thee, which are not of the cities of these nations.

(16) But of the cities of these people, which the Lord thy God doth give thee for an inheritance, thou shalt save alive nothing that breatheth:

(17) But thou shalt utterly destroy them; namely, the Hittites, and the Amorites, the Canaanites, and the Perissites, the Hivites and the Jebusites; as the Lord thy God hath commanded thee.

(18) That they teach you not to do after all their abominations, which they have done unto their gods; so should ye sin against the Lord your God. (Deut. 20: 15-18)

Note: As in quite a few other verses throughout Deuteronomy and the OT, there also are verses in Chapter 20 (including Deut. 20: 19-20) that command followers to destroy certain kinds of trees, while sparing other kinds of trees and animals on the lands of the people whom the Israelites have conquered. By the way, these verses are not registered in Table 9 because our focus is on physical violence against *human beings*.

Chapter 21 on Executions of Men Who Have Sinned, on Violent Treatment of "Rebellious Sons," And on Capturing and Mating with Beautiful Women

Chapter 21 generally deals with rules for operating Israelite households and domestic relations. However, there are three sets of verses in the chapter that are noteworthy regarding physical violence. One set of verses commands followers on how to deal with "stubborn and rebellious" sons— specifically with lethal punishment.

> *(18) If a man have a stubborn and rebellious son, which will not obey the voice of his father, or the voice of his mother, and that when they have chastened him, will not hearken unto them:
>
> (19) Then shall his father and his mother lay hold on him, and bring him out unto the elders of his city, and unto the gate of his place;
>
> (20) And they shall say unto the elders of his city, This our son is stubborn and rebellious, he will not obey our voice; he is a glutton, and a drunkard.
>
> (21) And all the men of his city shall stone him with stones, that he die: so shalt thou put evil away from among you; and all Israel shall hear, and fear. (Deut. 21: 18-21)

The very next verse rather abruptly instructs followers on how to execute "a man" who has "committed a sin worthy of death"—namely by hanging him on a tree: *"And if a man have committed a sin worthy of death, and he be put to death, and thou hang him on a tree," (Deut. 21: 22).

Another set of verses in Chapter 21 instructs male followers on how to deal with captives in war who are beautiful women. Whether the procedures constitute physical violence might be debated, given the differences between social norms of that time and contemporary social norms.

Note: I have not registered these verses in Table 9 mainly because the captives are allowed to survive, and it is not obvious that they are to be subjected to sexual assault against their will, even though that could be the case.

> *(10) When thou goest forth to war against thine enemies, and the Lord thy God hath delivered them into thine hands, and thou hast taken them captive,

> (11) And seest among the captives a beautiful woman, and hast a desire unto her, that thou wouldest have her to thy wife;
>
> (12) Then thou shalt bring her home to thine house; and she shall shave her head, and pare her nails... (Deut. 21: 10-12)

The subsequent verses instruct followers to allow this woman to have one month to *"bewail her mother and her father" after which "thou shalt go in unto her, and be her husband, and she shall be thy wife," (Deut. 21: 13). The next verse (Deut. 21: 14) commands followers *"if thou have no delight in her, then thou shalt let her go whither she will." However, it prohibits followers from selling her, "because thou hast humbled her."

Some Commands for Violence against Adulterers, Thieves, and Others

Chapters 22-25 have quite a few verses that demand violence against adulterers, thieves, and a variety of other miscreants. It is not obvious whether these are being commanded by God (according to Moses), by Moses, or by some other author of these verses. In Table 9, these verses are registered as being commanded by Moses, in contrast to many of the verses in earlier chapters of Deuteronomy in which the commandments were more obviously attributed to God. Also noteworthy is that some of these verses do not specify whether the violence is restricted to people of specific tribes or religious orientations. They seem to pertain to any and all miscreants, regardless of religion, ethnicity, or other social characteristics.

Taken as a set, Deuteronomy 22: 21, 22, 24, and 25 essentially command followers to kill both male and female adulterers by stoning them. Deuteronomy 22: 21 is most explicit in explaining why female adulteresses should be killed:

> *(20) But if this thing be true, and the tokens of virginity be not found for the damsel:

Portrayals of Violence in the Old Testament

(21) Then they shall bring out the damsel to the door of her father's house, and the men of her city shall stone her with stones that she die: because she hath wrought folly in Israel, to play the whore in her father's house: so shalt thou put evil away from among you.

There are many other verses of interest. Deuteronomy 24: 7 commands followers to kill thieves. Deuteronomy 24: 16 commands that *"everyman shall be put to death for his own sin" (not for the sins of others). Verses 2 and 3 in Chapter 25 command judges to allow the beating of miscreants with forty stripes:

*(2) And it shall be, if the wicked man be worthy to be beaten, that the judge shall cause him to lie down, and to be beaten before his face, according to his fault, by a certain number.

(3) Forty stripes he may give him, and not exceed: lest, if he should exceed, and beat him above these with many stripes, then thy brother should seem vile unto thee.

Deuteronomy 25: 11 (for context) and 12 command followers to cut off the hands of women who commit a specific offense:

*(11) When men strive together one with another, and the wife of the one draweth near for to deliver her husband out of the hand of him that smiteth him, and puteth forth her hand, and taketh him by the secrets:

(12) Then thou shalt cut off her hand, thine eye shall not pity her.

By the way, Chapter 26 of Deuteronomy is quite remarkable in that there are no verses that clearly refer to or portray violence against humans. This is another reason why it is invalid to claim that violence pervades all of Deuteronomy (or of any other book in the OT, for that matter).

Two Prohibitions against Certain Kinds of Violence

Chapter 27 conveys more than a dozen "curses." Among them are two verses that *prohibit* certain kinds of violence:

> *Cursed be he that smiteth his neighbor secretly: and all the people shall say, Amen. Cursed be he that taketh reward to slay an innocent person: and all the people shall say, Amen. (Deut. 27: 24-25)

The Final Verses of Deuteronomy

Chapter 34 concludes Deuteronomy with only twelve verses. The verses indicate that the Lord has chosen Joshua, Moses' military leader, to succeed Moses at his death. Then Verses 10-12 conclude Deuteronomy and the Pentateuch with no mention of violence but with reference to the "great terror which Moses showed in the sight of Israel."

> *(10) And there arose not a prophet since in Israel like unto Moses, whom the Lord knew face to face.
>
> (11) In all the signs and the wonders, which the Lord sent him to do in the land of Egypt to Pharaoh, and to all his servants, and to all his land.
>
> (12) And in all that, mighty hand, and in all the great *terror* which Moses showed in the sight of all Israel. (Deut. 34: 10-12)

Comment: It is not clear to me that the word "terror," as it is used here, is intended to refer to physical violence. But, as mentioned so many times in this book, our interest is in how a variety of contemporary people, including actual and potential terrorists, might react to verses and words such as these in the English language version of the OT. Do some of these people assume that the word "terror" means to engage in violent terrorist activities such as car-bombings, suicide killings, and other acts of mayhem?

So, in sum, how much and what kinds of violence and warfare are portrayed in Deuteronomy? Table 9 summarizes my findings on this question.

Table 9. Violence and War as Portrayed or Referred to in Deuteronomy.

1	Number of verses that portray or refer to violence against humans	97
2	Violence by non-Israelites (when apparent)	5
3	Violence by Israelites (when apparent)	21
4	GOD (or Moses) portrayed or referred to as GOD (Moses):	
	a. Committing of having committed violence	11 (9)
	b. Threatening, promising, or warning about violence	36 (3)
	c. Demanding violence by others	25 (11)
	d. Rejecting or repudiating violence	6* (4*)
5	Repudiations by others of violence	0
6	Portrayals or references to doom, fire, and hellfire as violence	2
7	Portrayals or reference to military wars or battles	18
	a. Portrayals or references to violence in wars or battles	4

Note: As explained in the text below, in two of the verses the rejections of violence seem to be by God along with Moses. Four other rejections are by God alone. Two of Moses' rejections are by him alone.

An Explanation of Table 9

As shown in Row 1 of Table 9, I found that 97 (10.1%) of Deuteronomy's 959 verses refer to or portray physical violence against human beings. This is considerably higher than the comparable percentage I reported in the previous section of this chapter regarding the book of Genesis (1.4%). It is much higher than the percentage I report in the next chapter regarding the NT, taken as a whole (1.84%). It is somewhat lower than the percentage I report for the Qur'an (11.9%), as presented in an earlier chapter of this book. Whether these are significant differences is worth discussing objectively and in some detail. This will be done in the concluding chapter of this book. Then again, *qualitative* differences in portrayals of violence in the "holy books" could be much more important than *quantitative* differences.

Who commits the violence, whenever this is apparent, in these verses? Row 2 indicates that non-Israelite people (including the Egyptians under the Pharaoh) were portrayed in five verses as committing violence. Israelite people are portrayed in twenty-one of the verses as having committed violence.

Comment: It is worth noting that Israelites are portrayed this way four times as frequently as non-Israelites. In almost all of these verses, the Israelites are the aggressors, almost always as demanded by God, by Moses, or by both of them (as suggested by the entries of "25" and "(11)" in Row 4c).

Row 4 indicates the number of verses in which God and Moses are portrayed or referred to as committing or having committed violence. Once again it should be emphasized that it is not always easy to determine if it is God alone, or Moses in concert with God, who is committing the violence. Notice that both God (11 verses) and Moses (9 verses) are portrayed as committing violence. Row 4b indicates that God is portrayed in thirty-six of the verses as predicting, threatening, promising, or warning about violence. This is much more frequent than for portrayals of Moses (N = 3). Row 4c shows that God also is portrayed rather often (in twenty-five of the verses) as demanding violence by others. By the way, the "others" are Moses and his followers. Moses himself is portrayed as demanding violence in eleven of the verses although, once again, it is not always clear whether Moses alone is demanding violence or whether he is relaying God's demands to his followers.

Rows 4d and 5 indicate that I found very few rejections or repudiations of violence in Deuteronomy. One of these rejections is the famous commandment "Thou Shalt Not Kill." Six of the verses had rejections of violence by God, possibly in concert with Moses in two of the verses (this is the reason for the asterisks in Row 4d). There were no verses in Deuteronomy in which anyone but God or Moses rejects violence.

Row 6 indicates that only two verses portrayed doom, fire, and hellfire as violence in the future—on Judgment Day. This is in stark contrast to the Qur'an, as presented in an earlier chapter of this book. In the Qur'an, Allah is portrayed in at least ninety of the verses as promising doom, fire, or hellfire in the future.

Finally, Rows 7 and 7a indicate that eighteen verses in Deuteronomy portray or refer to battles or wars, but that violence is portrayed explicitly in only four of those verses.

An Interpretation: My interpretation of the data in Table 9 is that Deuteronomy is by no means a violent book or a book about battles or war, taken quantitatively. And yet the relatively few verses that portray violence and war certainly are worth recognizing and contemplating. Relatively few verses portray God as predicting, threatening, promising, or warning about violence (thirty-six verses), demanding violence by Moses and his followers (twenty-five verses), and committing violence (eleven verses).

Perhaps we could expect Deuteronomy to contain a lot more verses that portray violence and war. After all, it contains many verses about how Moses and the Israelites endured captivity in Egypt under the Pharaoh, how they escaped from captivity, how they spent many years confronting the many pagan and polytheistic tribes and clans that inhabited the lands between Egypt and Canaan, and how they destroyed or displaced those opponents.

Now let us consider the other books of the OT. Are violence and war portrayed very differently in those books than in Genesis and Deuteronomy?

Violence in the Other Books of the Old Testament

Are violence and war portrayed far more often and in significantly different ways in the other books of the OT? Generally speaking, and taken in their entirety, I have *not* found this to be the case based on the methods of analysis that I have been using throughout this book. And yet, some of the books, including Ruth, Song of Solomon, and Jonah have little or no violence. On the other hand, some of the other books, including the books of Judges, Jeremiah, Ezekiel, Amos, Obadiah, Nahum, Zephaniah, and Zechariah are rather astounding both in the frequency and characteristics of the violence portrayed in them. What follows is a compact analysis of what I found in the other books of the OT. This analysis follows the sequence of these books in the KJV and the usual classification scheme of the Pentateuch, the Historical Books, the Poetical Books, the Major Prophets, and the Minor Prophets. By the way, double plus signs (++) indicate which books portray violence and war about as frequently as Deuteronomy, if not more so. A single plus sign (+) indicates that a book portrays violence and war, but somewhat less frequently than Deuteronomy. The absence of a plus sign means that violence and war are absent or are portrayed rarely in a particular book.

Please consider that the *kinds* and *qualities* of the violence portrayed are no less important than the quantities of violence, if not far more important. This is why so much attention is given in the pages ahead to the kinds and qualities of violence. Who is threatening or committing what kinds of violence against whom, for what reasons, and with what consequences? Is the violence portrayed in the past tense, the present tense, or in the future? Do the targets of the violence still exist, as might be the case with places including Ammon, Damascus, Gaza, Persia, Judea, Jerusalem, and Jericho?

Are some forms of violence — such as slaying — demanded against anyone who angers or disobeys God's commandments, regardless of their ethnicity or religious orientation?

Portrayals of Violence in the Old Testament

When wars occur, who are the aggressors, the defenders, the winners, the losers, and the victims? These are some of the questions that are responded to in the pages that follow through examples of dozens of verses from the OT.

The Books of the Pentateuch ("The Five Books of Moses")

Besides Genesis (Gen.) and Deuteronomy (Deut.), the other three books of the Pentateuch are Exodus (Ex.), Leviticus (Lev.), and Numbers (Num.).

+Exodus (Ex.): As indicated in its title, Exodus refers to the way Moses and the Hebrews escaped from Egypt, its Pharaoh, and military forces after centuries of bondage and persecution. However, its rather long forty chapters and 1,213 verses cover a wide range of other topics. Exodus also describes the many years of bondage suffered by the Hebrews in Egypt after what had been a period of relative prosperity they experienced there under earlier regimes. It describes Moses' life, his special relationship to God, and his growth as a leader of the Hebrews. It conveys God's many efforts to force the Pharaoh to liberate the Hebrews. These efforts include the ten "plagues" (including blood, lice, boils, and the deaths of first-born male children) that God brought down upon the Egyptians. Exodus also describes the eventual escape of the Hebrews from Egypt, their miraculous crossing of the Red Sea thanks to God's parting of the waters for them and the subsequent drowning of the pursuing Egyptian army. Many verses in Exodus describe how Moses and the Hebrews settled into Sinai and how Moses received the covenant and commandments from God on Mt. Sinai, as well as the details of laws for every aspect of Hebrew daily life. There also is a description of a victorious war against the Amaleks. Many of these events also are referred to in the books of the OT that follow Exodus. This probably indicates the enormous influence that Exodus had on the prophets and people who succeeded Moses. According to the KJV,[10]

> Exodus relates the story of freedom for God's people from slavery and the beginning of national identity. The book is strategically

important to both Old Testament history and a proper understanding of Hebrew customs and institutions. It is a vital connecting link between the age of the patriarchs (Abraham, Isaac, Jacob, and Joseph) and the remaining books of the Law.... Moses was born about 1527 B.C. during the reign of Amenhotep I (1545-1525 B.C.) and fled into exile about 1487 B.C.... Based upon two key scriptural witnesses, the Exodus took place in approximately 1447 B.C.

Note: The dates, names, and details presented here are the ones in the KJV of the "Protestant" Bible that is fully identified in the Bibliography. As mentioned earlier in this chapter, some of the dates, names, verse numbers, and some other details are slightly different in other versions of the "Protestant" and "Catholic" Bibles, and in various versions of the Jewish holy books. I have not found these differences to be significant regarding how often and in what ways violence, terror, and warfare are portrayed in these books of the OT.

Exodus conveys some very original and distinctive qualities of violence and war, although, quantitatively, only about five percent (N = 58) of its 1,213 verses portray physical violence against humans. A strong case can be made that some of these portrayals of violence in Exodus served as models for portrayals of violence and war in many of the later books of the OT. What follows are some of the most important examples of violence in Exodus.

The first portrayal of violence in Exodus refers to an anti-Semitic decree of the new Pharaoh of Egypt:

> *And Pharaoh charged all his people saying, Every son that is born ye shall cast into the river, and every daughter ye shall save alive. (Ex. 1: 22)

Chapter 2 of Exodus provides verses that are well-known beyond Judaism and Christianity about how newborn baby Moses was secretly saved from drowning by the Pharaoh's daughter. The daughter's maidens discovered the baby in a basket hidden in bull rushes along the river's edge. The Pharaoh's daughter was so charmed by the baby Moses that

Portrayals of Violence in the Old Testament 131

she arranged for him to be nursed and protected until he was a young man. Other verses in Chapter 2 tell us about key events of violence when Moses had grown into a young man. Very candidly, the verses disclose that Moses slayed an Egyptian (and "hid him in the sand") who he observed "smiting a Hebrew." In effect, Moses avenged the slaying of a Hebrew by slaying the Egyptian who slayed him. Moses then escaped and went into exile outside Egypt in order to avoid likely recriminations against him by the Egyptians.

> *(11) And it came to pass in those days, when Moses was grown, that he went out unto his brethren, and looked on their burdens; and he spied an Egyptian smiting a Hebrew, one of his brethren.
>
> (12) And he looked this way and that way, and when he saw that there was no man, he slew the Egyptian, and hid him in the sand.
>
> (13) And when he went out the second day, behold, two men of the Hebrews strove together: and he said to him that did the wrong, Wherefore smites this fellow?
>
> (14) And he said, Who made thee a prince and a judge over us? Intendest thou to kill me, as thou killedst the Egyptian? And Moses feared, and said, Surely this thing is known.
>
> (15) Now when Pharaoh heard this thing, he sought to slay Moses. But Moses fled from the face of Pharaoh, and dwelt in the land of Midian.... (Ex. 2:11-15)

Chapter 3 of Exodus tells us how God eventually commissions Moses to return to Egypt and to lead the Israelites out of bondage, aided by rather violent miracles that God will wreak upon the Egyptians.

> *...and I will stretch out my hand, and smite Egypt with all my wonders which I will do in the midst thereof; and after that he will let you go. (Ex. 3: 20)

Chapters 7-12 include verses describing how God brought down ten "plagues" of various sorts against the Egyptians in order to force the

Pharaoh to allow Moses and the Hebrews to escape from bondage. The tenth and final plague is especially gruesome and effective in bringing about the freedom of Moses and the Hebrews.

> *(29) And it came to pass, that at midnight the Lord smote all the first-born in the land of Egypt, from the first-born of Pharaoh that sat on his throne unto the first-born of the captive that was in the dungeon; and all the first-born of cattle.
>
> (30) And Pharaoh rose up in the night, he, and all his servants, and all the Egyptians; and there was a great cry in Egypt; for there was not a house where there was not one dead.
>
> (31) And he called for Moses and Aaron by night, and said, Rise up, and get you forth from among my people, both ye and the children of Israel; and go, serve the Lord, as ye have said. (Ex. 12: 29-31)

Chapter 14 provides the famous verses that describe how the Lord parted the waters of the Red Sea long enough for Moses and the Hebrews to escape the Egyptian military forces that were pursuing them but would be destroyed when the Lord drowned them.

> *(27) And Moses stretched forth his hand over the sea, and the sea returned to his strength when the morning appeared; and the Egyptians fled against it; and the Lord overthrew the Egyptians in the midst of the sea.
>
> (28) And the waters returned and covered the chariots, and the horsemen, and all the host of Pharaoh that came into the sea after them, there remained not so much as one of them. (Ex. 14: 27-28)

Chapter 20 has seventeen verses about the commandments that God issued to Moses for the Hebrews. One of the verses (Verse 13) simply states "Thou shalt not kill," just as it appears in Deuteronomy and in quite a few other books of the OT.

Portrayals of Violence in the Old Testament

Laws Concerning Acts of Violence

One of the most relevant parts of Exodus is in Chapter 21 and is referred to in the KJV as "laws concerning acts of violence." Ten of the verses between Verses 12-25 require the death of those who commit various acts of violence, including an act so seemingly simple as a child cursing his father or mother. Verses 23-25 expound on the famous Biblical verses of reciprocity in kind for violence by others. Here is a sample of some of these verses:

> *He that smiteth a man, so that he die, shall by surely put to death. (Ex. 21: 12)
>
> *And he that curseth his father, or his mother, shall surely be put to death. (Ex. 21: 17)
>
> *(23) And if any mischief follow, then thou shalt give life for life,
>
> (24) Eye for eye, tooth for tooth, hand for hand, foot for foot,
>
> (25) Burning for burning, wound for wound, stripe for stripe. (Ex. 21: 23-25)

By way of comment, notice that these verses are eternal and universal. They are not limited to Hebrews or to people of any other religious orientation. It is also important to know that verses like these are found in several of the other books of the OT.

Also, as in many other books of the OT, Exodus has verses which portray Moses claiming that God demanded that his followers put idolaters to death, even as many as three thousand in one day.

> *(27) And he said unto them, Thus saith the Lord God of Israel, Put every man his sword by his side, and go in and out from gate to gate throughout the camp, and slay every man his brother, and every man his companion, and every man his neighbor.

(28) And the children of Levi did according to the word of Moses: and there fell of the people that day about three thousand men. (Ex. 32: 27-28)

+Leviticus (Lev.): Leviticus has hundreds of verses that convey God's laws for the daily life of Hebrews, according to Moses. These include laws for offering blood sacrifices of animals, purification rituals for bodily discharges, treatments for leprosy and plague, and standards of morality and immorality. References to physical violence occur in the sections on penalties for acts of immorality, punishments for blaspheming, and punishments for disobedience. Often these penalties and punishments require the death of the miscreant even for actions that are not violent in themselves. Here are some examples:

> *(8) And ye shall keep my statutes, and do them: I am the Lord which sanctify you.
>
> (9) For every one that curseth his father or his mother shall be surely put to death: he hath cursed his father or his mother; his blood shall be upon him.
>
> (10) And the man that, committeth adultery with another man's wife, even he that committeth adultery with his neighbor's wife, the adulterer and the adulteress shall surely be put to death. (Lev. 20: 8-10)

By way of comment, it should be noted that, according to Moses, God requires the death of anyone who curses his own mother or father. Surely this constitutes summary violence—death— for a behavior that is not in itself physically violent.

Other verses portray God demanding the deaths of anyone who engages in homosexuality (Lev. 20: 13), sexual relations with animals (Lev. 20: 15-16), or blasphemy (Lev. 20: 16).

Penalties for almost any type of disobedience often include physical violence from the Lord.

Portrayals of Violence in the Old Testament

*(14) But if ye will not hearken unto me, and will not do all these commandments;

(15) And if ye shall despise my statutes, or if your soul abhor my judgments, so that ye will not do all my commandments, but that ye break my covenant:

(16) I also will do this unto you; I will even appoint over you terror, consumption, and the burning ague, that shall consume the eyes, and cause sorrow of heart: and ye shall sow your seed in vain, for your enemies shall eat it.

(17) And I will set my face against you, and ye shall be slain before your enemies: they that hate you shall reign over you; and ye shall flee when none pursueth you. (Lev. 26: 14-17)

By the way, notice the verb "terror" in Verse 16, and that Verse 17 contends that anyone who disobeys the Lord will be slain and humiliated in front of his enemies.

+Numbers (Num.): Like Deuteronomy and many of the other books in the OT, Numbers has an abundance of verses that convey laws for the daily life of Hebrews, especially for the performance of religious rituals. There also are dozens of verses that portray violence and war. Verses portray the battle at Hormah, the defeat of the Amorites, war and destruction of Midian, the dividing of spoils of war, and the expulsion or destruction of many tribes from their homelands by God, Moses, and their followers.

Chapter 14 has verses in which God requires violence, including death for Israelites who are guilty of idolatry. Chapter 15 Verse 11 requires the stoning of those who do not observe the Sabbath. Chapter 21 describes how the Canaanites under King Arad fought against the Israelites who were moving towards them. The Canaanites take some of the Israelites as prisoners. The Israelites then plead with God to come to their aid.

136   Violence, Terror, Genocide, and War

> *(2) And Israel vowed a vow unto the Lord, and said, If thou wilt indeed deliver this people into my hand, then I will utterly destroy their cities.
>
> (3) And the Lord hearkened to the voice of Israel, and delivered up the Canaanites; and they utterly destroyed them and their cities; and he called the name of the place Hormah. (Num. 21: 2-3)

Numbers also has verses that present "laws concerning murder.[11]" As in similar verses about violence in Exodus, the laws generally demand violence in kind for violent acts, and they are not limited to Hebrews or to people of any religious orientation. Here are a few of them:

> *(18) Or if he smite him with a hand weapon or wood, wherewith he may die, and he die, he is a murderer: the murderer shall surely be put to death.
>
> (19) The revenger of blood himself shall slay the murderer: when he meeteth him, he shall slay him. (Num. 35: 18-19)

By way of comment, could it be that verses like these are still influential in interpersonal relations in the Middle East? Is it possible that they carry greater weight in the minds of some contemporary people than the modern laws of the judicial courts?

The Other Thirty-Four Books of the Old Testament

++Joshua (Josh.): This relatively short book of twenty-three chapters has many verses about the many battles that Joshua and his military forces waged as they entered Judah. They conquered many of the kings and tribes that resisted them. Verses portray the invasion of Canaan, the conquest of the southern tribes, the conquest of Jericho, the southern campaign, the northern campaign, the defeat of the Amorites, the Battle of the Waters of Meron, and the Battle of Gibeon, among other battles. In the KJV, maps graphically portray some of these battles.[12] Chapter 6 has twenty-seven verses that portray how Joshua and his forces conquered and destroyed all of Jericho, as commanded by the Lord. Here are two of the key verses:

> *And the Lord said unto Joshua, See, I have given into thine hand Jericho, and the king thereof, and the mighty men of valor. (Josh. 6: 2)
>
> *And they utterly destroyed all that was in the city, both man and woman, young and old, and ox, and sheep, and ass, with the edge of the sword. (Josh. 6: 21)

By the way, verses also convey that the only inhabitants of Jericho who were allowed to live were a harlot, Rahab, and members of her "father's household." This was allowed because Rahab had aided two spies who Joshua had sent into Jericho before the invasion.

> *And Joshua saved Rahab the harlot alive, and her father's household, and all that she had; and she dwelleth in Israel even unto this day; because she hid the messengers, which Joshua sent to spy out Jericho. (Josh. 6: 25)

By way of comment, could this verse and other verses like it continue to influence modern-day political leaders and others—Israelis as well as their opponents and others? Might some modern-day terrorists use verses such as this to try to justify their actions for or against Israelis? As a personal account, when I was in Jericho in 1992, the city was impoverished and badly damaged by warfare. The few inhabitants who remained there identified themselves as Palestinians. A walled fortress was at the edge of Jericho. It was occupied by Israeli Army forces and surrounded by barbed wire. I can't help but wonder whether verses in the OT about Jericho influenced contemporary beliefs and behaviors regarding violence and the occupancy of Jericho.

Chapter 8 of Joshua provides extraordinary details on how the Israelites under Joshua, as demanded by the Lord, planned and executed an attack on the people and the city of Ai. More than a dozen verses portray the extreme violence of the Israelites as they destroyed all of the 12,000 inhabitants. Joshua had particularly brutal violence reserved for their king.

> *(25) And so it was, that all that fell that day, both of men and women, were twelve thousand, even all the men of Ai.
>
> (26) For Joshua drew not his hand back, wherewith he stretched out the spear, until he had utterly destroyed all the inhabitants of Ai.
>
> (29) And the king of Ai, he hanged on a tree until eventide: and as soon as the sun was down, Joshua commanded that they should take his carcass down from the tree, and cast it at the entering of the gate of the city, and raise thereon a great heap of stones, that remaineth unto this day. (Josh. 8: 25-26, 29)

The last four chapters of Joshua describe how Joshua apportioned the conquered lands to various Israelite clans before he died of natural causes, supposedly at one hundred-ten years of age (Josh. 24: 29).

By way of a conclusion, the book of Joshua contains dozens of verses which portray battles and physical violence that the Israelites inflicted on the many tribes that resided in Canaan. I believe that a fair interpretation is that Joshua, in many ways, is a book of offensive military conquest, rampant destruction, and repeated genocides by Israelites against non-Israelites. These acts of violence are demanded by the God of the Israelites and they are executed by Joshua and his Israelite followers.

I found no verses that portrayed Israelites in defensive warfare. Furthermore, I found no verses that indicated that any of the non-Israelites tribes were exiled or that they were allowed to endure as captives or to convert to Judaism. So once again, I cannot help but wonder how contemporary Israelis and their opponents react to, and give meaning to, the many verses in Joshua that are extremely violent and belligerent. Do they ignore or dismiss these verses as fables or as historical anachronisms? If not, do they use these verses and others like them to justify acts of vengeance and violence now and in the future?

Portrayals of Violence in the Old Testament

++Judges (Judg.): In many ways, Judges is a sequel to Joshua both historically and in its descriptions of physical violence and warfare that involved the Israelites in the three hundred years after the death of Joshua in 1367 BCE. For context, here are some excerpts from the KJV about Judges.[13]

> The Book of Judges takes its name for the gifted leaders who guided the fortunes of Israel from the death of Joshua to the days of Samuel, Israel's last judge. These leaders were men especially raised up by God not only for their military prowess, but for their administrative abilities and spiritual discernment....
>
> The Book of Judges is an action-packed account of the failure of the children of Israel to maintain the high spiritual standards laid down by Moses and Joshua. They not only failed to conquer the land of Canaan as God had challenged them to do (Cf. 2: 1-3, 20-23) but they also fell into the idolatry and sinful practices of the Canaanites....

By the way, notice that the editorial board of the KJV interprets these verses as asserting that God challenged the Israelites to "conquer the land of Canaan." It was a command by God, according to this interpretation.

In contrast to most of the books in the OT, Judges begins with candid and rather shocking portrayals of violence and warfare:

> *(1) Now after the death of Joshua it came to pass, that the children of Israel asked the Lord saying, Who shall go up for us against the Canaanites first, to fight against them?
>
> (2) And the Lord said, Judah shall go up: behold, I have delivered the land into his hand.
>
> (5) And they found Adoni-bezek in Bezek: and they fought against him, and they slew the Canaanites and the Perissites.
>
> (6) But Adoni-bezek fled; and they pursued after him, and caught him, and cut off his thumbs and his great toes.

> (8) Now the children of Judah had fought against Jerusalem, and had taken it, and smitten it with the edge of the sword, and set the city on fire. (Judg. 1: 1, 2, 5, 6, and 8)

Judges describes in detail how the Israelites captured many parts of the hill country of Canaan but could not completely subdue, drive-out, or destroy the tribal inhabitants. It describes the "war of Ehud," the "war of Gideon," "Gideon capturing and slaying Midian's kings," and the "war of Jephthah." Also included in Judges are dozens of verses which portray other tribes of the Israelites being defeated in two violent battles against the Benjamites before they finally prevailed in the battles that totally destroyed the Benjamites and all of their cities.

Judges also is famous for its accounts of the great warrior Samson (and Delilah, among his many other conquests), the hero of the Hebrews who was known for his physical strength as well as his moral flaws.[14] Verses describe how Samson supposedly slew a thousand Philistines with *"a new jawbone of an ass," (Judg. 15: 15).

Thus, it seems fair to say that Judges might well be among the most violent and bellicose books in the OT even though only about 8.6% of its verses refer to or portray violence or war. Of course, historically speaking, Judges covers a very broad period of about three hundred years of Israelite expansion in Canaan, whereas many of the other books in the OT are more restricted in their timeframes.

Ruth: In stark contrast to the books of Joshua and Judges, the very concise four chapters of the book of Ruth do not portray wars or violence. This is so unusual in the OT books that precede Ruth that it is worth noting how the KJV portrays Ruth.[15]

> The Book of Ruth derives its name from its principal character. The biographical sketch of this godly young Moabitess contains much information concerning the customs of the ancient Near East and provides its readers with some valuable data regarding

the ancestry of King David. It also demonstrates God's gracious concern for all mankind, Jew and Gentile alike.

I mention this because it contradicts authors and other people who contend that the entire OT is rife with violence and war.

++**The First Book of Samuel (1 Sam.):** The thirty-one chapters of this book cover many events of violence between and among various Israelites as well as seemingly endless wars between Israelites and other nations, particularly the Philistines. Many sections of the First Book of Samuel include: "Saul's national victories and personal failures," " Israel defeated by the Philistines," "The Philistines smitten," "the arc captured," "Saul smites the Amorites," the Battle of Michmash," "Saul seeks to kill David," "David puts the murderer to death," and "Saul kills the priests of Nob." This book also presents one of several versions in the OT of the famous story of David slaying Goliath, the Philistine giant.

> *(51) Therefore David ran, and stood upon the Philistine, and took his sword, and drew it out of the sheath thereof, and slew him, and cut off his head therewith. And when the Philistines saw their champion was dead, they fled.

> (54) And David took the head of the Philistine, and brought it to Jerusalem; but he put his armor in his tent. (1 Sam. 17: 51, 54)

Many verses then portray how Saul attempts to use violence against David in a contest of authority over the Hebrew people. In the final chapter (31), Saul commits suicide by falling on his sword in order to avoid being captured by the Philistines.

> *(1) Now the Philistines fought against Israel: and the men of Israel fled from before the Philistines, and fell down slain in mount Gilboa.

> (4) Then said Saul unto his armor-bearer, Draw thy sword, and thrust me through therewith, lest these uncircumcised come and

thrust me through, and abuse me. But his armor-bearer would not; for he was sore afraid. Therefore Saul took a sword, and fell upon it.

(5) And then his armor-bearer saw that Saul was dead, he fell likewise upon his sword, and died with him.

(8) And it came to pass on the morrow, when the Philistines came to strip the slain, that they found Saul and his three sons fallen in mount Gilboa.

(9) And they cut off his head, and stripped off his armor, and sent into the land of the Philistines round about, to publish it in the house of their idols, ,and among the people. (1 Sam. 31: 1, 4-5, 8-9)

By way of comment, is it any wonder that some contemporary people who identify with Israel or with its opponents use or misuse of verses such as these to promote and justify violence against each other?

++**The Second Book of Samuel (2 Sam.):** The twenty-four short chapters of this book include verses about "David's capture of Jerusalem, " "The Civil War," "David putting the murderers to death," "Joab killing Abner," "The Defeat of the Ammonites and Syrians," "Seven Sons of Saul Hanged," and another version of the slaying of Philistine giants by David and his men.

+**The First Book of Kings (1 Kings):** There is a moderate amount of violence and war in this book, but the violence often is very bloody and shocking, involving feuds and plots between and among various Israelite leaders and their followers who compete for power, as well as numerous battles between Israelite and Syrian military forces. This book describes the reigns of various kings of Israel, especially King Solomon, and the many intriguing activities of Elijah and Ahab. Major events include "Joab is put to death," "Shimei is put to death," "Jezebel plots Nabob's death," and "Elijah pronounces Ahab's doom."

For example, in a section titled "The reigns of Elah and Zimri over Israel" we encounter these verses of violence between Israelite leaders:

Portrayals of Violence in the Old Testament 143

*(10) And Zimri went in and smote him, and killed him, in the twenty and seventh years of Asa king of Judah, and reigned in his stead.

(11) And it came to pass, when he began to reign, as soon as he sat on his throne, that he slew all the house of Baasha: he left him not one that pisseth against a wall, neither of his kinsfolk, nor of his friends. (1 Kings 16: 10-11)

While the Israelites usually initiate battles against Syrian military forces and win them, they occasionally are defeated. In the final chapter of 1 Kings, for example, the great Israelite leader Ahab plans an elaborate attack on the king of Syria and his army. But the king of Syria outwits Ahab and devises a clever plot that leads to Ahab's death.

*(34) And a certain man drew a bow at a venture, and smote the king of Israel between the joints of the harness: wherefore he said unto the driver of his chariot, Turn thine hand, and carry me out of the host; for I am wounded.

(35) And the battle increased that day: and the king was stayed up in his chariot against the Syrians, and died at even: and the blood ran out of the wound into the midst of the chariot. (1 Kings 22: 34-35)

+The Second Book of Kings (2 Kings): This Second Book of Kings covers the succession of one Israelite dynasty after another. Along the way, there are plenty of verses that refer to warfare and violence, including: "Moab Defeated," "The Siege of Samaria," "The Fight of the Syrians," "Jehu kills Joram the King of Israel," "The Fall of Jerusalem," "The Captivity of Judah," and "The Campaign of Nebuchadnezzar against Judah." It also has four verses which portray the cursing and the ghastly killing of Jezebel.

+The First Book of the Chronicles (1 Chron.): As suggested by its title, this book chronicles genealogies, reigns, and problems of dozens of Hebrew kings and their ministers. Major topics of interest regarding warfare and violence include the killing of Saul and his sons by the Philistines, "The Wars of God," "Reuben versus Manasseh," "David Defeats the Syrians," "Uzza is Smitten," "The Capture of Rabbah," and, once again, "The Slaying of Philistine Giants by King David and His Men."

An aside: It is very important to acknowledge that the majority of verses in 1 Chronicles, and in all the other books of the OT, do *not* refer to or portray violence and warfare; nor do most verses advocate warfare against external enemies or violence against Israelites who disobey God's many rules. For example, here is David's psalm of thanksgiving:

> *(7) Then on that day David delivered first this psalm to thank the Lord into the hand of Asaph and his brethren.
>
> (8) Give thanks unto the Lord, call upon his name, make known his deeds among the people.
>
> (9) Sing unto him, sing psalms unto him, talk ye of all his wondrous works. (1 Chron. 16: 7-9)

+The Second Book of Chronicles (2 Chron.): This book has many verses about King Solomon and major events during his reign. Topics include: "Shishank's Invasion of Judah," "Asa's Victory over Zerah," "Moab invades Judah," "The Philistines and Arabians Invade Judah," "Invading Armies Stricken with Death," "The War between Abiaz and Pekal," and "Cyrus's Capture of Judah."

Ezra: This very short book has very little violence and warfare. It is mainly about the Israelites who returned to Jerusalem from their long captivity in Babylon and the benevolent reign of Ezra as their king, despite external threats and challenges to Ezra's authority from other Hebrew leaders.

Nehemiah (Neh.): This is another short book that has very little warfare and violence. Among other things, it lists all the priests and exiles who returned to Judah over the years.

Portrayals of Violence in the Old Testament 145

++Esther: This book is primarily about how the Hebrew woman Esther was chosen by the King of Persia, Ahasuerus, to become his queen and how she aided and protected the Hebrew community in Persia during her life, despite considerable opposition and threats from other leaders. Many sections of this book describe "Haman's plot to destroy the Jews," "The courage of Esther," and "The Jews destroy their enemies." For example:

> *(2) The Jews gathered themselves together in their cities throughout all the provinces of the King Ahasuerus, to lay hand on such as sought their hurt: and not many could withstand them: for the fear of them fell upon all people....
>
> (5) Thus the Jews smote all their enemies with the stroke of the sword, and slaughter, and destruction, and did what they would unto those that hated them. (Esther 9: 2, 5)

Job: The book of Job conveys Job's many lamentations and complaints about his life and his feeling that God had abandoned him. It also conveys the reactions of God and of Elihu and other Hebrews to Job's fears and complaints. It has relatively few verses about wars or violence.

+Psalms (Ps.): Probably one of the most quoted books by Jews and Christians, Psalms' one hundred-fifty poetical "songs of praise to the Lord" often are very inspiring and non-violent. However, there are about seventy-two violent verses spread through about seventeen of the psalms. Psalms 79 and 83 have quite a few violent images as well as prayers for violence against adversaries. Some of the verses in Psalms can be rather shocking in their violence. Here is a sample of some of them:

Verse 9 of Psalm 2 calls on the Lord: "Thou shalt break them with a rod of iron; thou shalt dash them in pieces like a potter's vessel."

Psalm 18 provides a set of six verses that convey violence, including these four:

> *(37) I have pursued mine enemies, and overtaken them: neither did I turn again till they were consumed.
>
> (38) I have wounded them that they were not able to rise: they are fallen under my feet.
>
> (39) For thou hast girded me with strength unto the battle: thou hast subdued under me those that rose up against me.
>
> (40) Thou hast also given me the necks of mine enemies; that I might destroy them that hate me. (Ps. 18: 37-40)

Psalm 78 presents a set of eight verses that portray how God saved the Israelites in Egypt by wreaking all sorts of violence against the Egyptians. Here are just a few of those verses:

> *(44) And had turned their rivers into blood; and their floods, that they could not drink.
>
> (45) He sent divers sorts of flies among them, which devoured them; and frogs, which destroyed them. (Ps. 78: 44-45)

A number of verses in Psalm 118 portray promises of destructive violence against the enemies of the Israelites but without specifying the identity of the enemies or when the destruction will occur. Could the violence be in the future? Forever? Can these verses, and others like these in the "holy books" of some religions, continue to motivate some people to commit violence towards their enemies?

> *(10) All nations compassed me about, but in the name of the Lord will I destroy them.
>
> (12) They compassed me about like bees; they are quenched as the fire of thorns: for in the name of the Lord I will destroy them. (Ps. 118: 10, 12)

Portrayals of Violence in the Old Testament 147

Several verses regarding the "mourning of the Jewish exiles in Babylon" seem to be especially vengeful and violent. For example:

> *(8) O daughter of Babylon, who are to be destroyed; happy shall be he that rewardeth thee as thou hast served us.
>
> (9) Happy shall he be, that taketh and dasheth thy little ones against the stones. (Ps. 137: 8-9)

Psalm 144 "A psalm of David" starts with rather perplexing verses regarding war and fighting:

> *(1) Blessed be the Lord my strength, which teacheth my hands to war, and my fingers to fight.
>
> (2) My goodness, and my fortress; my high tower, and my deliverer, my shield, and he in whom I trust; who subdueth my people under me.
>
> (6) Cast forth lightning, and scatter them: shoot out thine arrows, and destroy them. (Ps. 144: 1, 2, and 6)

Even the next to the last Psalm (149) contains verses pleading with the Lord to bring violence against enemies of the Israelites:

> *(6) Let the high praises of God be in their mouth, and a two-edged sword in their hand;
>
> (7) To execute vengeance upon the heathen, and punishments upon the people;
>
> (8) To bind their kings with chains, and their nobles with fetters of iron;
>
> (9) To execute upon them the judgment written: this honor have all his saints. Praise ye the Lord. (Ps. 149: 6-9)

Of course, it is important to note that Psalms also has many verses that are *not* violent or bellicose. Among these are the verses of Psalm

23—a psalm that is arguably the most popular psalm at funeral services and burials for many Christians, and for many Jews.

> *The Lord is my shepherd; I shall not want. He maketh me to lie down in green pastures: he leadeth me beside the still waters. He restoreth my soul: he leadeth me in the paths of righteousness for his name's sake. Yea, though I walk through the valley of the shadow of death, I will fear no evil: for thou art with me; thy rod and thy staff they comfort me. Thou prepares a table before me in the presence of mine enemies: thou anointest my head with oil; my cup runneth over. Surely goodness and mercy shall follow me all the days of my life: and I will dwell in the house of the Lord forever. (Ps. 23)

By way of comment, allow me to note that even though Psalm 23 is so popular and so reassuring to so many people, it does mention "the presence of mine enemies." On the other hand, it does not convey sentiments of vengeance, violence, compromise, or peace towards them.

There also are a few verses in Psalms that refer positively to the end of violence and war, although they do so without telling us when this happened or might happen. Psalm 46 conveys that God can be a refuge and a source of strength for believers:

> *He maketh wars to cease unto the end of the earth; he breaketh the bow, and cutteth the spear in sunder; he burneth the chariot in the fire. (Ps. 46: 9)

Proverbs (Prov.): The book of Proverbs also is quoted often for the "spiritual and moral precepts" it offers. I found very little evidence of violence and war in Proverbs, except for some verses in Chapter 1 regarding "sinners" who entice Hebrews to ignore God's commandments.

> *(12) Let us swallow them up alive as the grave; and whole, as those that go down into the pit:

Portrayals of Violence in the Old Testament 149

(32) For the turning away of the simple shall slay them, and the prosperity of fools shall destroy them. (Prov.1: 12, 32)

By the way, Proverbs 20: 18 is not explicitly violent but it is of interest regarding war. *"Every purpose is established by counsel: and with good advice make war." Notice that this rather general advice about war does not prohibit war. Nor does it limit war to any particular time, place, or opponent. It also does not indicate whether war must be physically violent. It simply seems to advise anyone and everyone to use "counsel" and "with good advice make war."

Ecclesiastes (Ecc.): This book contains many proverbs, many of which are similar to those in the Book of Proverbs, which precedes this one. Also similar to verses in some of the other books, Ecclesiastes has the famous passages about "a time to kill" and a "time of war."

*(1) To every thing there is a season, and a time to every purpose under the heaven.

(3) A time to kill, and a time to heal; a time to break down, and a time to build up;

(8) A time to love, and a time to hate; a time of war, and a time of peace. (Ecc. 3: 1, 3, 8)

By way of comment, it is worth noting that these verses do not convey when, with whom, or why the killing and war will occur. Has the "time" occurred yet? Like the annual cycle of the seasons on many parts of Earth, do the "seasons" of war, killing, and peace reoccur annually or in some other way? Do some contemporary people who are oriented towards violence use these verses to justify their hatreds and their killings, disregarding the less violent verbs in the phrases?

Song of Solomon (Song of Sol.): I did not find verses about violence or war in this famous book about sexual attraction between a black woman and her actual or imagined lover, King Solomon.

++**Isaiah (Is.):** The KJV refers to Isaiah as the author and as the "prince of the prophets."[16] It also claims that this very long book of sixty-six chapters is "the peak of the literary genius of the Old Testament." Isaiah recounts and interprets much of the Jewish history that was described by Moses in the Pentateuch and by the other authors up to the reign of Isaiah. It provides an often-bewildering array of verses about violence and war as well as about peace and many other topics. Some verses of Isaiah portray God as "the Prince of Peace" while many other verses portray God as promising that he will destroy many different people and places that offend him, including his own chosen people—Israelites.

As a side note, and although it is tangential to our focus on violence and war, Isaiah also has a passage that is considered by some people to predict the coming of Jesus as a savior:

> *Therefore the Lord himself shall give you a sign; Behold, a virgin shall conceive, and bear a son, and shall call his name Immanuel. (Is. 7: 14)

As to violence and war, Isaiah includes the famous verse about beating swords into plowshares:

> *And he shall judge among the nations and shall rebuke many people: and they shall beat their swords into plowshares, and their spears into pruning hooks: nation shall not lift up sword against nation, neither shall they learn war any more. (Is. 2: 4)

And yet, so many of the chapters in Isaiah seem to provide contradictory images of God, Isaiah the prophet, and the Israelites regarding violence, war, and peace. Here is just a small sample of these verses.

First, from Chapter 9 which is given the title "The Birth of the Prince of Peace" in the KJV:

> *(4) For thou hast broken the yoke of his burden, and the staff of his shoulder, the rod of his oppressor, as in the day of Midian.

(5) For every battle of the warrior is with confused noise, and garments rolled in blood; but this shall be with burning and fuel of fire.

(6) For unto us a child is born, unto us a son is given: and the government shall be upon his shoulder: and his name shall be called Wonderful Counselor, The mighty God, The everlasting Father, The Prince of Peace. (Is. 9: 4-6)

Only five verses after this set of famous verses, Isaiah tells us that:

*(11) Therefore the Lord shall set up the adversaries of Rezin against him, and join his enemies together;

(12) The Syrians before, and the Philistines behind; and they shall devour Israel with open mouth. For all this his anger is turned away, but his hand is stretched out still.

(13) For the people turneth not unto him that smiteth them, neither do they seek the Lord of hosts.

(14) Therefore the Lord will cut off from Israel head and tail, branch and rush, in one day. (Is. 9: 11-14)

By way of comment, let me once again emphasize that our concern here is with how various kinds of contemporary people might interpret and react to these verses and to the seemingly violent images that they contain, regardless of what scholars, clerics, and others say about "context" and the supposedly "correct" way to understand these verses. As explained in the opening chapter of this book, a strong case can be made that, in the contemporary world, increasing percentages of the world's population have Internet access to electronic versions of the "holy books," often in a wide range of languages and translations. Increasing percentages of the world's population are literate in at least one language and they are relatively free to make their own interpretations of what they read—without regard to "context" or to what clerics, scholars, and experts try to tell them about what anything means.

Other chapters in Isaiah portray God predicting that he will wreak violence on a wide variety of people and places, including his own Israelites. For example, Chapter 13 abounds in verses that portray God promising to destroy Babylon and its people with shocking forms of violence.

> *(15) Everyone that is found shall be thrust through; and every one that is joined unto them shall fall by the sword.
>
> (16) Their children also shall be dashed to pieces before their eyes; their houses shall be spoiled, and their wives ravished. (Is. 13: 15-16)

Chapter 19 is titled "The Oracle Concerning Egypt." [17] It has more than twelve verses that threaten Egypt with violence. Here are three of those verses:

> *(2) And I will set the Egyptians against the Egyptians: and they shall fight every one against his brother, and every one against his neighbor; city against city, and kingdom against kingdom. (Is. 19: 2)
>
> *(17) And the land of Judah shall be a terror unto Egypt, every one that maketh mention thereof shall be afraid in himself, because of the counsel of the Lord of hosts, which he hath determined against it. (Is. 19: 17)
>
> *(22) And the Lord shall smite Egypt: he shall smite and heal it: and they shall return even to the Lord, and he shall be entreated of them, and shall heal them. (Is. 19: 22)

By way of comment, we should acknowledge that these verses were written more than two-thousand years ago. Also, apparently, they were written in the future tense—not in the past tense. Do some contemporary people believe that the promises of the Lord in these verses have not yet been fulfilled? Has the Lord smitten Egypt yet? Has he healed Egypt yet?

Portrayals of Violence in the Old Testament 153

Do some contemporary people react with violence to the phrase "Judah shall be a terror unto Egypt?" Can some people—Jews, Egyptians, and other people of no particular political or religious orientation—regard statements like this as an eternal command for Jews to terrorize Egypt or to try to convert its people to Judaism?

It also is important to note that the book of Isaiah has dozens of verses in which the Lord proclaims his special concerns for Israel and for Israelites who will fear and obey him. And yet, even in the final chapter (66) titled "Zion's Future Hope" [18] there are verses which portray violence and destruction:

> *For by fire and by his sword will the Lord plead with all flesh: and the slain of the Lord shall be many. (Is. 66: 16)

Even the very last verse of Isaiah might convey to some people images of violent destruction:

> *And they shall go forth, and look upon carcasses of the men that have transgressed against me: for their worm shall not die, neither shall their fire be quenched; and they shall be an abhorring unto all flesh. (Is. 66: 24)

In sum, while Isaiah covers many topics besides violence and war, it certainly has a considerable number of passages that convey rather shocking and explicit forms of violence. This is even more true of the book that follows it—Jeremiah.

++Jeremiah (Jer.): This book of fifty-two chapters is very similar to the book of Isaiah in its style, tone, and images of violence and war. Actually, at times, Jeremiah seems to exceed Isaiah in its violence. Verse after verse convey the Prophet Jeremiah's fears, lamentations, anger, and prophecies regarding the sinfulness of his fellow Israelites. Jeremiah repeatedly tells us how God has punished them and will punish them in the future with all sorts of violence and wars with scores of adversaries including Egypt, Babylon, and the Philistines.

Jeremiah also has many verses that depict violence and warfare in Babylon, Egypt, Damascus, and Gaza. The final chapters of Jeremiah prophesize the destruction of more than a dozen tribes and nations by God.

There also are verses in Jeremiah, as in some other books of the OT, that seem to be timeless and eternal in portraying God assuring Israelites that he joins them in battles that will destroy entire nations.

> *Thou are my battle axe and weapons of war: for with thee will I break in pieces the nations, and with thee will I destroy kingdoms. (Jer. 51: 20)

Here are some other rather distinctive verses in Jeremiah:

> *(3) And say, Hear ye the word of the Lord, O kings of Judah, and inhabitants of Jerusalem; Thus saith the Lord of hosts, the God of Israel; behold, I will bring evil upon this place, they which whosoever heareth, his ears shall tingle.
>
> (7) And I will make void the counsel of Judah and Jerusalem in this place; and I will cause them to fall by the sword before their enemies, and by the hands of them that seek their lives: and their carcasses will I give to the meat for the fowls of the heaven, and for the beasts of the earth.
>
> (8) And I will make this city desolate, and a hissing; every one that passeth thereby shall be astonished and hiss because of all the plagues thereof.
>
> (9) And I will cause them to eat the flesh of their sons and the flesh of their daughters, and they shall eat every one the flesh of his friend in the siege and straitness, wherewith their enemies, and they that seek their lives, shall straiten them. (Jer. 19: 3, 7-9)

By way of another comment, let me say that, to me, these verses portray a God of extreme malice and violence against his own followers who displease him. I do not believe that I have found in the Qur'an or in

Portrayals of Violence in the Old Testament

the NT verses so explicit in their portrayals of a deity who threatens or promises to commit such violent destruction of human beings.

++**Lamentations (Lam.):** As suggested by its title, this very brief book of only five chapters and 154 verses has more than two dozen verses that bemoan the capture of Jerusalem by adversaries as well as God's many acts of violence against the Israelites because of their sinfulness in violating so many of his commandments.

> *The Lord was as an enemy: he hath swallowed up Israel, he hath swallowed up all her palaces: he hath destroyed his strongholds, and hath increased in the daughter of Judah mourning and lamentation. (Lam. 2: 5)

> *Thou hast called as in a solemn day my terrors round about so that in the day of the Lord's anger none escaped nor remained: those that I have swaddled and brought up hath mine enemy consumed. (Lam 2: 22)

++**Ezekiel (Ez.):** According to the KJV[19] "... the author of this book was Ezekiel the priest, the son of Buzi. He was taken captive in 597 B.C. among the 10,000 deported by Nebuchadnezzar during his second campaign against Judah. As one of three priest-prophets in the OT (including Jeremiah and Zechariah), Ezekiel emphasized the concerns of a priest: the glory of the Lord, priestly duties, and both the present and future temples. The purpose of the book is essentially threefold: (1) to explain that Judah must be judged for disobedience; (2) to encourage the remnant of Judah through prophecies of the glorious future restoration; (3) to emphasize the preeminence of God's glory and character."

This material from the KJV provides no indication of the rather extraordinary number of curses and prophecies in Ezekiel regarding the violence that God will impose upon any and all tribes, nations, and people who do not fear him or that do not obey his commandments. This includes not just the people of Egypt, Ammon, Moab, Edom, Philistia, Tyre, and Babylon, but also of the Israelites themselves.

> *So will I send upon you famine and wild beasts, and they shall bereave thee; and pestilence and blood shall pass through thee; and I will bring the sword upon thee. I the Lord have spoken it. (Ez. 5: 17)

One set of verses in Chapter 9 indicates how God commanded some of his faithful followers to slaughter their fellow Israelites who were guilty of disobedience:

> *(8) And it came to pass, while they were slaying them, and I was left, that I fell upon my face, and cried, and said, Ah Lord God! Wilt thou destroy all the residue of Israel in thy pouring out of thy fury upon Jerusalem?
>
> (9) Then said he unto me, The iniquity of the house of Israel and Judah is exceeding great, and the land is full of blood, and the city full of perverseness: for they say, The Lord hath forsaken the earth, and the Lord seeth not. (Ez. 9: 8-9)

By way of another comment, notice how Verse 9 provides insight into God's reason for becoming so violent against some of his followers: namely, that they supposedly had "forsaken the earth" and apparently believed that "the Lord seeth not."

While Ezekiel repeats many of the curses and prophecies of violence that are found in other books of the OT, including Isaiah and Jeremiah, I found this book of Ezekiel to have many of the most vile, violent, and ghastly passages in the entire OT, even though only about 132 of the verses are explicitly violent. And while it is perhaps tangential to this report on violence, I found Ezekiel to be remarkably obsessed with idolatry, adultery, harlots, and "whoredoms." For example:

> *(7) Thus she committed her whoredoms with them, with all them that were the chosen men of Assyria, and with all on whom she doted: with all their idols she defiled herself.

Portrayals of Violence in the Old Testament 157

> (8) Neither left she her whoredoms brought from Egypt: for in her youth they lay with her, and they bruised the breasts of her virginity, and poured their whoredom upon her.
>
> (9) Wherefore I have delivered her into the hand of her lovers, into the hand of the Assyrians, upon whom she doted.
>
> (10) These discovered her nakedness: they took her sons and her daughters, and slew her with the sword: and she became famous among women; for they had executed judgment upon her. (Ez. 23: 7-10)

Also quite remarkable in Ezekiel is the frequency of the English words "slain," "terror," and "destruction." For example, these words occur more than thirty times in Chapter 32 and they repeatedly convey shocking images of violence.

And yet it also should be mentioned that the final eight chapters of Ezekiel's forty-eight chapters contain little or no violence. They provide "visions" and instructions for how Jerusalem should be resettled, the temple shall be rebuilt, how the lands of Judah should be divided, and how the priests should carry out their duties.

+Daniel: This book presents the Prophet Daniel's recordings of his captivity with his fellow Israelites in Babylon under various Persian kings including Darius. The verses describe many conflicts, intrigues, plots, and the famous story of "Daniel cast into the lion's den" [20] but surviving as though a miracle from God.

+Hosea: This short book is about various sins of the Israelites that enrage God to violence, although he ultimately allows them to return to Jerusalem and rebuild. For example:

> *For Israel hath forgotten his Maker, and buildeth temples; and Judah hath multiplied fenced cities: but I will send a fire upon his cities, and it shall devour the palaces thereof. (Hosea 8: 14)

> *Samaria shall become desolate; for she hath rebelled against her God: they shall fall by the sword; their infants shall be dashed in pieces, and their women with child shall be ripped up. (Hosea 13: 16)

By way of comment, please notice once again that verses such as these are presented in English in the future tense—not the past tense. Could some people, now or in the future, use or misuse verses such as these to try to justify violence or hateful attitudes towards other people in the Middle East?

+Joel: This is another short book in the OT. It has verses in which God taunts his enemies and urges the Israelites to prepare for war. It also has a rather surprising verse that reverses the famous verse in other books about beating swords into plowshares.

> *(9) Proclaim ye this among the Gentiles: Prepare war, wake up the mighty men, let all the men of war draw near; let them come up:
>
> (10) Beat your plowshares into swords, and your pruning hooks into spears: let the weak say, I am strong. (Joel 3: 9-10)

++Amos: This is another short book that presents many condemnations and judgments of God against various enemies of the Israelites including Damascus, Gaza, Tyrus, Ammon, Moab, and even Judah as well. Occasionally God is portrayed as imposing violence on all those who anger him.

> *But I will send a fire on the wall of Gaza, which shall devour the palaces thereof. (Amos 1: 7)
>
> *(4) Thus saith the Lord; For three transgressions of Judah, and for four, I will not turn away the punishment thereof; because they have despised the law of the Lord, and have not kept his commandments, and their lies caused them to err, after the which their fathers have walked:

Portrayals of Violence in the Old Testament

> (5) But I will send a fire upon Judah, and it shall devour the palaces of Jerusalem. (Amos 2: 4-5)

+Obadiah: This is a book of only one chapter and twenty-one verses, three of which are quite violent in predicting the destruction of Edom by the Israelites. It also portrays God promising the Israelites that they will inhabit Judah forever.

Jonah: This book of only four short chapters and forty-eight compact verses includes the famous tale of God punishing Jonah for disobedience by having him cast into the sea and swallowed up by a "great fish" for three days until he repented. *"And the Lord spake unto the fish, and it vomited out Jonah upon the dry land," (Jonah 2: 10). Jonah is one of the few books in the OT that does not portray lethal physical violence and war (unless we claim that casting Jonah into the sea and into the belly of a "fish" were violent actions by God).

+Micah (Mic.): The KJV observes that[21] "Much of Micah's prophecy is very severe in tone, though it does contain much poetic beauty similar to that of Isaiah. In many ways, the Book of Micah is a "sister-book" to Isaiah. It has been called "Isaiah in shorthand."

Like so many of the books that precede it, the book of Micah conveys many of God's judgments for and against various people, including "those who oppress the poor."[22] For example:

> *(12) For the rich men thereof are full of violence, and the inhabitants thereof have spoken lies, and their tongue is deceitful in their mouth.
>
> (13) Therefore also will I make thee sick in smiting thee, in making thee desolate because of thy sins. (Mic. 6: 12-13)

Micah also repeats the famous verse, found in some of the other books, in which God orders his followers to beat their swords into plowshares and their spears into pruning hooks:

> *And he shall judge among many people, and rebuke strong nations afar off; and they shall beat their swords into plowshares, and their spears into pruning hooks: nation shall not lift up a sword against nation, neither shall they learn war any more. (Mic. 5: 9)

By way of comment, this verse is presented in the future tense. It does not tell us when any of this will occur. We might ask ourselves whether this verse and others like this one, act as a restraint against violence and warfare in the contemporary world.

++Nahum (Nah.): This short book of three chapters of forty-seven verses portrays God promising that the city of Nineveh will be besieged and destroyed because of the licentious behavior of its inhabitants.

> *(5) Behold, I am against thee, saith the Lord of hosts; and I will discover thy skirts upon thy face, and I will show the nations thy nakedness, and the kingdoms thy shame.
>
> (6) And I will cast abominable filth upon thee, and make thee vile, and will set thee as a gazing stock. (Nah. 3: 5-6)

By way of comment, these verses might not seem to be particularly relevant to contemporary people who are oriented towards violence since the ancient city of Nineveh no longer exists. On the other hand, the "Plains of Nineveh," northeast of the major city of Mosul in Iraq, is the site of frequent battles between Iraqi military forces and forces claiming allegiance to ISIS. The area is governed by the "Nineveh Governorate."

+Habakkuk (Hab.): This short book presents God's warnings about drunkenness and other sins, but it does not portray much violence or warfare. One of its verses promises punishment against those who have "spoiled many nations."

> *Because thou hast spoiled many nations, all the remnant of the people shall spoil thee; because of men's blood, and for the violence of the land, of the city, and or all that dwell therein. (Hab. 2: 8)

++Zephaniah (Zeph.): This is another very short book of only fifty-three verses near the end of the OT. However, in contrast to some of the books that immediately precede it, Zephaniah has at least twelve verses which portray a very wrathful God threatening violence against a wide variety of people who anger him, including "inhabitants of the sea coast" and "Ethiopians."

> *Woe unto the inhabitants of the sea coast, the nation of the Cherethites! The word of the Lord is against you; O Canaan, the land of the Philistines, I will even destroy thee, that there shall be no inhabitant. (Zeph. 2: 5)
>
> *(11) The Lord will be terrible unto them: for he will famish all the gods of the earth; and men shall worship him, every one from its place, even all the isles of the heathen.
>
> (12) Ye Ethiopians also, ye shall be slain by my sword.
>
> (13) And he will stretch out his hand against the north, and destroy Assyria; and will make Nineveh a desolation, and dry like a wilderness. (Zeph. 2: 11-13)

By way of comment, and noting that these verses are written in the future tense, is it possible that some contemporary people would notice verses like these and use them to try to justify violence against current day Ethiopia and Syria and the citizens of those countries?

In sum, the book of Zephaniah is remarkably violent in more than twenty percent of its verses, as short as it is and as close as it is to the end of the OT.

Haggai (Hag.): With only thirty-eight verses in only two chapters, Haggai follows Obadiah as the shortest book in the OT. Haggai was the first prophet to minister to Israel following the return from the Babylonian captivity. Most of the verses encourage the Israelites to rebuild the temple and the city. There are only two verses with violent images, both attributed to the Lord.

++**Zechariah (Zech.):** This book conveys many of Zechariah's messianic prophecies and visions. As in so many of the other books in the OT, Zechariah has verses that seem to be utterly contradictory regarding violence. Here are some examples:

> *(16) These are the things that ye shall do: Speak ye every man the truth to his neighbor, execute the judgment of truth and peace in your gates:
>
> (17) And let none of you imagine evil in your hearts against his neighbor; and love no false oath: for all these are things that I hate, saith the Lord. (Zech. 8: 16-17)

And yet, less than ten verses after this, Zechariah provides many verses in which the Lord identifies nations and places that he wants destroyed in order to accommodate his followers. These include Damascus, Hamath, Tyrus, Ashkelon, Gaza, and the land of the Philistines.

> *(4) Behold, the Lord will cast her out, and he will smite her power in the sea: and she shall be devoured with fire.
>
> (5) Ashkelon shall see it, and fear; Gaza also shall see it, and her expectation shall be ashamed; and the king shall perish from Gaza, and Ashkelon shall not be inhabited. (Zech. 9: 4-5)

By the way, notice that Gaza is one of the places identified for destruction. Can this verse motivate some contemporary people to inflict violence on modern-day Gaza even though this verse apparently was recorded more than two thousand years ago?

Chapter 14, "Jerusalem and the Nations," has more than ten verses in which the Lord predicts or promises that he will incite warfare and bestow violence against various people and nations, including his own Israelites.

> *(2) For I will gather all nations against Jerusalem to battle; and the city shall be taken, and the houses rifled, and the women ravished;

Portrayals of Violence in the Old Testament 163

and half of the city shall go forth into captivity, and the residue of the people shall not be cut off from the city.

(3) Then shall the Lord go forth and fight against those nations as when he fought in the day of battle. (Zech. 14: 2-3)

*And this shall be the plague wherewith the Lord will smite all the people that have fought against Jerusalem; Their flesh shall consume away while they stand upon their feet, and their eyes shall consume away in their holes, and their tongue shall consume away in their mouth. (Zech. 14: 12)

Even the last verse in Zechariah refers to the extermination of "the Canaanite" as the "Lord of hosts" promises eventual, eternal salvation to Jerusalem and Judah.

*Yes, every pot in Jerusalem and in Judah shall be holiness unto the Lord of hosts: and all they that sacrifice shall come and take of them, and seeth therein: and in that day there shall be no more the Canaanite in the house of the Lord of hosts. (Zech. 14: 21)

+**Malachi (Mal.):** This is the final book in the OT. The KJV claims that "After Malachi, the prophetic voice was silent for some four hundred years." The KJV also claims that Malachi's "theme is God's love for Israel in spite of the sins of the priests and people. "[23] And yet, its fifty-five verses include verses in which the Lord issues various warnings and curses at the Israelites.

*And ye shall tread down the wicked; for they shall be ashes under the soles of your feet in the day that I shall do this, saith the Lord of hosts. (Mal. 4: 3)

The very last verse of Malachi and the OT also ends with a warning of violence from God if the Israelites do not obey the prophet, Elijah:

*And he shall turn the heart of the fathers to the children, and the heart of the children to their fathers, lest I come and smite the earth with a curse. (Mal. 4: 6)

Regarding Portrayals of Genocide in the Old Testament

Does the OT portray or refer to acts of genocide, as the concept is defined and used in contemporary times? If so, how often and in what ways is genocide portrayed? Who are the perpetrators? The victims?

Let us first consider two definitions of genocide. A common definition of "genocide" is "*the deliberate mass murder of a race, people, or minority group.*" [24] A common example of genocide is the effort of the Nazis to exterminate the Jewish population of Europe in the Holocaust before and during WWII. In 1948, the United Nations established an "official" definition of genocide as part of the Genocide Convention which outlaws genocide. The definition is "acts committed with intent to destroy, in whole or in part, a national, ethnical, racial or religious group." [25]

The United Nations has formally declared that genocides were conducted or were attempted dozens of times since 1900. These included the Ottoman Empire Turks against predominantly Christian Armenians, 1915-1922; the Nazi Holocaust against Jews, gypsies, homosexuals, and other minorities, 1939-1945; the Khmer Rouge genocide in Cambodia, 1975-1979; the Ba'athist genocide against Kurdish people, 1986-1989; the "Bosnian Genocides" of Serbian Christians and Croat Muslims, 1992-1995; the Rwandan Genocide of 1994; and "ISIL's Genocides of Yazidis, Christians, and Shias, 2014-present." [26]

Also relevant to the concept of genocide is the long-standing Hebrew concept of "*herem.*" *The Oxford Handbook of Religion and Violence*[27] defines *herem* as "the utter annihilation of the enemy, combatants and non-combatants alike." The passage 1 Samuel 15: 1-3 is given as an example of *herem* in the OT. The "Lord of hosts" tells the Prophet Samuel to instruct military leader Saul to destroy a specific ethnic group, the Amaleks, and all their possessions, because the Amaleks ambushed the Israelites as they escaped from Egypt.

> *Samuel also said unto Saul, The Lord sent me to anoint thee to be king over his people, over Israel: now therefore hearken thou unto the voice of the words of the Lord. Thus saith the Lord of hosts, I remember that which Amalek did to Israel, how he laid wait for him in the way, when he came up from Egypt. Now go and smite Amalek, and utterly destroy all that they have, and spare them not; but slay both man and woman, infant and suckling, ox and sheep, camel and ass.

By the way, subsequent verses in Chapter 15 of 1 Samuel indicate that Saul did not fully comply with God's demand that he annihilate all of the Amaleks. Verses 15: 8-9 indicate that Saul had all of the Amaleks annihilated except for Agag, the king of the Amaleks. Saul also kept for himself *"the best of the sheep, and of the oxen, and of the fatlings, and the lambs, and all that was good." Additional verses in Chapter 15 indicate that God chastised Saul for failing to annihilate everything. Eventually, Samuel has King Agag of the Amaleks brought before him. He condemns Agag, then slays him in a brutal manner "before the Lord in Gilgal."

> *And Samuel said, "As thy sword hath made women childless so shall thy mother be childless among women." And Samuel hewed Agag in pieces before the Lord in Gilgal. (1 Samuel 15: 33)

Apparently, when taken as a whole, these verses in 1 Samuel convey that the God of the Israelites not only demanded the genocide of the Amaleks by the Israelites but that the genocide was complete when Samuel executed King Agag, the last Amalek. Thus, it seems to me that these passages describe actions that constitute "genocide" according to both the common and the United Nations definition of genocide, as well as the Hebrew concept of *herem*.

In considering verses that might refer to or portray genocide, we found that many verses portray forms of violence that do not obviously constitute genocide. Many verses call for or refer to the military conquests of cities, tribes, and nations. Some conquests result in the victors killing some or all of the members of their enemies' military forces. Some conquests result in the victors expelling the surviving enemies from their homelands. Other conquests result in the victors occupying the enemies' homelands, enslaving members of the defeated population, or allowing the defeated people to remain in some capacity or another. One example of expulsion is in Exodus 23: 23, 25, 27-28, and 30-31. Taken as a whole, these verses portray the God of the Israelites prophesizing or promising that he will help his followers expel all the non-Israelite inhabitants between the Red Sea and the Sea of the Philistines so that the Israelites can inhabit that land.

Earlier in this chapter, at various places, we presented fifteen passages with a total of twenty-eight verses in the OT which seem to portray or refer to genocide, according to both the common definition and the official definition established by the United Nations. These passages include Genesis 6: 17; 7: 4, 21-23 and 19: 24-25; Deuteronomy 3: 6; 7: 12, and 13: 15-16; Joshua 6: 2 and 21; 8: 25-26, 29; Hosea 13: 16; Nahum 3: 5-6; Zephaniah 2: 5, 12, 13; Zechariah 9: 4-5 and 14: 21; and Jeremiah 19: 7-9. Some of these verses are identified by noted author and historian of religion Philip Jenkins when he contends that the OT has many verses that describe acts of genocide by Israelites, as commanded by their God.[28]

However, these are not the only passages in the OT that portray or refer to genocide. There are dozens more, although it is important to note that portrayals of genocide appear in only twenty of the thirty-nine books (51%) of the OT. So, it would not be accurate to claim that genocide permeates or characterizes the OT. Then again, it would not be accurate to claim that the OT ignores or dismisses genocide, either. All of the passages and verses that portray genocide in the OT can be organized into six categories. Some of the verses and passages fit into more than one category. For example, Deuteronomy 9: 3 asserts that God will destroy many of the "children of the Anakim" and that God demands that the Israelites "drive them out, and destroy them quickly, as the Lord hath said unto thee."

Category 1: God of the Israelites committed genocide or attempted to do so.

Genesis 6: 17; 7: 4, 21-23 portrays God proclaiming that he flooded the Earth and destroyed all living things except for Noah, Noah's family, and mated pairs of various species of animals. Genesis 19: 24-25 portrays God proclaiming that he destroyed the cities of Sodom and Gomorrah so thoroughly that no inhabitants or vegetation remained. Zephaniah 3: 6 portrays God proclaiming that he destroyed many nations so thoroughly that no inhabitants survived.

Category 2: Israelites committed genocide or tried to commit genocide, with or without God's approval.

An example of this has already been presented. It is the case of Saul and the Israelites committing genocide against the Amaleks (1 Sam. 15: 1-3). Other passages in the OT that fit in this category include: 1 Samuel 15: 8-9; Numbers 21: 3; Deuteronomy 3: 3-7 and 7: 12; Joshua 6: 2, 21-27 and 8: 25, 26 and 29; 10: 35-42; 11: 11-12; Kings 10: 11, 17, and 25-28.

Category 3: Genocides committed by or attempted by non-Israelites.

I did not find any examples of this in the OT. In other words, every act of genocide, every threat of genocide, and every demand for genocide in the OT is by the God of the Israelites, by the Israelites, or by both the Israelites and their God.

Category 4: God of the Israelites declares that He will commit genocide against one or more nations, tribes, ethnic, religious, or minority groups that displease Him.
One of the many examples of this is Isaiah 17: 1-3. It portrays God declaring that He will destroy Damascus and other places. By the way, might verses like this be especially relevant now, and in the decades to come? At the time of this writing, Damascus is the huge, conflict-ridden capital. It is a badly damaged center of religious and political warfare in the Middle East, as it has been so often since Biblical times. Notice that the following verses assert that the Israelite God will not only destroy Damascus and other places but that "the children of Israel" will possess it.

> *The burden of Damascus. Behold, Damascus is taken away from being a city, and it shall be a ruinous heap. The cities of Aroer are forsaken: they shall be for flocks which shall lie down, and none shall make them afraid. The fortress also shall cease from Ephraim, and the Kingdom from Damascus, and the remnant of Syria: they shall be as the glory of the children of Israel, saith the Lord of hosts. (Is. 17: 1-3)

There are many other passages and verses in the OT in which the God of the Israelites declares that he will commit genocide against one or more nations, tribes, ethnic, religious or minority groups: Genesis 6: 13, 17 and 7: 4; Leviticus 26: 29-33; Deuteronomy 9: 3; Hosea 13: 16; Joel 3: 19; Amos 1: 7-9, 12, 14 and 2: 3, 5; Micah 1: 6-7; Nahum 1: 8; 2: 13 and 3: 5-7, 15; Zephaniah 1: 2-4 and 2: 4-5, 9, 11-13; Zechariah 9: 4-6 and 14: 2; Isaiah: 13: 15, 16, 18-20; 14: 22-23, 25; 16: 7, and 19: 22; Jeremiah 7: 32-33 and 19: 7-9; as well as Ezekiel 6: 3-7.

Category 5: God demands that His Israelites commit genocide.
An example of this is Deuteronomy 20: 17:

> *But thou shalt utterly destroy them; namely, the Hittites, and the Amorites, the Canaanites, and the Perizzites, the Hivites, and the Jebusites; as the Lord thy God hath commanded thee.

Portrayals of Violence in the Old Testament 169

Other examples of this are Deuteronomy 3: 2-7; 7: 2, 5, 24; 12: 2-3; 13: 15-16, and 20: 13-16; Joshua 6: 1-2 and 8: 1-2; 1 Samuel 4: 1 and 15: 3.

Category 6: Israelites call upon their God to commit genocide on their behalf.

While there are hundreds of verses in the OT which portray Israelites asking God for help, mercy, and forgiveness, I found only one passage that portrays an Israelite calling upon God to commit genocide on behalf of all Israelites. Psalm 83 is attributed to the musician Asaph. In the first set of verses, Asaph identifies a number of tribes and nations that supposedly "have consulted together with one consent: they are confederate against thee." Asaph mentions Edom, Moab, Ammon, Amalek, the Philistines of Tyre, and others. Then, in Verses 13-17 Asaph calls upon God:

> *O my God, make them like a wheel, as the stubble before the wind. As the fire burneth a wood, and as the flame setteth the mountains on fire. So persecute them with thy tempest, and make them afraid with thy storm. Fill their faces with shame; that they may seek thy name, O Lord. Let them be confounded and troubled forever; let them be put to shame, and perish.

By way of summary, we found a total of 114 verses in 45 of the passages in the OT that portray or refer to genocide. Recalling that the OT has a total of 23,145 verses, the percentage of verses that portray or refer to genocide is very small–less than one-half of a percent (0.49%). Whether that is significant is a matter for you to decide. To me, it is quite significant, and for a number of reasons. One reason is that the OT is in stark contrast to the Qur'an (as presented in Chapter 2) and the New Testament (as presented in Chapter 4) regarding genocide. As best as I can determine, there are *no* references to or portrayals of genocide in the Qur'an or in the New Testament. Furthermore, in the OT, all of the verses that portray genocide are presented as being righteous actions, threats, or demands by the God of the Israelites, by the Israelites, or both. And, of course, it is very important to acknowledge that *only* Israelites and their God are portrayed as perpetrators of genocide. None of the many non-Israelite nations, tribes, and entities are portrayed as committing genocide against the Israelites—not the Egyptians, the Babylonians, nor any other nations that defeated Israelites in battles, that exploited them, that enslaved them, or that dominated them in other ways. In addition to this, as shown in many of the verses in the OT that are presented in this chapter, the verses often call for genocides in the *future* tense—not genocides of the past. What is more, many of the portrayals are extremely graphic and absolute (i.e.: to destroy every living thing and all property of some other nation, religious group, or ethnic group so thoroughly that the land will never be inhabited again.)

SUMMARY OF VERSES IN THE OLD TESTAMENT THAT PORTRAY VIOLENCE

Table 10 presents a summary of the number (and percentage) of verses that convey violence in each of the books of the OT.

Portrayals of Violence in the Old Testament

Table 10a. Verses in the Old Testament That Convey Violence.

	Book Title	# Chapters	# Verses	# (%) of verses that convey violence against humans
1	Genesis	50	1533	22 (1.4%)
2	Exodus	40	1213	58 (4.8%)
3	Leviticus	27	859	22 (2.6%)
4	Numbers	36	1288	44 (3.4%)
5	Deuteronomy	34	959	97 (10.1%)
6	Joshua	23	658	51 (7.8%)
7	Judges	21	618	53 (8.6%)
8	Ruth	4	85	0 (0%)
9	1 Samuel	31	810	77 (9.5%)
10	2 Samuel	24	695	68 (9.8%)
11	1 Kings	22	816	27 (3.1%)
12	2 Kings	25	719	43 (6%)
13	1 Chronicles	29	942	33 (3.5%)
14	2 Chronicles	36	822	35 (5.2%)
15	Ezra	10	280	2 (0.7%)
16	Nehemiah	13	406	3 (0.7%)
17	Esther	10	167	15 (9%)
18	Job	42	1070	16 (1.5%)
19	Psalms	150	2461	72 (3%)

Note: The OT also includes one hundred thirty-seven unnumbered verses. If these are added to the 23,145 numbered verses, the total verses in the OT is 23,282 verses and the percentage of verses that were found to portray violence shift slightly from 5.16% to 5.13%—hardly a significant difference.

Table 10b. Verses in the Old Testament That Convey Violence (Cont).

	Book Title	# Chapters	# Verses	# (%) of verses that convey violence against humans
20	Proverbs	31	915	3 (0.3%)
21	Ecclesiastes	12	222	2 (0.9%)
22	Song of Solomon	8	117	0 (0%)
23	Isaiah	66	1292	52 (4%)
24	Jeremiah	52	1364	122 (8.9%)
25	Lamentations	5	154	26 (16.8%)
26	Ezekiel	48	1273	132 (10.3%)
27	Daniel	12	357	8 (2.2%)
28	Hosea	14	197	13 (6.5%)
29	Joel	3	73	6 (8.2%)
30	Amos	9	146	26 (17.8%)
31	Obadiah	1	21	3 (14.2%)
32	Jonah	4	48	0 (0%)
33	Micah	7	105	8 (7.6%)
34	Nahum	3	47	13 (27.6%)
35	Habakkuk	3	56	4 (7.1%)
36	Zephaniah	3	53	12 (22.6%)
37	Haggai	2	38	2 (0.3%)
38	Zechariah	14	211	19 (9.0%)
39	Malachi	4	55	5 (9.0%)
40	**OLD TESTAMENT TOTALS**	929	23,145*	1,194 (5.16%)

Note: The OT also includes one hundred thirty-seven unnumbered verses. If these are added to the 23,145 numbered verses, the total verses in the OT is 23,282 verses and the percentage of verses that were found to portray violence shift slightly from 5.16% to 5.13%—hardly a significant difference.

Portrayals of Violence in the Old Testament 173

SUMMARY AND CONCLUSIONS REGARDING THE OLD TESTAMENT

As shown in Table 10 regarding the quantities of violent verses in the OT, we found that about five percent (5.16%) of the OT's 23,145 verses portray or refer to physical violence. We also found considerable variations among its thirty-nine books in this regard. A few of the books (Ruth, Song of Solomon, and Jonah) have no verses that convey physical violence against humans. All of the other thirty-six books have at least a few violent verses, although in some books less than 1% of the verses convey violence. This is the case with the books of Ezra (0.7%), Proverbs (0.3%), Ecclesiastes (0.9%), and Haggai (0.3%). Books with the highest percentages of violent verses are Nahum (27.6%) and Zephaniah (22.6%).

Now, in terms of the kinds and qualities of violence portrayed in the OT, when violence is portrayed, often it is portrayed very explicitly, absolutely, timelessly, vehemently, and lethally. There are quite a few different victims and targets—both Jews and non-Jews. We found that the books of Isaiah, Jeremiah, Lamentations, Ezekiel, Amos, and Zephaniah are often rather shocking and noteworthy in this regard. These books contain more than a few verses in which God is portrayed as asserting that he has committed, or that he will commit in the future, many kinds of the most painful, lethal violence against any and all people who anger him or disobey his many rules—not just his well-known commandments. God's targets include the Israelites (His "chosen people") at different times and places. Verses also identify the targets of His violence as Egypt, Ethiopia, Gaza, Syria, Assyria, Persia (Iran), Damascus, Jerusalem, and Babylon. Repeatedly, God is portrayed as targeting dozens of various tribes, clans, and "nations," particularly the Philistines and Amorites.

Some of the verses depicting these targets of violence are presented as epigraphs at the head of this chapter. For convenience, here are two examples. In the first one, the Hebrew prophet and military leader Jeremiah claims that God proclaims to his Israelites that the Israelites are his "weapons of war" and that with them he will "break in pieces the nations, and with thee will I destroy kingdoms." Notice that the verbs are in the future tense.

> *Thou are my battle axe and weapons of war: for with thee will I break in pieces the nations, and with thee will I destroy kingdoms. (Jer. 51: 20)

But, as noted earlier in this chapter, at other times Jeremiah indicates that God also proclaims that He will deliver extraordinary lethal violence against His *own* people—the Israelites in Jerusalem.

> *And say, Hear ye the word of the Lord, O kings of Judah, and inhabitants of Jerusalem; Thus saith the Lord of hosts, the God of Israel; behold, I will bring evil upon this place, they which whosoever heareth, his ears shall tingle.
>
> And I will make void the counsel of Judah and Jerusalem in this place; and I will cause them to fall by the sword before their enemies, and by the hand of them that seek their lives: and their carcasses will I give to be meat for the fowls of the heaven, and for the beasts of the earth. (Jer. 19: 3, 7-8)

We also found that even in the first book of the OT—Genesis—God is portrayed repeatedly as committing, threatening, and demanding violence. This continues to be the case through most of the books including the last one—Malachi. Early in Genesis, God is portrayed as destroying the cities of Sodom and Gomorrah. Also in Genesis, Abram, the first of the prophets and rulers of the Hebrew people, is portrayed as using his trained servants to smite the guards who captured his brother Lot. In Deuteronomy, God commands Moses to take his Israelites into battles and to utterly destroy all living things, including the children, livestock, and trees, in many different cities that are occupied by Hittites, Amorites, and other nations. Young man Moses is portrayed as killing an Egyptian soldier who killed a Hebrew. Deuteronomy even has verses in which God commands Israelites to commit lethal violence against their own brothers, sons, daughters, wives, and close friends if they try to entice Israelites to worship some other god.

We also found that many of the famous Hebrew prophets served as military leaders who led their Israelites in offensive battles against non-Israelites, and occasionally against each other. Joshua, Samuel, Ezra, Nehemiah, Isaiah, Jeremiah, Ezekiel, Hosea, Joel, Amos, Micah, Nahum, Zephaniah, and Zechariah are among these prophets who engaged in lethal violence. Some verses even portray God as commanding that these leaders destroy entire cities and nations so completely that they will cease to exist and will never be occupied again. If we accept that verses such as these portray "genocide," using contemporary definitions of "genocide," then it can be said that we found a total of one-hundred fourteen verses in forty-five of the passages in the OT that portray or refer to genocide. Recalling that the OT has a total of 23,145 verses, the percentage of verses that portray or refer to genocide is very small –less than one-half of a percent (0.49%). While this might seem to be insignificant, the verses often are extremely graphic, absolute, and timeless. And they are in stark contrast to the Qur'an, as presented in Chapter 2, and in stark contrast to the NT, as presented in the next chapter.

In sum, then, there are more than enough explicitly violent verses in the Old Testament to incite violence for many decades to come—if not forever—between Jewish and non-Jewish people in Israel, Egypt, Gaza, Syria, Ethiopia, and other places in the Middle East, if not the world. There also are enough explicitly violent verses in the Old Testament to incite disagreements, misunderstandings, conflicts, and violence for decades to come between and among various factions of Israeli people within Israeli communities. This is just one of the reasons it is not difficult to understand why there seem to be so many bloody confrontations within Israel between and among extreme right-wing Jews, orthodox Jews, liberal Jews, and members of other ethnicities and religious orientations.

Now let us turn to the New Testament. Are its verses fundamentally different from the Qur'an and the Old Testament regarding violence, terror, and war? Is the New Testament completely "free" of the demands for genocide that are found in many of the books of the Old Testament? If so, what are some implications of this difference for world peace in the decades ahead?

Notes

1. *The King James Study Bible*. Nashville: Thomas Nelson Publishers. 1988. 1.
2. Ross, Floyd. H. and Tyrette Hills. *The Great Religions by Which We Live*. Greenwich, CT: Fawcett Publishing, Inc. 1959. 110-111.
3. Google search: https:// www.google.com/?gws.the+most+violent+books + in+the+Bible+Koran+holy books.
4. *The King James Study Bible*. Nashville: Thomas Nelson Publishers. 1988. 3.
5. Op. cit., 40.
6. Op. cit., 3.
7. Op. cit., 294.
8. Op. cit., 295.
9. Jenkins, *Laying Down the Sword*, 36-37.
10. *The King James Study Bible*, 99.
11. Op. cit., 291-292.
12. Op. cit., 374-375, 378.
13. Op. cit., 401.
14. Op. cit., 421.
15. Op. cit., 445.
16. Op. cit., 1019.
17. Ibid.
18. Op. cit., 1097.
19. Op. cit., 1193.
20. Op. cit., 1282.
21. Op. cit., 1335.
22. Op. cit., 1336.
23. Op. cit., 1375.
24. *Webster's New Encyclopedic Dictionary*, 405.
25. "United Nations Office on Genocide Prevention and the Responsibility to Protect." United Nations. http://www.un.org/en/genocideprevention/genocide.html.
26. "List of Genocides by Death-toll." Wikipedia. https://en.wikipedia.org/wiki/List_of_genocides_by _death-toll.
27. *The Oxford Handbook of Religion and Violence*. NY: Oxford University Press. 2013, 263.

28. Jenkins, *Laying Down the Sword*, 36-37.

Chapter 4

Portrayals of Violence in the New Testament

Epigraphs

Jesus's instructions to the twelve disciples he has just chosen:

> *Heal the sick, cleanse the lepers, raise the dead, cast out devils: freely ye have received, freely give. (Matt. 10: 8)

Jesus warns his disciples of persecutions to come:

> *But beware of men: for they will deliver you up to the councils, and they will scourge you in their synagogues. And the brother shall deliver up the brother to death, and the father the child: and the children shall rise up against their parents, and cause them to be put to death. And ye shall be hated of all men for my name's sake: but he that endureth to the end shall be saved. But when they persecute you in this city, flee ye into another: for verily I say unto you, Ye shall not have gone over the cities of Israel, till the Son of man come. (Matt. 10: 17, 18, 21-23)

Jesus's condemnation of some people who will not believe in his ministry (said by Jesus after a Roman centurion expresses his faith in Jesus's ability to cure his servant of palsy in Capernaum):

> *And I say unto you, that many shall come from the east and west, and shall sit down with Abraham, and Isaac, and Jacob, in the kingdom of heaven. But the children of the kingdom shall be cast out into darkness: there shall be weeping and gnashing of teeth. (Matt. 8: 11-12)

John's message to the church at Thyatira regarding the protection some people provided to Jezebel, a woman suspected of fornication and other sins:

> *...and I gave her space to repent of her fornication: and she repented not. Behold, I will cast her into a bed, and them that commit adultery with her into great tribulation, except they repent of their deeds. And I will kill her children with death; and all the churches shall know that I am he which searcheth the reins and hearts: and I will give unto every one of you according to your works. (Rev. 2: 21-23)

God shall add the plagues to anyone who adds anything to the Bible:

> *For I testify unto every man that heareth the words of the prophecy of this book, If any man shall add unto these things, God shall add unto him the plagues that are written in this book. And if any man shall take away from the words of the book of this prophecy, God shall take away his part out of the book of life, and out of the holy city, and from the things which are written in this book. (Rev. 22: 18-19)

INTRODUCTION TO THE NEW TESTAMENT

This chapter analyzes the New Testament (NT) by using the same analytic and coding procedures that I used to analyze the Qur'an and the Old Testament (OT) in the previous chapters. As with the Qur'an and the OT,

Portrayals of Violence in the New Testament

I have read every word of the NT many times for this sociological study. I have also read many analyses of these holy books by a number of members of the clergy and by esteemed religious scholars, particularly Philip Jenkins's *Laying Down the Sword: Why We Can't Ignore the Bible's Violent Verses* (2011), as indicated in earlier chapters of this book. Other influential books consulted include Mark Juergensmeyer's *Terror in the Mind of God: The Global Rise of Religious Violence* (2003); Jack Nelson-Pallmeyer's *Is Religion Killing Us? Violence in the Bible and the Quran* (2003); Madawi Al-Rasheed and Marat Shterins' *Dying for Faith: Religiously Motivated Violence in the Contemporary World* (2009); Juergensmeyer, Kitts, and Jerrysons' *The Oxford Handbook of Religion and Violence* (2013); and Karen Armstrong's *Fields of Blood: Religion and the History of Violence* (2014).

As mentioned in Chapter 1, I have no thesis, "argument," or predisposition regarding the NT or any other "holy books" other than to say that I obviously think they have been, and continue to be, very influential to many people, groups, and organizations. My analysis is meant to be as objective and sociological as possible. Like Philip Jenkins, I analyzed the widely respected, traditional, conservative, and readily available King James Version (KJV), specifically *The King James Study Bible,* although I also read a number of other versions of the Bible and the Qur'an for comparative purposes.

Once again, let me emphasize that I've written this book primarily for a *general audience* of interested, relatively unbiased, open-minded people who have not studied these three holy books systematically and for their psychological and sociological insights. While I have not written this book for members of the clergy, religious scholars, or others who are not interested in psychological and sociological insights, or for whom the background information that follows is unnecessary, I certainly hope they will find my new analysis of violence in all verses in all three books to be more objective, thorough, and incisive than anything they have read until now.

My understanding[1] is that the NT is widely regarded as being the recorded testaments, statements, letters, visions, and revelations of some of the disciples and successive followers of Jesus. It provides some of their recollections of, and beliefs about, what Jesus did and said to them and to others. It also provides statements about what some of them did during their lives with him and after his death. Some of the disciples and their associates traveled by land and sea throughout the Eastern Mediterranean as far as Rome to spread the story of Jesus Christ, to make conversions, and to encourage, guide, and expand groups of believers. Many of them suffered persecution, and several of them were executed for their beliefs and actions, including the disciples Peter and Paul. Additionally, the NT provides statements and beliefs about events that occurred before Jesus was born. It also recounts quite a few of the "biblical stories" in the OT. The NT also presents many guidelines for Christian worship and daily life, including the "Ten Commandments."

While some people believe that the NT is the "word of God," others believe that it is more directly the spoken and written words of the various disciples, as translated into various languages and disseminated widely over nearly two thousand years. I do not favor one position over the other. Our interest is in how violence, terror, and war are portrayed in the NT and other "holy books," rather than in whether the portrayals are authentic, credible, truthful, or moral.

The KJV of the Bible that I analyze consists of twenty-seven "books" by at least seven disciples of Jesus and some of their followers. Each book has a varying number of chapters, verses, and passages within each chapter. As in the preceding chapters on the Qur'an and the OT, I focus on the quantities and qualities of physical violence against human beings as portrayed or referred to in the verses of the NT. While doing this, I also suggest how these verses might influence some people towards or away from violent behaviors now and in the future.

In contrast to a common procedure in many books that *gradually* move towards major findings, I will now present what I believe to be my

Portrayals of Violence in the New Testament

most important findings regarding the *number* of portrayals of violence in the NT. Then I will present other important findings and detailed information about how I arrived at these findings. Table 11 presents a summary of the number of verses in each of the books of the NT that refer to or portray actual physical violence against human beings.

Regarding Table 11

As shown in Table 11, only about 1.84% (147) of the 7,956 verses in the NT refer to or portray actual physical violence against human beings. By contrast, as indicated in the preceding chapters of this book, the OT (5.16 %) and the Qur'an (11.9%) have considerably higher percentages of verses that refer to or portray actual physical violence against human beings. One implication of this finding for contemporary world affairs and issues about violence and terrorism is that people who are looking to find portrayals of physical violence in these "holy books" will find considerable more portrayals in the OT and in the Qur'an than in the NT. This is true both absolutely and proportionately. The OT has more than three times as many chapters (929) verses (23,145*) and words (645,117) as the NT (260 chapters; 7,956 verses; 138,020 words). The Qur'an has considerably fewer chapters/surahs (114), verses (6,204-6,236 — depending on the languages and translations), and words (77,449). Also, as explained in Chapter 2, in the Qur'an it is much easier for even the most casual viewer to find surahs, verses, and passages that portray actual physical violence towards humans. This is because the Qur'an is considerably shorter than the OT and the NT, and portrayals of violence tend to be concentrated in the first ten surahs (chapters) of the Qur'an. Additionally, as explained in Chapter 2, some of the surah titles, including "Spoils of War" (Surah 8), "The Troops" (Surah 39), and "Victory" (Surah 48), make it easier for readers to find passages that portray violence.

Table 11a. Summary of Portrayals of Actual Physical Violence against Humans in the Books of the New Testament.

	A*	B**
GOSPELS (A.D. 40s-70s)		
MATTHEW Jewish, apostle of Jesus. Tax collector.	27	1071
MARK Jewish, disciple of Peter. Missionary.	16	678
LUKE Greek, disciple of Paul. Physician.	30	1151
JOHN Jewish, apostle of Jesus. Fisherman.	19	879
ACTS OF THE APOSTLES. LUKE. (Same author as the Gospel).	23	1006
13 EPISTLES OF PAUL Jewish tentmaker. Former Pharisee.		
ROMANS	? 2 ?	433
1 CORINTHIANS	5	437
2 CORINTHIANS	2	256
GALATIANS	0	149
EPHESIANS	0	155
PHILIPPIANS	0	104
COLOSSIANS	0	95
1 THESSALONIANS	2	89
2 THESSALONIANS	2	47
1 TIMOTHY	0	113
2 TIMOTHY	0	83
TITUS	0	46
PHILEMON	0	25

Portrayals of Violence in the New Testament 185

Table 11b. Summary of Portrayals of Actual Physical Violence against Humans in the Books of the New Testament (Cont.).

	A*	B**
HEBREWS Author unknown, possibly Paul, Timothy, or others.	7	303
JAMES Jewish half-brother of Jesus. Pastor.	? 2 ?	108
1 PETER Jewish apostle of Jesus. Fisherman.	0	105
2 PETER Jewish apostle of Jesus. Fisherman.	2	61
JUDE Jewish half-brother of Jesus. Carpenter.	3	25
1 JOHN Jewish apostle of Jesus, fisherman (also authored the Gospel John).	1	105
2 JOHN Jewish apostle of Jesus, fisherman (").	0	13
3 JOHN Jewish apostle of Jesus, fisherman (").	0	15
REVELATION (Author generally considered to be John (in Patmos).	3	404
***TOTAL:	147 (1.84%)	7,956

* COLUMN A: The number of verses in each book of the New Testament that refer to or portray actual physical violence against human beings.

** COLUMN B: The approximate total number of verses in each book of the New Testament (the exact number can vary slightly among different versions).

*** Only about 1.84% (147/ 7,956) of the 7,956 verses in the New Testament refer to or portray actual physical violence against human beings.

There are many other findings of importance regarding the quantities and qualities of violence portrayed in the NT. But first, let me explain how I arrived at the calculations that are presented in Table 12. I start by discussing the first book of the NT, the Gospel of Matthew.

PORTRAYALS OF VIOLENCE IN THE GOSPEL OF MATTHEW

According to the introduction to this gospel by the editors of the KJV,[2] Matthew is generally considered to have been one of the closest disciples of Jesus. He was a Jewish tax collector. He composed this gospel of the life of Christ between 40-70 A.D. It is one of the longest books in the NT, with twenty-eight chapters and more than one thousand verses.

The portrayals of violence in Matthew cover a number of topics and events, including the plot to kill Jesus, the scourging, and his death by crucifixion.

Portrayals of Violence in the New Testament

Table 12. Violence as Portrayed in Matthew's Gospel.

1	Number of verses that portray violence against humans	27
2	Violence by non-Christians (when apparent)	8
3	Violence by Christian people other than Jesus (when apparent)	2
4	Jesus (GOD) portrayed as:	
	a. Committing violence	(0) ? 2 ?
	b. Predicting, threatening, or warning about violence	(0) 15
	c. Demanding violence by others	(0) ? 1 ?
	d. Rejecting violence	(0) 3
5	Other repudiations of violence	2
6	Portrayals and references to doom, fire, and hellfire as violence	11
7	Portrayals of military wars or battles	3
	a. Portrayals of violence in wars or battles	2

Regarding Table 12

Row 1 indicates that I found twenty-seven verses in Matthew that portray or refer to actual physical violence against humans. This does not include the many parables or stories that portray violence symbolically or metaphorically against nature, humans, animals, evil spirits, or other elements. It includes the very first portrayal of actual violence in the NT in which Herod demands the slaying of all children two years of age or younger (Matt. 2: 16). It also includes quite a few verses that describe the torture and killing of Jesus. Let me suggest that 27 verses with violence is a very small percentage (less than 3%) of the 1,071 verses in Matthew (indicated in Table 12).

Row 2 conveys that eight verses in Matthew (Matt.) portray violence by non-Christians. These include the verse that refers to Herod ordering the beheading of John the Baptist (Matt. 14: 10) and a verse that portrays the crucifixion of Jesus and the two thieves. Speaking for myself, I was rather surprised that so few verses depict violence by non-Christians.

Row 3 conveys that two verses portray violence by Christians other than Jesus. One of these verses has already been referred to as an instance in which Jesus repudiated this violence by his disciple who smites off the ear of a soldier (Matt. 26: 51). The other instance is the famous verse (Matt. 27:5) of the suicide of Judas—essentially lethal violence done to oneself.

Row 4 conveys the number of verses that portray Jesus and God (in parentheses) as committing violence (4a), predicting, threatening, or warning others about violence (4b), demanding violence by others (4c), and rejecting violence (4d). Notice that God is *not* portrayed in any of these ways in any of the verses. This is in stark contrast to how Allah is often portrayed in the Qur'an, and how God is often portrayed in the OT, as explained in the preceding chapters of this book. God is *not* violent in Mathew's Gospel. Nor is Jesus portrayed very often in relation to violence. There are only two verses in which Jesus seems to be portrayed as committing violence—and both of these are debatable and controversial. In Matthew 8: 32, Jesus casts devils into a herd of swine. Then the swine run into a river and drown. This is not violence against human beings. For this reason, I have placed question marks around the entries in Table 12. The second instance is in Matthew 21: 12; Jesus is portrayed as overturning tables of rabbis and merchants in a temple. Then he chases them out of the temple. I placed questions marks in Table 12 to acknowledge that this action may not have done any physical damage to any of the people.

Row 4b conveys that Jesus is portrayed fifteen times in Matthew as predicting, threatening, or warning about violence. For example, in Matthew 8: 13 Jesus predicts gnashing of teeth and other violence. In Matthew 17: 23, Jesus predicts that he will be killed.

Row 4c conveys that there is one verse (Matt. 10: 8) in which Jesus demands violence. However, he actually demands that his disciples "cast-out" "devils"—not humans. So, it is debatable as to whether this constitutes our working definition of physical violence. Even if it does, it is not against humans but only against "devils."

Row 4d indicates that Jesus rejects violence in three of the verses. This includes Jesus reprimanding his disciple for cutting off the ear of a soldier who was trying to arrest Jesus the night before the crucifixion (Matt. 26: 67).

By way of comment, then, Matthew's Gospel does not portray God as violent and it only occasionally relates Jesus to violence, often in the form of Jesus predicting violence against himself or against others.

Row 5 conveys that there are two verses in which violence is repudiated or rejected by people other than by God the Father or by Jesus. One of these is a verse that rejects the Hammurabi Code of "an eye for an eye" (Matt. 5: 38-39). Another verse instructs believers to "do no murder" (Matt. 19: 18).

Row 6 conveys that I found eleven verses that threaten, promise, or describe violent fire, "hellfire," doom, or burning for people who violate various Christian principles. These include verses Matthew 5: 22 and 13: 40-42. It is worth noting that, in contrast to the Qur'an, which often portrays Allah as condemning miscreants to hellfire, none of these verses portray God as doing so.

And finally, Row 7 shows that I found three verses that portray or refer to war. These are the famous verses (Matt. 24: 6, 7, 9) which convey that there will be wars and "rumors of war" and that some people will be killed before more peaceful times ensue. Only two of these three verses portray physical violence in war, however. That is the reason for the "2" in row 7a. It is worth noting that these verses do not convey who the combatants will be or why they will engage in warfare. There is no suggestion that the wars will pit Christians against non-Christians or that they will be religious in nature. As presented by Matthew, Jesus tells his disciples about the coming of these wars after he is angered by his observations of commercial activity and other perceived violations of Jewish law in a temple that they visited.

By way of conclusion, I believe that the more than 1,000 verses in the Gospel of Matthew do not often portray violence, wars, or violence in wars. None of the actual violence is by God. Jesus is not portrayed as committing lethal physical violence against any human beings or as demanding that any humans should be damaged, injured, or slain. In three verses he is portrayed as rejecting violence. Furthermore, the relatively few portrayals of violence in Matthew's Gospel usually portray Jesus, his disciples, or other followers as being the victims of violence —not the perpetrators of violence.

Violence as Portrayed in the Gospel of Mark

Portrayals of violence in Mark are similar to those in Matthew but there are fewer of them, as one might expect, given that Mark's Gospel is much shorter than Matthew's. Mark's Gospel consists of sixteen chapters and 678 verses.

By way of background, Mark is described as a Jewish missionary and close disciple of Peter.[3] He probably wrote his Gospel in the 60's A.D. "The book bears the stamp of the early and authentic written witness to Jesus's ministry. It is thought that Mark wrote primarily for a largely Gentile audience that resided in Rome." Much of this Gospel deals with the miracles attributed to Jesus and his disciples as well as with his crucifixion and ascension.

Table 13. Portrayals of Violence in Mark's Gospel.

1	Number of verses that portray violence against humans	17
2	Violence by non-Christians (when apparent)	10
3	Violence by Christian people other than Jesus (when apparent)	1
4	Jesus (GOD) portrayed as:	
	a. Committing violence	(0) ? 1 ?
	b. Predicting, threatening, or warning about violence	(0) 3
	c. Demanding violence by others	(0) 0
	d. Rejecting violence	(0) 0
5	Other repudiations of violence	1
6	Portrayals and references to doom, fire, and hellfire as violence	? 1 ?
7	Portrayals of military wars or battles	4
	a. Portrayals of violence in wars or battles	3

Regarding Table 13

Row 1 shows that I found seventeen verses that portray or refer to actual violence against humans. Most of the portrayals of violence in Mark's Gospel are the same or very similar to the portrayals in Matthew's Gospel. For example, Mark 6: 16 and 27 refer to Herod ordering the beheading of John the Baptist. Mark 14: 65 refers to the crowds striking and spitting on Jesus. Several other verses refer to the scourging of Jesus.

Row 2 shows that I found ten verses that portray violence by non-Christians. Most of these relate to the crucifixion of Jesus. Row 3 indicates that one verse was found in which a Christian other than Jesus committed violence (Mark 14: 47). This is essentially the same incident reported in Matthew in which one disciple cuts off the ear of a servant of a high priest. However, it is interesting that Mark does not portray Jesus reacting to this violence by repudiating it, as did Matthew.

Row 4 shows that, once again, God the Father is never portrayed in relation to violence. Only in a few verses is Jesus related to violence. Similar to a verse in Matthew, Mark 11: 15 portrays Jesus casting out merchants from the temple. Question marks are placed in row 4a because it is debatable as to whether this constitutes physical violence that damaged anyone. Row 4b shows that there are three verses in which Jesus predicts, threatens or warns about violence. These are Mark 9: 31; 10: 34, and 14: 27. Rows 4c and 4d show that I did not find any verses in which Jesus is portrayed as demanding violence or rejecting violence. Row 5 shows that one verse in Mark repudiates violence.

The entry in Row 6 is noteworthy. It is based on Mark 16: 16, a verse that is only four verses from the end of Mark's Gospel. In this verse Mark portrays Jesus as saying, *"He that believeth and is baptized shall be saved; but he that believeth not shall be damned." I placed question marks adjacent to this entry in Table 13 to indicate that it is not clear to me that being "damned" constitutes physical violence. Readers are encouraged to decide for themselves. As indicated in an earlier chapter of this book, Allah is often portrayed as personally condemning unbelievers and other miscreants to fire, hellfire, and other types of very explicit violence. Whereas, in this verse in Mark, it is Mark claiming that Jesus said, "He that believeth..." It is not a direct quote by Jesus or by God the Father—nor is it portrayed that way.

And finally, Rows 7 and 7a indicate that military wars and battles are referred to in four verses of Mark (13: 7, 8, 9, and 13) and that physical violence is conveyed in three of these verses (13: 8, 9, 13). These verses are very similar to those in Matthew's Gospel. Jesus tells his disciples that there will be wars and rumors of wars and that some people will suffer various types of violence, although, eventually, these wars will pass.

Violence as Portrayed in the Gospel of Luke

Considerable attention is given to Luke here, and for many reasons that are explained at length in the KJV.[4] A highly literate, educated, and dedicated Greek physician, Luke is widely considered to be the author, not only of the Third Gospel but of the voluminous "Acts of the Apostles."

> Modern scholarship has rightly drawn attention to Luke as the author of the companion volume of Acts, the two works were certainly written by the same author. Together they make up over half of the New Testament, so by sheer volume of output alone Luke takes on special significance.
>
> While Luke was not himself an eyewitness of the gospel events (1: 2), he had access to writings about them, and eyewitnesses to them. He had sifted sources carefully.... He presents both the meaning of the gospel saga and its factual ground. He produces what is, by the reckoning of many, the gospel most attractive in style and poignant in messages that we possess.

Luke's Gospel describes many of the events in Jesus's life and crucifixion that also are portrayed in the Gospels of Matthew, Mark, and John, but Luke's versions sometimes are somewhat different than theirs. Luke's Gospel also includes a considerable number of additional topics and interpretations.

Table 14. Violence Portrayed in Luke's Gospel.

1	Number of verses that portray violence against humans	30
2	Violence by non-Christians (when apparent)	8
3	Violence by Christian people other than Jesus (when apparent)	1
4	Jesus (GOD) portrayed as:	
	a. Committing violence	(0) ? 3 ?
	b. Predicting, threatening, or warning about violence	(0) 15
	c. Demanding violence by others	(0) 0
	d. Rejecting violence	(0) 5
5	Other repudiations of violence	1
6	Portrayals and references to doom, fire, and hellfire as violence	3
7	Portrayals of military wars or battles	6
	a. Portrayals of violence in wars or battles	3

Some Distinctive Aspects of Violence Portrayed in Luke's Gospel

Row 1 shows that I found thirty portrayals or references to actual physical violence in Luke's Gospel. This is somewhat higher than in the Gospels of Matthew and Mark.

In Luke 4: 29, Jews cast Jesus out of the temple. In Luke 9: 42 the devil throws down a boy, but Jesus then saves the boy.

Luke's Gospel has quite a few portrayals of Jesus predicting or warning about violence (Row 4b). In Chapters 11 and 12, Jesus warns the Pharisees and lawyers of God's power. Jesus also warns the Pharisees of doom (Luke 19: 43). In Luke 21: 20, 22, and 24, Jesus warns that Gentiles will capture Jerusalem. In Luke 12: 49, Jesus warns that "I came to send fire on the Earth." In Luke 13: 3-5, Jesus warns people to repent or perish, but without saying who will make them perish, or when this will occur.

Portrayals of Violence in the New Testament 195

There also are several verses in which Jesus is portrayed as referring to violent events in the past, including the destruction by the flood which spared Noah (Luke 17: 27) and the destruction of Sodom (Luke 17: 29).

Other entries in Table 14 indicate that, compared to the other books of the NT, Luke's Gospel has a number of verses in which Jesus rejects violence (Row 4d), hellfire is portrayed as violence against humans (Row 6), and military wars and battles are portrayed (Row 7), and are portrayed as being violent (Row 7a). Then again, as with the Gospels of Matthew and Mark, violence is not portrayed very often in Luke's Gospel if we consider that his Gospel has more verses (1151) than any other book in the NT. Once again, however, it is noteworthy that, just as in the Gospels of Matthew, Mark, and John, Luke's Gospel never portrays God the Father as committing, predicting, threatening, warning, demanding, or rejecting violence (Rows 4a, b, c, and d).

VIOLENCE AS PORTRAYED IN THE GOSPEL OF JOHN

According to the KJV,[5] "John's Gospel is noticeably distinct from the other three gospels.... John's purpose is unique and consequently, so is his interpretation of the life of Jesus."

As shown in Table 15, John's Gospel is also quite distinctive in providing a relatively large number of verses (14 in Row 2) that portray violence by non-Christians, particularly by Jews and Pharisees against Jesus and the disciples. For example, in verses John 5: 16, John 7: 1, and John 7: 19, Jews are portrayed as persecuting Jesus and seeking to slay him on several occasions, months before the crucifixion. There also are three verses in which Jews or Pharisees are portrayed as trying to stone Jesus, although he escapes from them (John 8: 59; 10: 39, and 11: 45-48).

John's Gospel also has more verses that provide violent details about the crucifixion of Jesus and the thieves (including John 18: 12 and 22, and John 19: 1, 2, 3, 18, 29, 32, and 34). The entries in rows 3, 4a, 4d, and 5 are similar to the same entries in the tables related to the Gospels of Matthew,

Mark, and Luke. For example, in Row 4a the question marks around the entry indicates that it is questionable whether physical violence actually is portrayed in the verse about Jesus overturning the tables in the temple and casting-out the merchants. By the way, the entry in Row 3 is the same event reported in the other Gospels, except John's version is more explicit in identifying the perpetrator (Peter) and the recipient (Malchus) of the violence in which a sword was used to cut-off the ear of a servant—Malchus, in this case. Row 4d refers to the same two instances of rejections of violence; both are by Jesus. In John 8: 5-11, Jesus refuses to approve the stoning of an adulterous woman. In John 18: 11, Jesus rebukes Peter for cutting off the ear of Malchus.

Perhaps even more noteworthy with John's Gospel than with those of the other three disciples, I did not find any verses in which Jesus or God the Father is portrayed as predicting, threatening, or warning of violence, or of demanding violence by others. This is indicated in rows 4b, 4c, 6, 7, and 7a. Nor did I find verses which portrayed doom, fire, or hellfire as violence (row 6), or of military wars or violence in wars (rows 7 and 7a).

By way of comment, contemporary people who are oriented towards violence are not likely to find in John's Gospel many, if any, verses that promote the use of violence. Then again, some contemporary people might be offended by the violence that was used against Jesus and his disciples in the relatively few verses that portray this in John's Gospel and the Gospels of the other three disciples. And, once again, I mention that God the Father is *never* portrayed as violent in any way in the Gospel of John, as best as I could tell from my effort to read every word as objectively and literally as possible.

As you might have guessed by now, my analysis of the Qur'an and of the NT is leading me to conclude that portrayals of Allah in the Qur'an are considerably more violent than are portrayals of God the Father and of Jesus in the NT. We often hear well-meaning religious leaders, scholars, and believers of different religions say that they are worshipping "the same God." We also hear it said that there is "only one God" and that the

Portrayals of Violence in the New Testament

one God has many different names including Allah, God, Jesus, The Holy Spirit, Jehovah, etc. It is not for me to question whether these claims are true. However, I believe that my analysis is demonstrating that *portrayals* of Allah, of God the Father, and of Jesus certainly are quite different in the Qur'an, in the OT, and in the NT, at least as far as violence is concerned. The God might be the same—but the portrayals certainly are not the same, or even close to the same regarding violence. Admittedly the portrayals might be much closer—possibly even identical—regarding some other quality, such as justice, forgiveness, sin, love, and redemption.

Table 15. Violence Portrayed in John's Gospel.

1	Number of verses that portray violence against humans	19
2	Violence by non-Christians (when apparent)	14
3	Violence by Christian people other than Jesus (when apparent)	1
4	Jesus (GOD) portrayed as:	
	a. Committing violence	(0) ? 1 ?
	b. Predicting, threatening, or warning about violence	(0) 0
	c. Demanding violence by others	(0) 0
	d. Rejecting violence	(0) 2
5	Other repudiations of violence	0
6	Portrayals and references to doom, fire, and hellfire as violence	0
7	Portrayals of military wars or battles	0
	a. Portrayals of violence in wars or battles	0

Acts of the Apostles

According to the KJV,[6] Acts "is a unique and therefore crucial book of the New Testament. It alone presents an extensive picture of early church life and history." It is widely assumed that Luke wrote it and completed it by 62 A.D. Luke's purpose was to bring unity to early Christian groups and to "show to the Roman world that Christianity is not a subversive political movement." Most of Acts tells the stories of the travels of Peter and Paul around the eastern coast of the Mediterranean trying to spread Christianity through conversions, miracles (e.g. Dorcas is restored to life by Peter at Joppa) despite facing frequent persecution, arrests, trials, and violence by various religious and ethnic groups. Acts also includes a number of verses about how Saul converted to Christianity and assumed the name of Paul. By the way, we do not assume that arrests and imprisonment are necessarily physically violent unless they are portrayed that way. For example, Acts 5: 26 conveys that a high priest had the disciples arrested for doing miracles, but that this was done "without violence." It is worth keeping in mind that verses that portray violence against humans (Row 1) include verses that refer to historical acts of violence including the torturing and crucifixion of Jesus, as well as to acts of violence that occurred during the travels of the apostles in the decades after Jesus's death.

Portrayals of Violence in the New Testament

Table 16. Violence Portrayed in Acts of the Apostles.

1	Number of verses that portray violence against humans	23
2	Violence by non-Christians (when apparent)	18
3	Violence by Christian people other than Jesus (when apparent)	? 3 ?
4	Jesus (GOD) portrayed as:	
	a. Committing violence	(0) 0
	b. Predicting, threatening, or warning about violence	(0) 0
	c. Demanding violence by others	(0) 0
	d. Rejecting violence	(0) 0
5	Other repudiations of violence	0
6	Portrayals and references to doom, fire, and hellfire as violence	1
7	Portrayals of military wars or battles	0
	a. Portrayals of violence in wars or battles	0

Row 1 of Table 16 indicates that only 23 verses were found in Acts of the Apostles (Acts) that convey violence. Row 2 indicates that eighteen of these verses portray violence by non-Christians. This includes verses that refer to events in the distant past, but also to events that occurred during the conversion missions of Peter and Paul. Some of the examples include verses in which high priests have the apostles beaten (Acts 5: 40), the stoning of Stephen the Greek convert to Christianity (Acts 7: 58-59), and Herod having a prison guard put to death because Peter escaped during his watch in the midst of an earthquake (Acts 12: 19). Other verses that portray violence by non-Christians include a situation in which a chief captain has Paul beaten as *"gentiles violently protest that Jews and soldiers are doing this" (Acts 21: 32-35); Paul being bound and beaten violently (Acts 24:7); and a verse in which Ananias has Paul smitten in the mouth because of his preaching (Acts 23: 4). Even more explicit is the violence portrayed in Acts 16: 22-24:

> *And the multitude rose up together against them: and the magistrates rent-off their clothes and commanded to beat them. And when they had laid many stripes upon them, they cast them into prison, charging the jailer to keep them safely: Who, have received such a charge, thrust them into the inner prison, and made their feet fast in the stocks.

Row 3 indicates that there are possibly three verses in Acts which portray Christians other than Jesus and God the Father as committing violence, although inclusion might be debatable. Acts 13: 8 portrays Paul condemning a sorcerer and blinding him for a season. Acts 12: 23 claims that an *"angel of the Lord smote him (Herod) and had him eaten by worms." Verse 17 in Chapter 18 of Acts conveys that Greeks in Corinth beat the chief ruler of the synagogue in defense of Paul and Christianity. However, it is not clear that these Greeks had already converted to Christianity. In any case, this is a relatively rare instance of the NT portraying Christians or Christian sympathizers as using violence against non-Christians.

Possibly the most significant numbers in Table 16 are the many "zero" entries. They indicate that I did not find any verses in Acts that portray Jesus or God the Father as committing, predicting, threatening, warning of, demanding, or rejecting violence (Rows 4a, b, c, d). Nor did I find any portrayals of anyone explicitly rejecting violence (Row 5).

Row 6 indicates that I found one verse of doom being invoked. In Acts 3: 23, Peter threatens doom on those who will not hear the Prophet: *"And it shall come to pass, that every soul, which will not hear that Prophet, shall be destroyed from among the people."

And finally, as indicated in Rows 7 and 7a, I did not find any portrayals of military war or of violence in military wars or battles.

By way of conclusion, it seems to me that Acts of the Apostles does not portray a lot of violence and that the violence that it does portray is decidedly by non-Christians against Christians, Paul and Peter in particular.

THE EPISTLE OF PAUL TO THE ROMANS

According to the KJV,[7] Paul, the 13th apostle of Christ, was a convert to Christianity after having been born a Jew (named Saul) and a former Pharisee. He also had vigorously opposed and persecuted Christians before his conversion. Like Peter, Paul traveled much of the Eastern Mediterranean on three or four conversion missions, often with his favorite protégé, Timothy. Paul resided in Rome for two years before he was executed for his preaching of Christianity. Paul generally is considered to be the author of the thirteen epistles attributed to him, of which Romans (Rom.) is the longest and most influential.

According to the KJV,[8] "Romans has been called 'The Constitution of Christianity,' 'The Christian Manifesto,' and 'The Cathedral of the Christian Faith.' It is noteworthy for being the most complete compendium of Christian doctrine.'" It is generally believed that Paul wrote it between 56-58 A.D., during the two years he was in Corinth. Paul's purpose was to inspire and unify the small groups of Christians who were trying to practice their faith in Rome, in anticipation of his visiting Rome. As important as it is in these ways, the Epistle of Paul to the Romans is relatively short. Paul often claims that God the Father is vengeful and wrathful, as well as merciful and forgiving (not unlike many passages in the Qur'an regarding Allah—as I described in the chapter on the Qur'an). But Paul does not make it clear that vengefulness and wrathfulness are physically violent to humans in terms of inflicting physical pain, damage, or death upon them. Because of this, there are very few positive numbers in Table 17 regarding portrayals of physical violence.

Table 17. Violence Portrayed in Paul's Epistle to the Romans.

1	Number of verses that portray violence against humans	? 2 ?
2	Violence by non-Christians (when apparent)	1
3	Violence by Christian people other than Jesus (when apparent)	0
4	Jesus (GOD) portrayed as:	
	a. Committing violence	(? 2 ?) 0
	b. Predicting, threatening, or warning about violence	(0) 0
	c. Demanding violence by others	(0) 0
	d. Rejecting violence	(0) 0
5	Other repudiations of violence	2
6	Portrayals and references to doom, fire, and hellfire as violence	0
7	Portrayals of military wars or battles	0
	a. Portrayals of violence in wars or battles	0

By way of explanation of the entries in Table 17, Row 1 has question marks adjacent to the entry because the verses they refer to (Rom. 10: 3 and 12: 20) might be more figurative than literal in terms of violence. "Lord they have killed thy prophets," is the essence of Verse 3 of Chapter 10. "Thou shall heap coals on his head," is the essence of Verse 20 of Chapter 12. In Row 4a the two entries also have question marks because it is Paul —not God the Father—who claims that God the Father is violent or can be violent. In Romans 12: 19-20, Paul asserts that "only God can be vengeful, wrathful." This does not explicitly state that God commits wrathful or vengeful acts that are necessarily violent physically. In Romans 16: 20, Paul proclaims that *"The God of Peace shall bruise Satan under your feet shortly." The target of the violence here seems to be Satan, rather than any human being. The question marks indicate these differences.

Portrayals of Violence in the New Testament

Row 5 indicates that there are two verses in Romans which reject violence. These are Romans 12: 18 and 13: 8 (*"Thou shalt not kill.").

By way of conclusion, Paul's letter to the Romans portrays very little violence by anyone against anyone despite the persecutions of Christians, including Paul, that were occurring during this time.

VIOLENCE PORTRAYED IN PAUL'S OTHER TWELVE EPISTLES

The KJV[9] indicates that Paul probably composed these other twelve epistles while he was residing for two years in various provinces, principally the Macedonian city of Corinth. The epistles diminish in length and in Paul's near obsession and frequent rages about human lusts. His later epistles are not so insistent on strict obedience to Christian and Jewish commandments and daily rules to counter human frailties and to avoid sin. In the epistles to the Corinthians and Thessalonians, Paul also provides many verses about proper gender roles, marriage, consumption of food and beverages, circumcision, virginity, and other topics. He also provides some of the most famous quotes from the NT, including *"When I was a child I spake as a child," (1 Cor. 13: 11). As the epistles get shorter, Paul seems to age noticeably. He becomes calmer, less imperative and harsh, and more inclined to ask for help, friendship, brotherly love, and peace among all people. More central to our analysis, however, is that there is relatively little physical violence referred to and portrayed in Paul's epistles. This is rather remarkable, given the severe persecution that he and many other Christians were experiencing, including beatings. Paul was executed by the Romans two years after he moved to Rome to continue his conversions. It can be helpful to consider how the KJV portrays Corinth in Paul's time.[10]

> When Paul came to Corinth in about A.D. 51, it was again a thriving metropolis, the capital of the senatorial province of Achaia.... Religiously, the city had every type of cult its pluralistic society could bring to it. There was also a synagogue and a large contingent of Jews. From such a diverse cultural hub, a strong

gospel witness might well be heard all over the world. No wonder Paul felt constrained to bear a testimony to such a city.

The moral depravity of Corinth, legendary even in the ancient pagan world, vividly reflected the spiritual need of the city, which was known as a seaman's paradise and moral cesspool.

Table 18 summarizes the relatively few verses in all twelve of Paul's Epistles that refer to or portray actual physical violence against humans (once again, *not* including violent figures of speech, metaphors, and symbols).

Table 18. Violence Portrayed in Paul's Other Twelve Epistles.

1	Number of verses that portray violence against humans	13
2	Violence by non-Christians (when apparent)	7
3	Violence by Christian people other than Jesus (when apparent)	0
4	Jesus (GOD) portrayed as:	
	a. Committing violence	(0) 0
	b. Predicting, threatening, or warning about violence	(0) 0
	c. Demanding violence by others	(0) 0
	d. Rejecting violence	(0) 0
5	Other repudiations of violence	1
6	Portrayals and references to doom, fire, and hellfire as violence	4
7	Portrayals of military wars or battles	0
	a. Portrayals of violence in wars or battles	0

Some Distinctive Aspects of the Entries in Table 18

Row 1 shows that I found only thirteen verses in all twelve of Paul's epistles that refer to or portray physical violence against humans. Many of these refer to violence in historical events and to the crucifixion of Jesus (1 Cor. 10: 8, 9, and 10, 2 Cor. 13: 4, and 1 Thes. 2: 14-15). In one verse (1 Cor. 3: 17), Paul warns of possible violence by God: *"If any man defile the temple of God, him shall God destroy; for the temple of God is holy, which temple ye are."

Of course, this is a claim by Paul—not by God; but it certainly does warn of physical violence—the defiler will be destroyed.

Row 2 shows that I found seven verses that portray violence by non-Christians, usually Jews, against Christians or converts to Christianity, including Paul himself. For example, 2 Corinthians 11: 23-25 portray Paul himself claiming to have suffered physical violence by Jews even though he was born a Jew:

> *Are they ministers of Christ? (I speak as a fool) I am more; in labors more abundant, in stripes above measure, in prisons more frequent, in deaths oft.
>
> Of the Jews five times received I forty stripes save one.
>
> Thrice was I beaten with rods, once was I stoned, thrice I suffered shipwreck, a night and a day I have been in the deep.

The remainder of the rows in Table 18 show "0" as entries except for row 5 and 6. Row 5 has one entry. It is based on Titus 3: 2. This is a verse which warns people to not be brawlers. The four entries in Row 6 are based on four verses that portray the doom of hell for various kinds of offenses. Here are a few of those verses:

> *In flaming fire taking vengeance on them that know not God, and that obey not the gospel of our Lord Jesus Christ:
>
> Who shall be punished with everlasting destruction from the presence of the Lord, and from the Glory of his power; (2 Thes. 1: 8, 9)

> *And then shall the wicked be revealed, whom the Lord shall consume with the spirit of his mouth, and shall destroy with the brightness of his coming. (2 Thes. 2: 8)

Once again, we should note that these are portrayals by Paul about the Lord rather than by the Lord. And once again I mention that this is in contrast to quite a few verses in the Qur'an which portray Allah as the perpetrator, demander, threatener, and warner of doom for unbelievers and sinners.

Along this same line of thought, there is a verse (2 Cor. 5: 11) in which Paul refers to the "terror of the Lord." *"Knowing therefore the terror of the Lord, we persuade men; but we are made manifest unto God; and I trust also are made manifest in your consciences." Notice that there is no indication that this "terror" necessarily includes physical violence. For this reason, this verse is not included as an entry in Table 18.

Before leaving the Epistles of Paul, we note that, in his later epistles, Paul often portrays himself as an old man who has "fought the good fight." He advises his beloved protégé, Timothy, to drink no water but just a little wine.[11] At times, the verses seem to convey that Paul anticipates his own death, possibly by execution, because of his preaching. And yet, in the final verses in the final epistle, Philemon, Paul is a prisoner in Rome, but he mentions in his letters that he is preparing to be released from prison, without realizing he will be beheaded very soon. Paul's last words and testament appear as follows in the KJV.[12]

> *Paul's Last Testament*
>
> *For I am now ready to be offered, and the time of my departure is at hand.
>
> I have fought a good fight, I have finished my courses, and I have kept the faith. (2 Timothy 4: 6-7)

The Epistle to the Hebrews

According to the KJV:[13]

> For some unknown reason the author remains anonymous to us, though he was known to his original readers.... The exhortations and warnings of Hebrews indicate that the recipients were Jewish Christians who were in danger of returning to Judaism. By returning, these early Christians could avoid persecution. Judaism was sanctioned and protected by Roman law; Christianity was not.

Hebrews has thirteen chapters and occupies about twenty pages in the KJV, including footnotes. Many of the verses in Hebrews (Heb.) are similar to verses in the OT in their abundance of harsh warnings, curses, and references to sacrificing beasts in religious rituals (Heb. 13: 11). As shown in Row 1 of Table 19, I found seven verses that portrayed or referred to actual violence against humans (Heb. 3: 17; Heb. 11: 34-37; Heb. 12: 2; and Heb. 12: 6). Four verses in Chapter 11 are particularly violent in referring to bloody conflicts involving Moses, other Prophets, and their adversaries.

> *Quenched the violence of fire, escaped the edge of the sword, out of weakness were made strong, waxed valiant in fight, turned to fight the armies of the aliens.
>
> Women received their dead raised to life again; and others were tortured, not accepting deliverance; that they might obtain a better resurrection:
>
> And others had trial of cruel mockings and scourgings, yes, moreover of bonds and imprisonment:
>
> They were stoned, they were sawn asunder, were tempted, were slain with the sword; they wandered about in sheepskins and goatskins; being destitute, afflicted, tormented. (Heb. 11: 34-37)

Table 19. Violence Portrayed in Hebrews.

1	Number of verses that portray violence against humans	7
2	Violence by non-Christians (when apparent)	6
3	Violence by Christian people other than Jesus (when apparent)	0
4	Jesus (GOD) portrayed as:	
	a. Committing violence	(0) 0
	b. Predicting, threatening, or warning about violence	(0) 0
	c. Demanding violence by others	(0) 0
	d. Rejecting violence	(0) 0
5	Other repudiations of violence	0
6	Portrayals and references to doom, fire, and hellfire as violence	0
7	Portrayals of military wars or battles	1
	a. Portrayals of violence in wars or battles	1

Most significant for us, once again, is that relatively little violence is portrayed or referred to in Hebrews, just as in so many of the other books of the NT. What little violence is portrayed there refers to historical events long before the time of Jesus. None of it is conveyed by God or by Jesus. There are no demands by anyone to be violent towards anyone else. There are just references to violent events in the distant past.

THE GENERAL EPISTLE OF JAMES

The KJV[14] indicates that it is likely that James was a half-brother of Jesus. He grew up in a carpenter's home in Nazareth and later moved to Capernaum when Jesus began his ministry there, eventually becoming a believer. The KJV also states that "everything about the Epistle of

James suggests that it was one of the first New Testament books written probably before 49 A.D. James might have been martyred about A.D. 62."

The verses in James (Jas.) generally are very merciful, encouraging, and non-violent. They include the commandments, including *"Do not kill" (Jas. 2: 11), as well as some of the most often quoted verses in the NT including *"Not by faith alone" (Jas. 2: 24), *"Don't swear or covet," and to *"sing psalms" (Jas. 5: 13). As indicated in Table 20 there are just a few exceptions, among them:

> *From whence come wars and fightings among you? Come they not hence, even of your lusts that war in your members?
>
> Ye lust, and have not: ye kill, and desire to have, and cannot obtain; ye fight and war, yet ye have not, because ye ask not. (Jas. 4: 1-2)

The only two verses that I found that refer to violence portray it as a human sin. In James 5: 6, James asserts that rich men are corrupt and that they kill people who are just. James 4: 2 tells us why wars occur and people are killed. These are not specific references to actual people being killed, so I have marked the entries in Row 1 with question marks. For example: *"Ye have condemned and killed the just; and he doeth not resist you."

Table 20. Violence Portrayed in the Epistle of James.

1	Number of verses that portray violence against humans	? 2 ?
2	Violence by non-Christians (when apparent)	0
3	Violence by Christian people other than Jesus (when apparent)	0
4	Jesus (GOD) portrayed as:	
	a. Committing violence	(0) 0
	b. Predicting, threatening, or warning about violence	(0) 0
	c. Demanding violence by others	(0) 0
	d. Rejecting violence	(0) 0
5	Other repudiations of violence	1
6	Portrayals and references to doom, fire, and hellfire as violence	0
7	Portrayals of military wars or battles	2
	a. Portrayals of violence in wars or battles	1

1st and 2nd Epistles Attributed to Peter

According to the KJV,[15] there is considerable debate as to whether both epistles named for Peter were actually authored by the same person. There is more agreement that the 2nd Epistle (2 Pet.) is more clearly the work of the disciple Peter. Most of the verses in the 1st Epistle (1 Pet.) are very mild and soothing in content. The content of the 2nd Epistle has considerably more negative images and it is more critical, sometimes even harsh. For example, 2 Peter 2: 22 conveys an image of dogs consuming their own vomit. Yet, the 2nd Epistle usually receives more attention, in part because it is thought to have been written by Peter just a year or so before he was martyred in Rome for his preaching. According to the KJV,[16] "By its sheer endurance, 2 Peter demonstrates the truth of 1 Peter 1: 25a 'The word of the Lord endureth for ever.'"

Portrayals of Violence in the New Testament

I found no verses in 1 Peter that portrayed violence, war, doom, or any of the other topics in Table 21. And while there are plenty of rather negative and repulsive passages in the verses of the 2nd Epistle, the very few entries in Table 21 reflect the very few violent verses that I found in Peter's 2nd Epistle.

Table 21. Violence Portrayed in Peter's Two Epistles.

1	Number of verses that portray violence against humans	2
2	Violence by non-Christians (when apparent)	0
3	Violence by Christian people other than Jesus (when apparent)	0
4	Jesus (GOD) portrayed as:	
	a. Committing violence	(? 2 ?) 0
	b. Predicting, threatening, or warning about violence	(0) 0
	c. Demanding violence by others	(0) 0
	d. Rejecting violence	(0) 0
5	Other repudiations of violence	0
6	Portrayals and references to doom, fire, and hellfire as violence	1
7	Portrayals of military wars or battles	0
	a. Portrayals of violence in wars or battles	0

The two entries in Row 1 of Table 21 are based on two verses (2: 5-6) in Peter's 2nd Epistle:

> *And spared not the old world, but saved Noah the eighth person, a preacher of righteousness, bringing in the flood upon the world of the ungodly.

> And turning the cities of Sodom and Gomorrah into ashes condemned them with an overthrow; making them an example unto those that after should live ungodly.

By the way, the entry in Row 4a is based on Peter claiming that God was violent (as distinct from God making such a claim). This is the same entry that is registered in Row 1 above (2 Pet. 2: 4-6).

The entry in Row 6 is based on 2 Peter 2: 12 regarding how sinners will be doomed on Judgment Day:

> *But these, as natural brute beasts, made to be taken and destroyed, speak evil of the things that they understand not; and shall utterly perish in their own corruption.

There also are two verses (2 Pet. 3: 10, 12) that refer to the *"heavens being on fire and other calamities" on Judgment Day, but they do not convey that any humans will suffer physical violence then or because of it. For this reason, these verses were not included as entries.

THE GENERAL EPISTLE OF JUDE

The KJV indicates that Jude probably was a half-brother of James and Jesus. Jude's epistle has only one chapter and 25 verses, quite a few of which are rather fearsome in their depicting events in nature such as of *"raging waves of the sea, foaming out their own shame" (Jude 13). These images seem to be figurative and metaphorical. They do not obviously indicate the physical destruction of humans. However, there are three continuous verses in which Jude refers to violence before Jesus's time (thus the entries in Row 1 of Table 22) and contend that "the Lord" committed these actions (the entries in Row 4a). Two of these verses also convey violent doom on Judgment Day, although one of them asserts that the Lord doomed "angels"— apparently not humans (thus the question marks around the entry in Row 6).

Portrayals of Violence in the New Testament

Here are the three verses, Jude 1: 5-7:

> *I will therefore put you in remembrance, though ye once knew this, how that the Lord, having saved the people out of the land of Egypt, afterward destroyed them that believed not.
>
> And the angels which kept not their first estate, but left their own habitation, he hath reserved in everlasting chains under darkness until the judgment of the great day.
>
> Even as Sodom and Gomorrah, and the cities about them in like manner, giving themselves over to fornication, and going after strange flesh, and set forth for an example, suffering the vengeance of eternal fire.

And yet, like the vast majority of endings in the books of the NT, Jude's final verse (Jude 25) is very spiritual and positive:

> *To the only wise God our Savior, be glory and majesty, dominion and power, both now and ever. Amen.

Table 22. Violence Portrayed in the Epistle of Jude.

1	Number of verses that portray violence against humans	3
2	Violence by non-Christians (when apparent)	0
3	Violence by Christian people other than Jesus (when apparent)	0
4	Jesus (GOD) portrayed as:	
	a. Committing violence	(?3?) 0
	b. Predicting, threatening, or warning about violence	(0) 0
	c. Demanding violence by others	(0) 0
	d. Rejecting violence	(0) 0
5	Other repudiations of violence	0
6	Portrayals and references to doom, fire, and hellfire as violence	?2?
7	Portrayals of military wars or battles	0
	a. Portrayals of violence in wars or battles	0

John's 1st, 2nd, and 3rd Epistles

The KJV[17] indicates that these three very short epistles were authored by the same John whose Gospel bears his name. The verses in these three epistles emphasize brotherly love and love by, and for, God and Jesus and the entire Christian tradition. The 1st Epistle (1 John) has five chapters and nine pages. The 2nd Epistle (2 John) has only thirteen verses. John addresses it to an *"elect lady and her children, whom I love in the truth" (2 John: 1). The 3rd Epistle (3 John) has only fourteen verses. It is written to John's "beloved" colleague Gaius. John continually extends his love and hope for peace to his many colleagues.

As one might expect, there are almost no references to violence in these three epistles. The only entry indicated in Row 1 is based on a verse that claims that Cain slew his brother Abel long before the time of Jesus (1 John 3: 12). There is also a reference to Jesus having *"destroyed the works of the devil" (1 John 3: 3), but there is no indication that this was violence towards any human being. The verse also might be figurative or metaphorical. For this reason, it was not included as an entry in Table 23.

John does warn his readers to avoid fratricide. This is indicated by the entry in Row 5:

> *Whosoever hateth his brother is a murderer: and ye know that no murderer hath eternal life abiding in him. (1 John 3: 15)

Table 23. Violence Portrayed in John's Three Epistles.

1	Number of verses that portray violence against humans	1
2	Violence by non-Christians (when apparent)	0
3	Violence by Christian people other than Jesus (when apparent)	0
4	Jesus (GOD) portrayed as:	
	a. Committing violence	(0) 0
	b. Predicting, threatening, or warning about violence	(0) 0
	c. Demanding violence by others	(0) 0
	d. Rejecting violence	(0) 0
5	Other repudiations of violence	1
6	Portrayals and references to doom, fire, and hellfire as violence	0
7	Portrayals of military wars or battles	0
	a. Portrayals of violence in wars or battles	0

By way of comment, to me, these three epistles of John are remarkably loving, peaceful, and devoid of violence. This is in contrast to the final book of the NT, Revelation, which often is attributed to the same John who wrote the three epistles and one of the Gospels. Personally, I find this to be very doubtful because Revelation is loaded with violent images and many figures of speech and references that seem to be more like the OT than the NT. Then again, some experts[18] claim that Revelation essentially is only the report of a dream, dreams, or visions that someone —possibly John—had about Judgment Day.

THE REVELATION OF JESUS CHRIST TO JOHN

Because I am not an ordained minister, nor an esteemed scholar of religion, let me once again rely on the authors of the KJV[19] to provide some background information about this, the final book, and perhaps the most unusual and controversial book in the NT.

> The Book of Revelation was probably written near the end of the reign of the Roman emperor Domitian —A.D... 95-96. John had been exiled to Patmos for preaching the gospel of Christ (R 1: 9). (It) was designed to close the New Testament revelation and to be the final inspired statement from God until the return of Christ Himself. John may have distributed copies of the book upon his return from exile.... John reports that he saw his visions and was told to write them down while he was on the island of Patmos, and send them to seven churches in the province of Asia (western Asia Minor).
>
> In Revelation Christ and His eternal program are fully revealed, so that the book provides a fitting capstone to the New Testament revelation.
>
> Revelation is apocalyptic in form: that is, it is principally prophetical. Written during a time of persecution, the book abounds with visions (similar to Daniel and Zechariah) and the style is generally figurative and symbolic.

Let us consider the title "Revelation" (Rev.) as it is explained in the KJV. It suggests that John believed that he received this "revelation" from Jesus, perhaps while John was dreaming or meditating. "Twelve times throughout the book John reports that he was told to write down what he saw."[20] A footnote in the KJV[21] goes even further to assert that "God gave the revelation to Christ to be shown to John by means of an angel (messenger). The word 'revelation' (Greek: *Apokalypsis*) refers to an unveiling or exposure of God's program for the world through Christ."

We might also recall that the Qur'an is often thought to have been produced through revelations from Allah through the angel Gabriel to Muhammad while he meditated late at night. It is widely claimed that Muhammad could not read or write. The common belief is that he orally transmitted and revealed the recitations he received to his followers over

Portrayals of Violence in the New Testament

a number of years. In time, those revelations were recorded, translated, and interpreted by an untold number of others. And, of course, devout Muslims throughout the world are obligated to read, recite, or listen to a number of verses in the Qur'an at least five times every day of their lives. To the best of my knowledge, no other religion is so demanding of its followers in this regard.

Going a little further on this matter, while it might be tangential to this report on violence in the holy books, it seems interesting to me that there is this parallelism between the belief systems of Christianity and Islam as to how the Christian "Revelation" and the Muslim Qur'an originated and were created.

Now, in terms of content, the vast majority of passages and verses in Revelation convey what John said he saw (i.e. "I saw...") in the revelation that he received from Jesus regarding events that would occur in the future. Many of these verses refer to Judgment Day and the horrible fates to be suffered by sinners, in contrast to the salvation of righteous Christians. These verses abound in metaphors and symbols (e.g. *"washed us in His own Blood" in Rev. 1: 5). There are many verses in which John claims that in his dreams he saw the tormenting and slaying of all sorts of beasts, dragons, demons, and sinners (harlots and fornicators in particular). So, there are a lot of violent images in Revelation. However, the vast majority of them are *imagined* images of violence—not actual violence in the real world. Table 24 shows that I only found three verses which refer to or portray violence against humans in the real world. Two of these (Rev. 1: 7 and Rev. 11: 8) refer to the actual crucifixion of Jesus. Another verse (Rev. 2: 13) mentions that Antipas was slain at Pergamum. These verses are the ones signified in Row 1 of Table 24. They also are signified in Row 2 because the violence was by non-Christians.

The remainder of the rows have "0" as entries except for Row 4b. That entry has questions marks adjacent to the number "2" for both God the Father and for Jesus. The reason for this entry, and this uncertainty is because the verses are rather ambiguous as to whether it is John or Jesus or God the Father who is portrayed as threatening or warning that they will be violent. Revelation 2: 22-23 conveys ("to the church in Pergamos") that, regarding the woman Jezebel:

> *Behold, I will cast her into a bed, and them that commit adultery with her into great tribulation, except they repent of their deeds.
>
> And I will kill her children with death; and all the churches shall know that I am he which searcheth the reins and hearts; and I will give unto every one of you according to your works.

In Revelation 22: 16, John wrote that, in his revelation from Jesus: *"I Jesus have sent my angels to testify unto you these things in the churches...." Among the things that he testifies to is this in Romans 22: 18: *"For I testify unto every man that heareth the words of the prophets of this book, If any man shall add unto these things, God shall add unto him the plagues that are written in this book."

Portrayals of Violence in the New Testament

Table 24. Violence Referred to or Portrayed in "The Revelation of Jesus Christ to John"

1	Number of verses that portray violence against humans	3
2	Violence by non-Christians (when apparent)	3
3	Violence by Christian people other than Jesus (when apparent)	0
4	Jesus (GOD) portrayed as:	
	a. Committing violence	(0) 0
	b. Predicting, threatening, or warning about violence	(? 2 ?) ? 2 ?
	c. Demanding violence by others	(0) 0
	d. Rejecting violence	(0) 0
5	Other repudiations of violence	0
6	Portrayals and references to doom, fire, and hellfire as violence	0
7	Portrayals of military wars or battles	0
	a. Portrayals of violence in wars or battles	0

And so, while Revelation often is recognized as having many violent images that John recalled from his dreams, few of those images pertain to *actual* violent events against human beings in the real world. It seems appropriate to mention that, despite the many vile and daunting images conveyed in John's Revelation, the final verse in Revelation—and thus in the NT—is devoid of violence, suspicion, intimidation, or any other negative quality. It also extends "grace" to "all." Surely this is not violent, and it does not portray violence: *"The grace of our Lord Jesus Christ be with you all. Amen," (Rev. 22: 21).

Table 25. Summary of the Quantities and Qualities of Violence Portrayed in all Books of the New Testament (as presented in the previous fourteen tables).

	TOTAL number of verses in the New Testament	7,956
1	Number of verses that portray violence against humans	147 – 4 ?
2	Violence by non-Christians (when apparent)	57
3	Violence by Christian people other than Jesus (when apparent)	8 – 3 ?
4	Jesus (GOD) portrayed as:	
	a. Committing violence	(7 – 7 ?) 7 – 7 ?
	b. Predicting, threatening, or warning about violence	(4 – 4 ?) 35 – 2 ?
	c. Demanding violence by others	(0) 1 – 1 ?
	d. Rejecting violence	(0) 10
5	Other repudiations of violence	9
6	Portrayals and references to doom, fire, and hellfire as violence	23
7	Portrayals of military wars or battles	16
	a. Portrayals of violence in wars or battles	10
8	Portrayals of "terror" as physical violence	0
9	Portrayals of genocide as the extermination of all human beings in specific settlements, cities, clans, or nations	0

Regarding Table 25

Table 25 serves as a summary of various types of violence as portrayed in verses in the NT, as presented in the previous fourteen tables. Moving from the top row to the bottom row of Table 25, first consider that many versions of the NT have 7,956 verses. Notice that the numbers in Rows 1-7 in Table 25 are quite small in contrast to the total numbers of verses. The largest number, 147, might even be reduced by 4 (for reasons explained earlier in this chapter—namely that the violence might not have been against human beings at all). Consider that the numbers in the rows would be in the hundreds or thousands if the NT frequently portrayed

Portrayals of Violence in the New Testament 221

or referred to actual violence against humans, by non-Christians, or by Christians. The numbers also would be considerably larger if the NT frequently portrayed Jesus or God the Father in relation to violence (Rows 4a-d). And, of course, the numbers also would be larger if the NT frequently portrayed other repudiations of violence (Row 5); doom, fire, and hellfire as physical violence against humans (Row 6); and military wars, battles, and violence in wars or battles (Rows 7 and 7a).

Now let us consider in more detail the entries in some of the rows. Row 3 has the entry "8 - 3?" This is because there are some ambiguities in three of the eight verses as to whether the punishments were physically violent.

The entries in Row 4, "(7 - 7?)" and "7-7?" indicate that the verses are somewhat ambiguous as to whether God the Father, Jesus, or someone else actually committed violent actions against human beings. Similar reasoning applies to the entries in Row 4b. There are four verses that are somewhat ambiguous as to whether it is actually God the Father, rather than one of the disciples, who is predicting, threatening, or warning about violence. The entry "35 - 2?" indicates that there is some ambiguity about whether Jesus is portrayed as doing any of these three things in two of the thirty-five verses. Row 4c indicates that I did not find any verses which portrayed God the Father as demanding violence against human beings. One verse might portray Jesus demanding violence, but this is not totally clear. Less ambiguous are the entries in Row 4d. As indicated earlier in the fourteen previous tables, I found ten verses in which Jesus is portrayed as explicitly rejecting violence, but no verses in which God the Father is portrayed this way (or in a contrary way, for that matter).

Row 5 shows that I found nine other verses that reject violence, but that these are by people other than Jesus. The entry in Row 6 is somewhat surprising to me in that I expected that actual physical violence (excluding images of physical violence that are dreamed or imagined by John) of sinners burning in hellfire on Doomsday would be much more frequent in the NT (Perhaps I was thinking of the OT at the time!).

Rows 7 and 7a indicate that I found only sixteen verses that mention battles or war, and that only ten of these verses portray violence in battles or war. Recall that in the OT, relevant verses identify and focus on specific battles that involved Israelite military forces, such as battles against the Philistines and Amorites. By contrast, in the NT, the references are much less specific. Examples of this are the verses in Matthew that quote Jesus as saying that there will be times of war and of killing without providing any more information as to who the adversaries will be, when and where the battles will occur, and what the outcomes will be. Furthermore, the NT has nothing comparable to the verses in the Qur'an in which Allah refers to specific battles such as Badr or calls on his followers to engage in specific battles.

Row 8 of Table 25 shows that I did not find any verses in the NT that specify "terror" as physical violence against human beings. Recall from previous chapters that I found "terror" to be portrayed as physical violence twelve times in the Qur'an and more than fifty times in the OT.

Row 9 shows that I did not find any verses in the NT that portray or refer to the genocide of all human beings in specific settlements, clans, or nations—not to just the extermination of an adversary's military forces. This also contrasts with the OT, where I found more than forty verses that portrayed or referred to genocide by Israelite forces against both the military forces and the civilian populations of their adversaries.

Some Concluding Comments about Violence in the New Testament

By way of conclusion, let me suggest that the NT is not really a very violent book in its portrayals and references, so long as we discount quite a few parables, metaphors, and visions that have some rather violent images and symbols in a few of its parts—Revelation in particular. This general point is even more noteworthy because many of the NT authors —the disciples and their successors—mention the crucifixion of Jesus

Portrayals of Violence in the New Testament

and the persecution of Jesus and of some of his disciples, Peter and Paul among them. In sum, the NT is about many topics, but very little of it is about actual physical violence or about war or violence in war.

Please allow me to speculate a little about possible implications of these aspects of the NT for some people throughout the world, now and in the future. It seems to me that the NT does not lend itself to new acts of violence, at least not by non-Christians. Its portrayals of God, Jesus, the disciples, and their followers are benign and forgiving, with very few exceptions, most of which are in the final book, Revelation. Furthermore, the NT is not highly critical or frequently critical of non-Christians, even though non-Christians are portrayed as having persecuted and killed Jesus and quite a few of his followers. And of course, neither the OT nor the NT portrays violence against or by Muslims, presumably because Islam did not emerge until Muhammad experienced his own revelations that started in 610 CE, many centuries after the birth and death of Jesus Christ. It is widely accepted that all of the passages in the Bible predate Muhammad and the emergence of Islam as a religion.

As a final note on violence as portrayed in the verses of the New Testament, this chapter is much shorter than the previous chapters on the Qur'an and on the Old Testament because there are far fewer verses that portray violence in the New Testament than in the two other holy books.

In the next chapter, we consider how the findings of this chapter and the previous chapters relate to the observations and claims about religious violence in the published books of a number of well-known religious scholars and other authors who have published controversial books on this topic.

Notes

1. *The King James Study Bible*, 1399-1400.
2. Op. cit., 1401-1404.
3. Op. cit., 1489.
4. Op. cit., 1531-32.
5. Op. cit., 1602.
6. Op. cit., 1656-57.
7. Op. cit., 1399-1400.
8. Op. cit., 1727-28.
9. Op. cit., 1761-62.
10. Op. cit., 1761.
11. Op. cit., 1893.
12. Op. cit., 1901.
13. Op. cit., 1910.
14. Op. cit., 1936-37.
15. Op. cit., 1946.
16. Op. cit., 1954.
17. Op. cit., 1961.
18. Op. cit., 1978.
19. Op. cit., 1978-80.
20. Op. cit., 1980.
21. Op. cit., 1981.

CHAPTER 5

SUMMARY OF FINDINGS, AND CLAIMS OF OTHER AUTHORS

EPIGRAPHS

> Despite the inclusion of some verses that ostensibly counsel tolerance, the Koran's overall message is that Infidels should be converted to Islam, subjugated as legal inferiors to Muslims, or killed. Consequently, for Infidels, the Koran is a dangerous book.
> — Author Robert Spencer

> The violence inherent in the Hebrew image of God is particularly significant because the divine serves as a model for human emulation (*imiatio dei*). The Hebrew God is a "Lord of Hosts," vengeful and militant. He ruthlessly kills individuals, annihilates groups, and punishes humanity with plagues, brutal wars, and natural disasters. He also commands killing on a "chauvinist" basis. His chosen people are instructed to implement his fury against inferior peoples that are accursed from the moment of their inception, like the Ishmaelites, Moabites, Ammonites, and Edomites.
> — Ron E. Hassner and Gideon Aran, "Religion and Violence in the Jewish Traditions."

226 VIOLENCE, TERROR, GENOCIDE, AND WAR

> If the Qur'an urges believers to fight, as it undoubtedly does, it also commands that enemies be shown mercy if they surrender. Some frightful portions of the Bible, by contrast, order the total extermination of enemies, of whole families and races—of men, women, and children, and even their livestock, with no quarter granted....The Bible overflows with 'texts of terror,' to borrow a phrase coined by American theologian Phyllis Trible, and biblical violence is often marked by indiscriminate savagery.... But in terms of the violent and unacceptable faces of their fundamental scripture, differences between the faiths are minimal.
>
> —Author and religious scholar Philip Jenkins [1]

INTRODUCTION

In this chapter, first we summarize our major findings as presented in Chapters 2 through 4. Then we consider how the findings relate to the claims made by a number of authors in their well-known, but somewhat controversial books about violence, terror, war, and genocide, as portrayed in the three holy books.

How similar or different do you expect these three holy books to be on these matters? Which books are most and least violent in terms of quantities of verses that portray violence? Which one portrays a supreme being as the most or the least frequent source of violence? Which one portrays adversaries as being the most violent? Which one most frequently demands that its followers commit genocide against adversaries?

SUMMARY OF MAJOR FINDINGS IN CHAPTERS 2 - 4

Let us start by considering the information in Table 26. Notice that the Qur'an has the largest percentage (11.9%) of verses that convey violence, followed by the Old Testament (5.15%), and then the New Testament (1.84%). The Qur'an's percentage (11.9%) is a little more than twice as

Summary of Findings, and Claims of Other Authors   227

large as the percentage for the Old Testament (5.15%) and about six times as large as the percentage for the New Testament (1.84%). However, the Old Testament's (OT) percentage is more than twice as large as the percentage for the New Testament (NT). Clearly, then, the OT is significantly more violent than the NT in this regard. They are not the same, by any means. Also, it is clear that the Qur'an has proportionately more violent verses than either the OT or the NT, and of the Bible taken as a whole (4.3%). And yet, it seems very important that we acknowledge that *none of the three holy books are dominated by violent verses, taken quantitatively.* In none of the three books do the percentages of violent verses reach even 15%, let alone 25% or 50%.

Table 26. Verses that Convey Violence in the Old Testament, the New Testament, and the Qur'an.

		A	B	C
		# of chapters	# of verses	# (%) of verses that convey violence
1	Old Testament TOTALS	929	23,145*	1,194 (5.16%)
2	New Testament TOTALS	260	7,958	147 (1.84%)
3	Bible TOTALS	1,189	31,107*	1,341 (4.3%)
4	Qur'an TOTALS	114	6,220	741 (11.9%)

Note. The OT also includes one hundred thirty-seven unnumbered verses. If these are added to the 23,145 numbered verses, the total verses in the OT is 23,282 verses and the percentage of verses that were found to portray violence shift slightly from 5.16% to 5.13%. This is a very minor difference, isn't it?

Now let us consider the percentages in the three books regarding terror, battles, war, and genocide. Table 27 summarizes our findings.

Table 27. Percentages of Verses in the Three Books that Convey Terror, Genocide, Wars, and Battles.

		Terror	Genocide	Wars and Battles
1	Old Testament TOTALS	1.50%	0.50%	3.00%
2	New Testament TOTALS	0%	0%	< 0.2%
3	Bible TOTALS	< 1.0%	0.40%	< 2.8%
4	Qur'an TOTALS	0.10%	0%	4.00%

Regarding Table 27

First, please notice that all of the percentages in Table 27 are extremely low or they are zero. None exceed 4%. Thus, it seems fair to say that none of the three holy books are fundamentally, predominantly, or significantly books about terror, genocide, wars, or battles. To me, this is one of the most significant findings in this book. It should allow us to dismiss, as exaggerations, any and all claims by anyone, anywhere, that one or more of these holy books essentially are books of terror, genocide, wars, battles or, as shown in Table 27, about physical violence against human beings. Unfortunately, exaggerations such as these are sometimes made by very influential religious scholars, members of the clergy, antagonists, atheists, agnostics, columnists, government leaders, and members of other religions.

Second, please notice that even though all the percentages in Table 27 are extremely low, the OT has the most verses and the highest percentages of verses that portray terror as genocide. In fact, the OT is the only one of the three books that portrays genocide. As you might recall from Chapter 3 on the OT, all of these verses describe, demand, or predict that Israelite forces commit genocide against entire settlements, clans, or nations of non-Israelite people. Also, as shown in Table 27, the Qur'an has the

Summary of Findings, and Claims of Other Authors 229

highest percentage of verses that portray or refer to war or battles (4%). But, as explained in Chapter 2 on the Qur'an, only about 25% of these verses actually portray physical violence in wars and battles.

Moving beyond Tables 26 and 27 to consider the qualities of physical violence portrayed in the three holy books, let us simply recall that the Qur'an and the NT have no verses that explicitly advocate lethal violence as timeless, absolute, and total as in the following verses in the OT that also are discussed in Chapter 3.

> *For every one that curseth his father or his mother shall be surely put to death: he hath cursed his father or his mother; his blood shall be upon him. (Lev. 20: 9)

> *The Lord will be terrible unto them: for he will famish all the gods of the earth; and men shall worship him, everyone from its place, even all the isles of the heathen. Ye Ethiopians also, ye shall be slain by my sword. And he will stretch out his hand against the north, and destroy Assyria; and will make Nineveh a desolation, and dry like a wilderness. (Zeph. 2: 11-13)

> *Thou shalt surely smite the inhabitants of that city with the edge of the sword, destroying it utterly, and all that is therein, and the cattle thereof, with the edge of the sword. And thou shalt gather all the spoil of it into the midst of the street thereof, and shalt burn with fire the city, and all the spoil thereof every whit, of the Lord the God: and it shall be a heap forever; it shall not be built again. (Deut. 13: 15-16)

As indicated throughout the previous chapters of this book, I have not found any verses anywhere in the NT or in the Qur'an that approach these verses in the OT in portraying a deity demanding and promising violence as brutal and as lethal as this. Stated in another way, no verses in the NT or the Qur'an come close to matching the violence of the God of the Israelites as portrayed in the OT. By the way, I offer this conclusion as objectively as I can. I realize that it is probably extremely disturbing to some readers.

Claims Made by Other Authors about Violence in the Three Holy Books

How do our findings, as reported in the previous chapters, relate to the claims that authors, experts, and political leaders have made about the influence of each of the three holy books on violence, terrorism, war, and genocide? Let us now consider the claims made by influential authors Robert Spencer, Rabbi Jonathan Sacks, Mark Juergensmeyer, Jessica Stern, and Karen Armstrong, Philip Jenkins, and others. Please understand that this is an effort to describe their major assertions about violence in the holy books and in religions. Our purpose, is to build upon their insights, so long as their insights are accurate and unbiased, rather than to criticize their work.

Robert Spencer's *The Complete Infidel's Guide to the Koran*

> Despite the inclusion of some verses that ostensibly counsel tolerance, the Koran's overall message is that Infidels should be converted to Islam, subjugated as legal inferiors to Muslims, or killed. Consequently, for Infidels, the Koran is a dangerous book.
>
> Whatever policy prescriptions Infidel lawmakers choose to adopt in the face of that fact will determine whether or not their Infidel polity survives as such, or becomes an Islamic Sharia polity.[2]

So writes Robert Spencer on the concluding page of his provocatively-titled interpretation of the Qur'an. Spencer is identified this way on the back cover of the paperback version of his book:

> Robert Spencer is the Director of Jihad Watch, a program of the David Horowitz Freedom Center. He is the author of nine books on Islam and jihad, a weekly columnist for Human Events and the website FrontPage Magazine, and has led numerous seminars for the U.S. military and intelligence communities.

Summary of Findings, and Claims of Other Authors 231

Also, on the back cover of Spencer's book is an endorsement by Geert Wilders, as a member of the Parliament of the Netherlands and as Chairman of the Party for Freedom (PVV):

> Governing officials and media spokesmen may ignore Spencer's warnings, but they do so at their own risk, because Islamic jihadists are not ignoring what's in the Koran, and are working to destroy our freedoms in obedience to Koranic dictates. In illuminating for Westerners exactly what the Koran teaches, Spencer has performed a valuable service in the defense of Western civilization against the Islamic jihad.

Another endorsement of Spencer's book is by Andrew C. McCarthy. He is identified as a senior fellow at the National Review Institute and author of *Willful Blindness: A Memoir of the Jihad*:

> Unlike most of today's self-styled experts, Robert Spencer won't tell you that 'slay the idolaters wherever you find them' really means 'love your enemies and pray for those who persecute you.' In *The Complete Infidel's Guide to the Koran*, Spencer shows once again that he is America's most informed, fearless, and compelling voice on modern jihadism, insisting that we come to grips with the words behind the ideology that fuels international terror.

As we might expect from these endorsements, Spencer provides scathing indictments of the Qur'an as being a thoroughly violent book and the cornerstone of Islamic terrorism. According to Spencer, "An infidel, as far as the Koran is concerned, is anyone who refuses to submit to Allah as the one true God and to recognize Muhammad as his prophet." Spencer often ridicules a number of famous defenses of the Qur'an as a book of peace—not violence and war. For example, Spencer writes that:

> The U.S.—based Council on American-Islamic Relations (CAIR) claims that the book reveals the true, peaceful nature of Islam and promotes interfaith harmony. As CAIR's "Explore the Quran" campaign urges, "In today's climate of heightened religious sensitivities and apparent cultural clashes, now is the time for people

of all faiths to better acquaint themselves with Islam's sacred text, the Holy Qur'an." CAIR indicates that this campaign is a response to those who dare to claim that Islam has something to do with terrorism.[3]

Spencer also takes exception with a number of Muslim scholars who claim that the Qur'an is about peace.

> Muslims often insist vociferously that the Koran teaches peace. Adil Salahi, the Muslim author of a biography of Muhammad maintains, "You only need to open the Koran and read to realize that what it calls for is peace, not war." [4]

Former British Prime Minister Tony Blair also receives Spencer's scorn for claiming that

> ...the authentic basis of Islam, as laid down in the Koran, is progressive, humanitarian, and sees knowledge and scientific advance as a duty, which is why for centuries Islam was the front of so much invention innovation. Fundamental Islam is actually the opposite of what the extremists preach.[5]

Spencer contends that defenses like these are totally unrealistic because they are contradicted by the violent behaviors and testimonies of infamous jihadists who readily admit that the Qur'an is their inspiration and justification for violence. Spencer claims that this includes the now deceased Jihadists Khalid Sheik Mohammed and Osama bin Laden, as well as numerous "rank and file" terrorists.[6] Often, Spencer implies that the Qur'an is the basis for Jihad—that it is, in fact, a manual for Jihadist warfare. Using a clipping from a newspaper as his evidence, Spencer cites the case of Mohammed Taheri-Azar (whom I report on extensively in this book and I interviewed more than twenty-five times) as an example of how passages of the Qur'an turned him into a jihadist. Spencer then concludes that "Overall, it is extremely rare—if not impossible—to find a jihadist who does not cite the Koran to justify his actions." [7]

Summary of Findings, and Claims of Other Authors

To support his thesis, Spencer selects several dozen rather violent passages (not necessarily entire verses) from the Qur'an and contrasts them against a few dozen of the least violent passages in the Bible. Spencer's book features quarter-page panels such as this one: [8]

BIBLE vs. KORAN

*"Slay the idolaters wherever you find them..."
—Koran 9:5 (cf. 4: 89 and 2: 191)

*"Thou shall not kill."
—Exodus 20: 13

Spencer never tells us whether he read all of the verses in all of the surahs of the Qur'an and, if he did so, how or why he selected only a few dozen verses from the more than 6,000 verses in the Qur'an. He also does not tell us why he skipped over the hundreds of verses in the OT in which God is portrayed as killing those people who anger him, or where God is portrayed as demanding that his Israelite followers exterminate the Philistines and so many other tribes.

Some Comments about Spencer's Book

I did not find any errors in Spencer's quoting from the Qur'an or the Bible. His quotations are accurate. Unfortunately—and in contrast to what I present throughout this book—Spencer never acknowledges that there are hundreds of verses in the OT of the Bible that portray violence, terror, genocide, and war by God, and by many of his Israelite prophets, military leaders, and their many Israelite followers. Furthermore, Spencer usually presents only parts of some verses that are the most absolute and inflammatory in portraying Allah demanding violence by his followers against *non*-Muslims. Spencer portrays all non-Muslims as being "infidels" even though the verses in the Qur'an often refer to them in other ways, including "unbelievers," "non-believers," "idolaters," "polytheists," and "People of the Scripture." Spencer also does not acknowledge that, as shown in Chapter 2 of this book, quite a few verses in the Qur'an portray

Allah demanding or threatening violence against anyone—Muslims as well as non-Muslims— who anger Allah or seem to violate his rules, such as his prohibition of adultery.

Also, in contrast to our findings as presented in Chapters 2-4 of this book, Spencer does not tell us how he determined that a passage is violent, and he does not provide any quantifications or the percentages of verses that are "violent" to him. Nor does he examine variations in the *qualities* of the violence as portrayed in the Bible and in the Qur'an in terms of the sources, targets, and kinds of violence. As presented by Spencer in his book, it is as if all of the passages in both the OT and the NT oppose violence while none of the passages in the Qur'an do so. Spencer routinely presents passages from the Qur'an that advocate violence by Muslims against "Infidels"—meaning anyone and everyone who is not a Muslim.

Of course, neither Spencer nor his publisher, Regnery Publishers of the Salem Media Group in Washington, D.C., claim that his purpose is to provide an objective, scholarly analysis of the Qur'an or of the Bible. So, we should not be surprised that he has not done so.

After reading Spencer's book, it occurs to me that someone could easily write and publish a book whose title and contents counter Spencer's book or "turn it on its head," so to speak. The title could be *The Complete Infidel's Guide to the Old Testament.* In it, the author could select a few dozen or more of the most violent verses in the OT and then contrast them against a few dozen of the most anti-violent verses in the Qur'an. Here is just one example of many examples that contradict Spencer's theme:

> A Peaceful Passage in the Qur'an vs. a Violent Passage in the Bible
>
> *And if they incline to peace, incline thou also to it, and trust in Allah. Lo! He is the Hearer, the Knower. (Surah 8, Verse 61)

> *Thou shalt surely smite the inhabitants of that city with the edge of the sword, destroying it utterly, and all that is therein, and the cattle thereof, with the edge of the sword.
>
> And thou shalt gather all the spoil of it into the midst of the street thereof, and shalt burn with fire the city, and all the spoil thereof every whit, for the Lord the God: and it shall be a heap for ever; it shall not be built again. (Deut. 13: 15-16)

Going further, a troubling thought occurs to me. Could Spencer's book increase the likelihood of violence between and among Jews, Christians, and Muslims because it is so one-sided in presenting only violence in the Qur'an and presenting only non-violence in the Bible? Could Spencer's book actually increase misunderstandings, bigotry, prejudice, and discrimination by non-Muslims towards Muslims? It seems to me that Spencer seems to take delight in needlessly ridiculing and insulting Allah, Islam, Muslims, and the Qur'an.

Spencer's Recommendations

Spencer's book was first published in 2009, so it might not be as current or relevant as it was when it was published. However, it still sells well, and Spencer still is quoted often in the mass media.

Spencer very directly calls for major changes in U.S. policy and in the attitudes of U.S. citizens regarding Islam and the Qur'an.

> America clearly needs a dramatic change in policy. But what measures would most effectively protect us from the jihadist threat? First, we must recognize the contents of the Koran have implications for public policy. The fact that significant numbers of Muslims worldwide consider the book to be a mandate for violence should concern government and law enforcement authorities who should prevent Koran-inspired violence. Officials should refuse to accept the deceptions and half-truths that U.S.-based Islamic groups routinely offer regarding the Koran's violent teachings.

By the way, Spencer does not provide any evidence that "significant numbers of Muslims worldwide consider the book to be a mandate for violence." He goes on to write that:

> U.S. officials should also monitor mosques and Islamic schools in America, demanding that they institute large-scale, transparent programs, open to full and comprehensive inspections that teach against the doctrines of violence, subjugation, and hatred that we have examined in this book. Such programs should unambiguously tell Muslims that any and all passages in the Koran that mandate contempt for, violence against, and the subjugation of Infidels are not to be regarded as having any literal application—not now and not at any time in the future.[9]

Spencer also goes so far as to recommend drastic changes in immigration policy.[10] He states, "Since there is no reliable way to tell if any given Muslim believer takes the Koran's dictates about warfare against Infidels literally, immigration of Muslims into the United States should be halted."[11] Spencer also suggests that "immigration officials should at the very least adopt procedures to screen prospective immigrants for jihadist sentiments."

Of course, you are free to form your own opinion about Spencer's suggestions. My own reaction is that Spencer's recommendations are not informed by the findings presented in the previous chapters of this book. Spencer's recommendations are ill-informed, prejudicial, impractical, and probably in violation of the First Amendment and many other laws that demand the separation of state government from religion. At the same time, I would hope that our immigration officials, policies, and procedures carefully screen prospective immigrants and refugees to the U.S. for jihadist sentiments and that they prohibit violent and violence-prone people from entering the U.S. By the way, whenever I review the details of the U.S. immigration screening process, I am impressed by how thorough it seems to be, especially for refugees who apply to immigrate to the U.S.

Summary of Findings, and Claims of Other Authors 237

Also let me admit that, given Spencer's prejudices, I am a little surprised that he did not recommend that prospective immigrants to the U.S. should be disqualified if they say that they believe all of the passages of the Qur'an or that they believe that the Qur'an requires all Muslims to be violent towards non-Muslims.

In sum, even though Spencer is accurate in presenting a few dozen direct quotes of verses in the Qur'an and in the Bible, he selects only the verses in the Qur'an that seem to advocate violence and he only selects verses in the Bible that seem to prohibit violence. He disregards hundreds of counter-examples in the process. Additionally, Spencer's interpretations and claims are almost always totally inflammatory and condemnatory against the Qur'an and Islam while they are totally complimentary towards Judaism, Christianity, and both the OT and the NT.

Rabbi Jonathan Sacks' *Not in God's Name: Confronting Religious Violence*

An epigraph from Rabbi Sacks' book:

> Too often in the history of religion, people have killed in the name of God of life, waged war in the name of the God of peace, hated in the name of the God of love and practiced cruelty in the name of the God of compassion. When this happens, God speaks, sometimes in a still, small voice almost inaudible beneath the clamour of those claiming to speak on this behalf. What he says at such times is: *Not in My Name.*[12]

According to material on the back cover of his book, Rabbi Jonathan Sacks is an esteemed author of nearly thirty books on religion, primarily on Judaism. He has won the esteemed Templeton Prize, among many other honors. Of particular relevance to our work is his book *Not in God's Name: Confronting Religious Violence*.

The back cover of the paperback version of the book states Sacks' thesis this way:

Rabbi Sacks shows that religiously inspired violence has as its source in the misreading of biblical texts at the heart of all three Abrahamic faiths. By looking anew at the book of Genesis, with its foundational stories of Judaism, Christianity, and Islam, Rabbi Sacks offers a radical re-reading of many of the Bible's seminal stories of sibling rivalry: Cain and Abel, Isaac and Ishmael, Jacob and Esau, Joseph and his brothers, Rachel and Leah.

Here is an eloquent call for people of goodwill from all faiths and none to stand together, confront the religious extremism that threatens to destroy us all, and declare: Not in God's Name.

Sacks' Main Points

As I understand them, Sacks principal assertions are as follows:

1. All three religions originate with the Hebrew Prophet Abram (Abraham). Sacks calls these the "Abrahamic Faiths." He writes that anyone who belongs to any of these three religions is spiritually related to Abraham.

2. Sacks contends that God is never violent in Genesis, the first book in the Jewish Torah and the Christian Bible, or in the rest of the books in the Torah. God has never been violent, and He has never endorsed violence. In the opening sentence of his book, Sacks writes: "When religion turns men into murderers, God weeps. So the book of Genesis tells us."[13]

3. It is humans who have created violence and who have perpetuated it, often claiming, falsely, that they are doing so "in God's Name." Sacks continually repudiates this, hence the title of his book *Not in God's Name*.

4. The origins of human violence are in the "sibling rivalry" of Adam and Eve's two sons: Cain and Abel. Cain killed Abel because Cain (a planter) was afraid that God preferred Abel (a shepherd). Much of Sacks' book recasts the stories of Cain and Abel, Isaac and

Summary of Findings, and Claims of Other Authors

Ishmael, Jacob and Esau, Joseph and his brothers, and Rachel and Leah as being cases of "sibling rivalry" that often turns violent.

5. It is time for members of all three religions to recognize the validity of points 1-4 above and to realize that violence originated as sibling rivalry among humans. According to Sacks, humans mistakenly believe that they must compete against each other for God's approval, when, in fact, God loves everyone, accepts everyone, and never condones violence. If we will acknowledge this, then all forms of violence will diminish and perhaps even cease to exist.

Near the end of his book, Sacks concedes that there are some violent passages in the holy books. But he does not identify them nor say much about them. He simply asserts that they are more or less irrelevant if we consider historical context and the overall theology of belief and faith. In his own words:

> And yes, there are hard texts. There are passages in the sacred scriptures of each of the Abrahamic monotheisms which, interpreted literally, can lead to hatred, cruelty and war.
>
> But Judaism, Christianity, and Islam all contain interpretive traditions that in the past have read them in the larger context of co-existence, respect for difference and the pursuit of peace, and can do so today. Fundamentalism—text without context, and application without interpretation—is not faith but an aberration of faith.[14]

Sacks' Suggestions to End Religious Violence

In the final pages of his book, Sacks predicts that terrorism will increase in the years ahead. But he does offer a number of suggestions to diminish this prospect:

> 1. Today Jews, Christians, and Muslims must stand together, in defence of humanity, the sanctity of life, religious freedom and the honour of God himself.[15]

2. We must put the same long-term planning into strengthening religious freedom as was put into the spread of religious extremism.

3. There must be an international campaign against the teaching and preaching of hate.

4. We need to recover the absolute values that make Abrahamic monotheism the humanizing force it has been at its best: the sanctity of life, the dignity of the individual, and so many other core values.

5. We need to insist on the simplest moral principle of all. The principle of reciprocal altruism, otherwise known as Tit-for-Tat. This says: as you behave to others, so will others behave to you.

Some Comment's on Sacks' Claims

Rabbi Sacks is obviously very sincere, compassionate, and tolerant of all three religions and their holy books. I doubt that any of us would object to any of his recommendations. Unfortunately, they are rather commonplace, and Sacks does not provide details as to how they could be implemented, nor by whom, where, or when. I am reluctant to be critical of his well-meaning and positive book. And yet, it seems to me that in many ways he is "whistling in the dark" by letting his deep faith in a compassionate God allow him to overlook so many verses and passages in the OT and the Qur'an that contradict his most general thesis that God is never violent and that it is, therefore, invalid to ever commit violence in God's name.

For whatever reason, Sacks repeatedly ignores the famous verses that are immediately adjacent to the "anti-violent" verses he emphasizes and that contradict those verses. It is as though Sacks has ignored or missed the dozens of verses in Genesis that portray God as being extremely violent, as well as the hundreds of verses throughout the OT that also do this, as shown in Chapter 3 of this book. For example, as mentioned previously, on page 3 of his book, Sacks makes a claim that he repeats

Summary of Findings, and Claims of Other Authors 241

throughout his book: "When religion turns men into murderers, God weeps. So the book of Genesis tells us."

And yet, the only evidence that Sacks provides from the Hebrew Torah to support his claim is this one from Genesis 6: 6: *"...the world was filled with violence. God 'saw how great the wickedness of the human race had become on the earth.'...God regretted that he had made man on the earth, and his heart was filled with pain."

Notice that the verse does not say that "God weeps." It says that "God was filled with pain." Notice that the tense is past tense—not current, or eternal in its tense. But this is a minor point. The much more important point is that Sacks stops at this verse. He does not include the next few verses in Genesis which portray God being so angry that he decides to flood the earth and kill all living things except for Noah, his immediate family, and mated pairs of animals of several species. Here are those verses from my copy of the Jewish Torah, specifically *The Jewish Study Bible* by Adel Berliner and Marc Zvi Brettler (editors). And, by the way, these verses are almost identical to the verses in the OT versions of the Bible that I have used throughout this book, as indicated in Chapter 3 and the Bibliography, except that the verse numbers sometimes vary.

> *The Lord saw how great was man's wickedness on earth, and how every plan devised by his mind was nothing but evil all the time. And the Lord regretted that He had made man on earth, and His heart was saddened. The Lord said, "I will blot out from the earth the men whom I created—men together with beasts, creeping things, and birds of the sky; for I regret that I made them." But Noah found favor with the Lord. (Gen. 6: 5-7)
>
> *God said to Noah, "I have decided to put an end to all flesh, for the earth is filled with lawlessness because of them: I am about to destroy them with the earth...." (Gen. 6: 13)
>
> *For My part, I am about to bring the Flood—waters upon the earth—to destroy all flesh under the sky in which there is breath of life; everything on earth shall perish. But I will establish my covenant

with you, and you shall enter the ark with your sons, your wife, and your sons' wives. (Gen. 6: 17)

And then, several verses later in Genesis, God is portrayed as doing exactly what he threatened to do—exterminate every living thing except for Noah, his family, and selected pairs of mated animals.

*The Flood continued for forty days on the earth.... (Gen. 7: 17)

*(21) And all flesh that stirred on earth perished—birds, cattle, beasts, and all the things that swarmed upon the earth, and all mankind.

(22) All in whose nostrils was the merest breath of life, all that was on dry land, died.

(23) All existence on earth was blotted out—man, cattle, creeping things, and birds of the sky; they were blotted out from the earth. Only Noah was left, and those with him in the ark. (Gen. 7: 21-23)

Surely these verses portray God as being so angry and violent that he not only used the flood to kill all human beings, except for Noah and his family, but God also killed "cattle, creeping things, and birds of the sky." We might ask why God would kill all of these non-human creatures, as well as the humans. Did they disappoint him? Were all of these creatures disobedient? It seems to me that these verses, and dozens more of them in Genesis and in the OT, portray God as being herbicidal, bio-cidal, as well as homicidal—so homicidal that it constitutes genocide of all groups, clans, and nations of people except for Noah and his family members. It seems to me that God's violence would only have been more total if he had exterminated Noah and his family, as well as all of the other animals on the Ark. And God's violence would have only been more violent and hurtful if he had first tortured everything so brutally that their agony was total, and their deaths were as slow and as agonizing as possible.

To put it more succinctly, Sacks seems to ignore all of the verses in Genesis that portray God as being violent and that portray God as

Summary of Findings, and Claims of Other Authors 243

demanding violence from his Israelites. Sacks only quotes from the book of Genesis. As shown in Chapter 3 of this book, violence and violence by an angry God are portrayed in all five of the books of the Pentateuch—not just in Genesis—and they also are found in almost all of the thirty-seven books of the OT. Why didn't Sacks at least acknowledge this? Perhaps it was just "wishful thinking" on his part.

Now, regarding Abram (Abraham) as the "Father of all people who are Jewish, Christian, or Muslim;" contrary to what Sacks writes about Abraham, he is portrayed in verses in Genesis as being both violent and anti-violent. For example:

> *When Abram heard that his kinsman had been taken captive, he mustered his retainers, born into his household numbering three hundred and eighteen, and went in pursuit as far as Dan. At night, he and his servants deployed against them and defeated them; and he pursued them as far as Hobah, which is north of Damascus. He brought back all the possessions; he also brought back his kinsman, Lot and his possessions, and the women and the rest of the people. (Gen. 14:13-15)

Then again, Abraham is also portrayed in some verses as convincing God to *not* be violent in one situation. At one point, he discourages God from destroying Sodom and Gomorrah, although eventually God goes ahead and does this.

> *Let not my Lord be angry if I speak but this last time: What if ten innocent people should be found there (in Sodom)? And he (God) answered, "I will not destroy for the sake of the ten." (Gen. 18:32)

Genesis does not tell us whether ten innocent people were found in Sodom. But it does tell us that God eventually destroyed both Sodom and Gomorrah, despite Abraham's plea.

> *As the sun rose upon the earth and Lot entered Zoar, the Lord rained upon Sodom and Gomorrah sulfurous fire from the Lord out of heaven. He annihilated those cities and the entire Plain, and

all the inhabitants of the cities and the vegetation of the ground. Lot's wife looked back, and she thereupon turned into a pillar of salt. (Gen. 19: 23-26)

*Thus it was that, when God destroyed the cities of the Plain and annihilated the cities where Lot dwelt, God was mindful of Abraham, and removed Lot from the midst of the upheaval. (Gen. 19: 29)

By way of a conclusion, sadly I must conclude that Rabbi Sacks is often mistaken in how he portrays violence and God in the book of Genesis. There certainly are plenty of verses that portray the God of Genesis as being totally anti-violent and totally compassionate and loving. Sadly, there are many other verses that contradict this. As shown in Chapter 3 of this book, in Genesis, God, Moses, many other prophets and various Israelite military and political leaders are often portrayed as being violent. They intentionally impose terror upon their enemies. They engage in countless devastating offensive battles, most of which they win decisively. They possess the spoils of their battles or they destroy everything, including the livestock, crops, and residences of their enemies. Sometimes they commit genocide, often as demanded by their God, as portrayed in Genesis.

Rabbi Sacks means well, but he acknowledges none of these facts. His work would be more valuable if he had done so.

Mark Juergensmeyer's *Terror in the Mind of God: The Global Rise of Religious Violence*

Mark Juergensmeyer is one of the more influential and current authors of books about religious violence. This book of his continues to be widely cited by policymakers, law enforcement leaders, news commentators, scholars, and members of the clergy. The timing of the book's first printing in 2000 made it readily available to worldwide audiences whose members were shocked by the 9-11-2001 terrorist attacks on the World

Summary of Findings, and Claims of Other Authors 245

Trade Center and the Pentagon. The book has been reprinted and revised in several editions and several languages since then.

Juergensmeyer was a practicing Methodist minister with a Doctor of Divinity degree from Union Theological Seminary prior to becoming a religious scholar and a professor, first at the University of California at Berkeley, and now at Santa Barbara. His book also became famous because of his primary research method. In the late 1980s and through the 1990s Juergensmeyer was able to correspond with, and occasionally conduct personal interviews with, a number of people who had been convicted of high-profile terrorist acts, allegedly because of their political and religious beliefs and affiliations with Judaism, Christianity, Islam, Sikh, Hinduism, and Buddhism and other religions. Among his interviewees were:

- Rabbi Meir Kahane, the founder of the radical Jewish Kach Party. Juergensmeyer interviewed Kahane in New York City in 1989. One year later, Kahane was assassinated by a radical Egyptian Muslim named El Sayyid Nosair after speaking to his supporters at a gathering in New York.
- Mahmud Abouhalima. An accomplice of Nosair, Mahmud was convicted and imprisoned for his role in the bombing of the World Trade Center in 1993, an act that was believed to be master-minded by Nosair.
- Abdul Aziz Rantisi, a founder of the Palestinian organization Hamas.
- Sheik Yassin, whom Juergensmeyer refers to as the "spiritual founder of Hamas."
- Reverend Michael Bray, who was convicted of participating in the destruction of seven abortion clinics in and around the District of Columbia in the 1980s.
- Irish Sinn Fein member Tom Hartley.
- Radical Sikh leader Harjap Singh.

- Takeshi Nakamura, an assistant to Shoko Asahari, the leader of the violent, apocalyptic Buddhist sect Aum Shinrikyo that allegedly bombed the Tokyo subway system in 1995.

In his book, Juergensmeyer seems to rely most heavily on his interviews with Bray and with Mahmud. Here are some relevant excerpts:

> Mahmud Abouhalima's religious influences began at an early age. He was raised in Kafir al-Darwat, a town in northern Egypt near Alexandria, where he attended a Muslim youth camp. It offered him the "first light for understanding what it is to be Muslim," Abouhalima said. He took courses at Alexandria University and became increasingly active in Islamic politics, especially the outlawed al Gamaa-I Islamiya, led by Sheik Omar Abdul Rahman.
>
> During his initial years in Germany, Abouhalima said, he lived a "life of corruption—girls, drugs, you name it." He went through the outward signs of Islamic reverence—daily prayers, fasting during the month of Ramadan—but he had left the real Islam behind. After a while he "got bored" with his wayward existence, began reading the Qur'an again, and returned to a committed religious life. "Islam is a mercy," Abouhalima told me, explaining that it rescued the fallen and gave meaning to one's personal life.[16]

Regarding his use of violence, Abouhalima told Juergensmeyer, "It is my job as a Muslim... to go wherever there is oppression and injustice and fight it." [17]

The seventeen years he had lived in the West, Abouhalima told me, "is a fair amount of time to understand what the hell is going on in the United States and in Europe about secularism or people, you know, who have no religion." He went on to say, "I lived their life, but they didn't live my life, so they will never understand the way I live or the way I think." [18]

Juergensmeyer writes that many contemporary Muslim terrorists, such as Abouhalima, have been influenced greatly by the Egyptian writer Abdu al-Salam Faraj.

Summary of Findings, and Claims of Other Authors 247

> ...Faraj stated more clearly than any other contemporary writer the religious justifications for radical Muslim acts. His booklet was published and first circulated in Cairo in the early 1980s. What is significant about this document is that it grounded the activities of modern Islamic terrorists firmly in Islamic tradition, specifically in the sacred text of the Qur'an and the biographical accounts of the prophet in the Hadith. Faraj argued that the Qur'an and the Hadith were fundamentally about warfare.... The true soldier of Islam is allowed to use virtually any means available to achieve a just goal. Deceit, trickery, and violence are specifically mentioned as options available to the desperate soldier.[19]

Juergensmeyer writes that he found that many other people convicted of terrorist activities also claimed to do so because of their religious beliefs, particularly their belief that modern governments and modern secular culture ignore and sometimes violate key moral principles that are established in the holy books of their religions. In the case of Reverend Michael Bray, Juergensmeyer reports that Bray was convicted in 1985, along with two other defendants, of destroying seven abortion clinics in 1984 in Delaware and three other states, with a total of over one million dollars in damages.

> When I talked with Reverend Bray in his suburban home in Bowie (Maryland) many years later, I found nothing sinister or intensely fanatical about him. He was a cheerful, charming, handsome man in his early 40s, who liked to be called Mike. Hardly the image of an ignorant, narrow-minded fundamentalist, Mike Bray enjoyed a glass of wine before dinner and talked knowledgeably about theology and political ideas.[20]

Juergensmeyer reports that Bray refused to admit to him that he was the author of The Army of God manual on how to stop abortions by attacking abortionists and abortion clinics.

> Bray clearly sympathized with the ideas in the manual. As a leader of the Defensive Action movement, Mike Bray has justified the

use of violence in anti-abortion activities, although his attacks on abortion clinics have been considered extreme even by members of the pro-life movement.

Juergensmeyer writes that Bray also

> ...was the spokesman for two activists who were convicted of murderous assaults on abortion clinic staff. Bray's friend, Reverend Paul Hill, killed Dr. John Britton and his volunteer escort James Barrett as they drove up to The Ladies Center, an abortion clinic in Pensacola, Florida in 1994.[21]

He also writes that Bray is the author of the book *A Time to Kill*, "which defended his own acts of terrorism, the murders of abortion clinic doctors," and the attempted murder of another provider of abortions.[22] In addition to this, Juergensmeyer writes that a favorite Biblical verse of Bray and his associates regarding using terror to stop abortions is Psalm 91: *"You will not be afraid of the terror by night, or of the arrow that flies by day." [23]

Juergensmeyer concludes that Reverend Bray and many of his colleagues encourage violence that can serve the purpose of reconstructing societies and governments based on the moral principles presented in various verses of the Bible.

> "There is a time to kill," Rev. Michael Bray wrote, paraphrasing a passage from the book of Ecclesiastes in the Bible. In his case, however, Bray was talking not about particular dates but about a period of history, a moment justifying what he called "defensive actions on behalf of the unborn" and what others have called terrorist acts against abortion clinics and their staffs.[24]

According to Juergensmeyer:

> Bray sees the legitimacy of using violence not only to resist what he regards as murder—abortion—but also to help bring about the Christian political order envisioned by Reconstruction thinkers such as Gary North. In Bray's mind, a little violence is a small price

to pay for the possibility of fulfilling God's laws and establishing His kingdom on earth."[25]

Juergensmeyer writes about quite a few other radical anti-abortion Christians who were convicted of terrorist actions. One of these is Kerry Noble, the leader of a group called Christian Identity. By the way, Kerry Noble was one of the key informants for author Jessica Stern, whose interviews with Noble are considered later in this chapter.

> "The Lord God is a man of War," Christian Identity leader Kerry Noble reminded his followers in the Arkansas compound of the Covenant, the Sword, and the Arm of the Lord. After he had served prison time and left the movement, Noble regretted his radical stance but explained that he then felt it necessary, since his group "needed to know that it was time to cross the line into violence," and that these actions would be "acceptable to the Lord." [26]

Juergensmeyer goes on to write that other members of the Christian Identity movement echo this sentiment. "The Bible is 'a book of war, a book of hate,' another Christian Identity activist remarked."

Juergensmeyer then relates these statements to the concept of "cosmic war" and to what other authors have called "mimetic violence."

> These images of divine warfare are persistent features of religious activism.... In a booklet entitled *Prepare War!*, for instance, Kerry Noble provided a scriptural rationale for his martial stance and for his involvement in the Christian Army of God. Because God was a "man of war" (Ex. 15: 3) and took vengeance on his enemies, Noble argued, it behooved his followers to do the same. Like many activists who have turned to terror, he has been driven by an image of cosmic war.[27]

Juergensmeyer explains his concept of "cosmic war" this way: "I call such images 'cosmic' because they are larger than life. They evoke great battles of the legendary past, and they relate to metaphysical conflicts between good and evil." [28]

In addition to these excerpts, Juergensmeyer also reports that violent passages in "Revelation" of the OT inspired Asahara, the Japanese leader of the violent Buddhist sect Aum Shinrikyo, to arrange the bombing of the Tokyo subway system in 1995.

> Asahara took the prophecies of Revelation and mixed them with visions from the Old Testament and sayings of the sixteenth-century French philosopher Nostradamus.... "Armageddon," Asahara said, must occur because the "inhabitants of the present human realm do not recognize that they are fated to die." [29]

Juergensmeyer's Major Findings and Interpretations

It is interesting that Juergensmeyer's epigraph at the beginning of his book is a quote from Exodus 25: 27 in the OT: *"I will send my terror before you, And will throw into confusion all the people."

From his interviews, Juergensmeyer claims that violent religious movements have three things in common: [30]

> First, they have rejected the compromises with liberal values and secular institutions that were made by most mainstream religious leaders and organizations. Second, they refuse to observe the boundaries that secular society has imposed around religion—keeping it private rather than allowing it to intrude into public spaces. And third, they have replaced what they regard as weak modern substitutes with the more vibrant and demanding forms of religion that they imagine to be a part of their tradition's beginnings.

In Chapter 7, titled "Theater of Terror," Juergensmeyer claims that the terrorists he studied have led him to believe that their terrorism can be called "performance violence." [31] Their terrorist acts "are products of an internal logic—not of random or crazy thinking." Their purpose is "to make a symbolic statement" by getting the attention of the mass media, the general public, and government leaders and agencies. Terrorist organizations violently oppose the legitimacy of modern governments,

Summary of Findings, and Claims of Other Authors 251

institutions, and popular culture so as to bring about a shift back to fundamental, traditional theocratic states.[32] Juergensmeyer contends that the world is now engaged in a "cosmic war" between "modernists" and regressive religious extremists who use terror in order to get noticed in the most theatrical ways possible. They commit the most sensational dramatic acts of violence in public places that will horrify the most people. Their goal is to shake the very foundations of secular society. Juergensmeyer writes that, because this it is a "cosmic war... compromise and negotiation is unlikely." [33] He notes that all wars end eventually, but he does not indicate how or when this one might end. He does not offer explicit solutions, but more or less implies that we should not give sensationalistic media exposure to terrorist events and organizations.[34]

Five "Possibilities"

Although Juergensmeyer does not offer explicit suggestions for reducing religious violence, he does identify and expound upon "five possibilities" regarding the future of religious violence.

> 1. "Destroying violence" with violence or extreme force. His example is the effort of U.S. military forces to kill all of the conspirators in the 9-11-2001 attacks on the World Trade Center and the Pentagon. He concludes that this kind of "possibility" is highly unlikely to be successful and for many reasons. He writes that "The destructive strategy can work only in limited circumstances." [35]

> 2. "Terrifying Terrorists." Juergensmeyer writes that this "second scenario is one in which the threat of violent reprisals or imprisonment so frightens religious activists that they hesitate to act." He mentions that terrorists sometimes become repelled by the carnage they have committed, and they desist from further carnage. He also mentions that some terrorists might desist because they fear that their actions will result in foreign military forces occupying their homeland. He asserts that this possibility rarely becomes a reality.

3. "Violence Wins." This occurs "when the violence is used as leverage in political negotiation and the causes behind the struggle are met." Juergensmeyer provides several examples of this but concludes that "negotiated compromise with activists involved in terrorism is fraught with difficulties" and rarely works.

4. "Separating Religion from Politics." Juergensmeyer writes that "the fourth scenario for peace is one in which the absolutism of the struggle is defused, and the religious aspects are taken out of politics and retired to the moral and metaphysical planes." He gives as examples "...the British reactions to the violence of the Irish Republican Army and at least one moment in the Israeli response to Palestinian activism." [36]

5. "Healing Politics with Religion." Juergensmeyer seems to prefer this "possibility," perhaps in part because he was a Methodist Minister and a graduate of a divinity school. But he does not express much optimism that it will become a reality.

"The most successful solutions are those that have been forged on a moral plane—those that have required the opponents in the conflict to summon at least a minimal level of mutual trust and respect." He writes that this occurs "when religious activists have perceived governmental authorities as having a moral integrity in keeping with, or accommodating of, religious values." He contends that "in some instances when religious violence has been quelled, religion has literally been subsumed under the aegis of governmental authorities."

As examples, Juergensmeyer mentions that this occurred in Sri Lanka and in the British response to Irish terrorism. He goes on to say that this also occurs when both government and religion provide society with "high-mindedness" but also a concern with the quality of life rather than just an emphasis on power and possessions.

Summary of Findings, and Claims of Other Authors 253

Juergensmeyer's Conclusion

On the final page, Juergensmeyer writes that one of history's ironies is that "although religion has been used to justify violence, violence can also empower religion." [37] He writes that religious violence won't end until there is "some moderation in religion's passion, and some acknowledgement of religion in elevating the spiritual and moral values of public life." He calls for "a renewed appreciation for religion itself."

A Few Comments on Juergensmeyer's Claims

It seems to me that Juergensmeyer's major claims do not contradict my findings about portrayals of violence, terror, war, and genocide in the three holy books, although many of his claims do not directly bear upon my findings. My focus is on the verses in the holy books that might be used and abused to promote violence. According to the title of his book, his subject is *Terror in the Mind of God*. He tries to address this topic primarily by relying on interviews he and some other researchers had with rather infamous people who were convicted of violent crimes. He also interviewed some well-known leaders of extremist religious groups and organizations that were alleged to promote and conduct terrorist activities. They may or may not have made reference to verses in the holy books in their interviews with Juergensmeyer. Apparently, only a few of them did so, based on what he reports in his book. None of them claimed that verses in the holy books were irrelevant. It is just that very few of them mentioned the holy books or verses in the holy books.

I have no major objections to any of Juergensmeyer's observations or claims. Obviously, his work inspires me and is of great value to me. I will simply mention a few ways his book could be even more valuable.

First, I don't believe that his interviews can tell us much if anything about "terror in the mind of God"—the title of his book. I'm not sure that anything, *by anyone*, can tell us anything about "the mind" of God. My book certainly does not try to do so. As mentioned so often throughout this book, a primary purpose of my book is to add to our understanding of how violence, terror, war, and genocide are *portrayed* in the OT, the NT, and the Qur'an. A second purpose is to explain how these portrayals might have been used and misused to incite violent acts in the past and *how they might be used in the decades ahead*—not just by terrorists, but by anyone or by any group, organization, or government, anywhere in the world.

Second, Juergensmeyer determined that the people he interviewed either sponsored or engaged in terrorist events between 1980-2000 in a number of nations. According to him, they did this primarily in order to shock and horrify as many people as possible, and to do so in such ways as to get a lot of sensationalistic, mass media coverage throughout the world. He contends that they believed that this would ultimately destabilize and destroy modern, secular governments and replace them with the kinds of traditional theocratic states that supposedly were based on the holy books of Judaism, Christianity, and Islam.

I believe that Juergensmeyer's book would be more valuable if he had asked each of his interviewees if any specific verses in the holy books inspired and motivated them to commit their violent actions and, if so, which verses, and how this occurred in terms of their reasoning. For example, when interviewee Abouhalima told Juergensmeyer that reading the Qur'an returned him to a life committed to Islam after he tired of his "dissolute life in Germany," [38] it would have been even more valuable to know which verses were most important to him, and why this was the case.

I also think it would have been worthwhile for Juergensmeyer to have interviewed and reported on the motivations, beliefs, and dispositions of lower-class, rank and file religious extremists and terrorists in addition to the upper-class, well-educated leaders and media celebrities that he interviewed. If he had done so, he might have discovered that the "rank and file," lower-level extremists were influenced far more than their leaders and propagandists by specific, violent passages in the holy books. The lower-level extremists might well have been recruited and motivated

Summary of Findings, and Claims of Other Authors   255

to engage in violence for religious reasons that were conveyed to them in the holy books—including salvation for fighting and dying for what they assumed to be their religions and their God. By contrast, the leaders, recruiters, and propagandists were motivated primarily by their political interests—to gain power and overthrow governments—rather than by religious beliefs. Of course, this is speculation on my part. But, as I have reported several times in this book, the many conversations I have had with convicted, alleged terrorist Mohammed Taheri-Azar in 2016 convince me that he was heavily and directly motivated and inspired to commit his vehicle-ramming attack in 2006 by at least forty very specific verses in the Qur'an, most of which portrayed Allah as demanding violence from his followers. Taheri-Azar identified many of those verses in a letter he wrote immediately before his attack. He repeated them several times in public letters after that attack. He did not call for the overthrow of any governments, although he did express his disapproval of how his fellow Muslims were being dealt with in their own countries by outsiders, including U.S. military forces. As mentioned several times in Chapters 1 and 2, Taheri-Azar also confirmed the importance of those verses to me a number of times in my conversations with him.

Finally, I believe that the title of Juergensmeyer's book, *Terror in the Mind of God*, is not very appropriate. His book does not really tell us about that subject. The title also is very unfortunate because it might well be blasphemous to many people who object to any claim, by any human being, that any human being could ever know "the mind of God." Furthermore, I did not find that Juergensmeyer ever illuminates the "mind of God," nor could he. I believe he has helped illuminate what probably was "in the minds" of some of his interviewees when he interviewed them. That was always many months or years after their terrorist acts.

But to be perfectly clear on this matter, once again, I emphasize that my book does not attempt to say anything about "the mind of God" or the "mind" of any deity or spiritual force. This book of mine is only about how violence, terror, war, and genocide *are portrayed*, if and when they are portrayed in any of the three holy books. Often the portrayals include statements about God or Allah or statements that are attributed to God, Allah, various prophets, disciples, and leaders as the originators of violence. Whether these portrayals tell us anything about "the mind of God," or the mind of anyone else, is not for me to say. You are of course free to decide this matter for yourself. But obviously I believe that Juergensmeyer's book tells us a lot about the behaviors of quite a few terrorists and propagandists who revealed their religious identities and some of their affiliations.

Jessica Stern's *Terror in the Name of God: Why Religious Militants Kill*

One of the most influential books on "religious militants who engage in terrorist events" is Jessica Stern's *Terror in the Name of God: Why Religious Militants Kill.* It was first published in 2003 by Ecco Books, an imprint of Harper/Collins Publishers. Here is how Jessica Stern is described on the back cover of the paperback edition of the book:

> Jessica Stern, the foremost U.S. expert on terrorism, is a lecturer at Harvard University's Kennedy School of Government. She has served as the "Superterrorism Fellow" (believe that title or not!) at the Council on Foreign Relations and as a senior Fellow at Stanford University's Hoover Institution.

Regarding her research method and her book, the back-cover states:

> For four years, Jessica Stern interviewed extremist members of three religions around the world: Christians, Jews, and Muslims. Traveling extensively—to refugee camps in Lebanon, to religious schools in Pakistan, to prisons in Amman, Ashqelon, and Pensacola—she discovered that the Islamic jihadi in the mountains of Pakistan and the Christian fundamentalist bomber in Oklahoma have much in common.

Summary of Findings, and Claims of Other Authors 257

Let us see what Stern has to say about these terrorists and whether they revealed that the holy books of their religions contributed to their violence.

Stern writes that her first interview was with Kerry Noble.

> Kerry Noble has been second-in-command of a violent apocalyptic cult active in the 1980s, whose members were convicted of murder, fire-bombing a synagogue and a church that accepted homosexuals, conspiracy to assassinate federal officials, and other crimes. They had stockpiled cyanide with the aim of poisoning major city water supplies and, like Timothy McVeigh ten years later, plotted to bomb the Oklahoma City Federal Building.[39]

Stern describes her first meeting by Noble this way:

> In March of 1998 I had my first extended conversation with a religious terrorist. He is an American who had been released from prison and was living in a Texas trailer park at the time we spoke. I called him in connection with an earlier project on terrorists' potential to use weapons of mass destruction. Although I had been studying and working on terrorism for many years by that time, none of what I had read or heard prepared me for that conversation, which was about faith at least as much as it was about violence....
>
> During our first conversation, Noble told me he spends a lot of time in meditation and prayer. He is an accomplished student of the Scriptures—he knows whole chapters of the Bible by heart. And he feels he has a personal relationship with God.[40]

To me this is an intriguing account by Stern. And yet, please notice that Stern does not indicate how she determined that Noble "is an accomplished student of Scriptures" or how she determined that Noble "knows whole chapters of the Bible by heart." Speaking for myself, while I have met people who can readily recite by heart quite a few passages from the Bible or Qur'an, I have never met anyone who "knows whole chapters of the Bible by heart." In addition to this, I wish that Stern and so many other authors would have determined which verses were most important to their interviewees, before, during, and after their acts of violence.

Psychological Doubling

Stern is justly acknowledged by many experts for a number of significant insights about violence and religion. One of these is that she believes most of her interviewees, including Kerry Noble, manifest what she calls "psychological doubling." [41]

Stern explains it this way:

> This is a group phenomenon. Once inside an organization whose goals include killing, ordinary people can commit seemingly demonic acts. According to psychiatrist Robert J. Lifton, who has studied Nazis and other violent, fanatical groups, cult members become two people: the self they were, and the new, morally disengaged killer self. Some people are more susceptible to such doubling than others, often in response to trauma. [42]

Stern focuses on terrorism and terrorists. As important as this is, as with so many other authors, she does not deal with interpersonal violence, genocide, nor war. I am also rather surprised that Stern makes few comments about the Bible and the Qur'an or other books considered holy in various religions. The Index only has eight references to the "Koran" in the book. The "Bible" only has three references in the Index. The scarcity of references to these books leaves me to wonder whether passages in these books were not, and are not significant, to the terrorists she interviewed? Or perhaps Stern simply did not pay attention to this matter. Then again, none of her interviewees seemed to blame their violent acts on any specific passages in the holy books or on any religion.

Stern's Suggestions for Reducing Terrorism in the Years Ahead

Although her book was first published in 2003, Stern makes a few suggestions that might have value now:

> The religious terrorists we face are fighting on every level—militarily, economically, psychologically, and spiritually. Their military weapons are powerful, but spiritual dread is the most dangerous weapon in their arsenal.... We need to respond—not just with guns—but by seeking to create confusion, conflict, and competition among terrorists and between terrorists and their sponsors and sympathizers.[43]

How should we do this? According to Stern:

> We should encourage the condemnation of extremist interpretations of religion by peace-loving practitioners. We should change policies that no longer serve out interests or are inconsistent with our values, even if those happen to be policies that the terrorists demand. In the end, however, what counts is what we fight *for*, not what we oppose. We need to avoid giving into spiritual dread, and to hold fast to the best of our principles, by emphasizing tolerance, empathy, and courage.[44]

Comment: These suggestions seem very tolerable but rather abstract to me, including Stern's term "spiritual dread." I have not found a definition of "spiritual dread," but I do not doubt that it is important to Stern.

Karen Armstrong's *Fields of Blood: Religion and the History of Violence*

This is one of the most often quoted books on this subject. Anchor Books, a division of the huge publishing house, Penguin Random House, LLC, published this massive book of more than 500 pages in 2014. The back cover of the book identifies Armstrong as a leading scholar of religion who has published "numerous books on religion" including *The Battle for God* and *Holy War*. It indicates that her work has been translated into forty-five languages and that she has won a number of prestigious prizes for her work including the Nayef Al-Rodham Prize for Transcultural Understanding. One of the endorsements for this book, inside the front cover, is from the Library Journal. It succinctly conveys Armstrong's major thesis that throughout history the many so-called "religious wars" were more the result of "political issues" than the result of differences in religions and their beliefs:

> A well-written historical summary of what have traditionally been viewed as "religious" wars, showing convincingly that in pretty much all cases it was not so much religion as it was political issues that fueled the conflict.[45]

I did not find anything in Armstrong's book that directly contradicts the findings that I present in this book. By the same token, Armstrong does not contend that verses in the OT, the NT, or the Qur'an have determined how, why, and when most so-called religious wars have been fought during the past three-thousand years. Nor does she contend that they were or are irrelevant. She mentions these three books hundreds of times in her book, and she quotes dozens of verses from them at various places, often indicating how they were interpreted differently by various religious and political leaders before or after specific wars including the Crusades, the 9-11-2001 jet airplane attacks in America, many other terrorist attacks, and the rise of Hamas, the PLO, the Taliban, al-Qaeda, ISIS, and ISUL.

Armstrong's focus is on what she calls "religious wars" of the last three thousand years, primarily but not exclusively in the Middle East and Europe. And, once again, her thesis is that we cannot blame or "scapegoat" (her term for it) religions for these wars even though they pitted people of different religions against each other. Her reason is that "political issues" were far more salient than "religious differences" in causing these wars and in determining their outcomes. As shown in the preceding chapter of this book, the focus of my book is on *violence of all types—not just on religious wars*—as portrayed in the verses of the OT, the NT, and the Qur'an. In other words, we have counted, coded, and analyzed every verse in these three books that portray interpersonal violence, violence by deities and other forces against human beings, acts of terror and genocide, as well as actual military battles and wars. Also worth noting is that our interest is not just in these portrayals, but in how these portrayals might be used and misused to perpetrate violence in the decades ahead. In the next chapter, we consider suggestions and recommendations by Armstrong and these other authors to reduce the risks of so-called "religious violence" in the decades ahead. But for now, I will present the passages in Armstrong's book that most directly relate to the material I present in Chapters 1-4 of this book.

Regarding the New Testament

Armstrong does not often distinguish between the OT and the NT in terms of the frequencies of portrayals of violence and the types of violence. In one of her relatively few efforts to give explanations for violent verses in the holy books, she provides this explanation as to why one book in the NT, Revelation, has what she considers to be many more references to violence than the other books of the NT. She writes that the book of Revelation was "probably written while the Jews of Palestine were fighting a desperate war against the Roman Empire."

> The author, John of Patmos, was convinced that the days of the Beast, the evil empire, were numbered. Jesus was about to return, ride into battle, slay the Beast, fling him into a pit of fire, and establish his kingdom for a thousand years. Paul has taught his converts that Jesus, the victim of imperial violence, had achieved a spiritual and cosmic victory over sin and death. John, however, depicted Jesus, who had taught his followers not to retaliate violently, as a ruthless warrior who would defeat Rome with massive slaughter and bloodshed. Revelation was admitted to the Christian canon only with great difficulty, but it would be scanned eagerly in times of social unrest when people were yearning for a more just and equitable world.[46]

Regarding the Qur'an

Armstrong provides relatively little attention to the Qur'an and its many verses. However, I believe that her interpretation of it is consistent with mine as presented in Chapter 2, in a general sense. As I did in Chapter 2, she writes that the Qur'an's verses, taken as a whole, are not consistent regarding violence.

> There is no univocal or systematic Quranic teaching about military violence. Sometimes God demands patience and restraint rather than fighting; sometimes he gives permission for defensive warfare and condemns aggression; but at other times he calls for offensive warfare within certain limits; and occasionally these restrictions are lifted. In some passages, Muslims are told to live at peace with the people of the book; in others, they are required to subdue them. These contradictory instructions occur throughout the Qur'an, and Muslims developed two exegetical strategies to rationalize them. The first linked each verse of the Qur'an with a historical event in Muhammad's life and used this context to establish a general principle.... The second strategy was to abrogate verses; scholars argued that while the ummah was still struggling for survival, God could only give Muslims temporary solutions to their difficulties, but once Islam was victorious, he could issue permanent commands. Thus, the later revelations—some of which call for unrestrained warfare—were God's definitive words and rescinded the earlier, more lenient directives.[47]

By way of comment, notice that Armstrong's interpretation is that some of the later revelations in the Qur'an "call for unrestrained warfare." And notice that the verb she uses is "call for"—not "called for." The "call" was timeless. Perhaps it still is timeless.

Regarding the Terrorist Attacks of 9-11-2001

Armstrong relies heavily on books published by other authors, rather than primarily on any data that she might have collected from any terrorists. One of the authors seems to rely on forensic psychiatrist Marc Sageman. In 2008, he published a book titled *Leaderless Jihad: Terror Networks in the Twenty-First Century*. Armstrong writes that Osama Bin Laden was very familiar with the Qur'an, that he quoted it often regarding violence, but that his motivations were essentially political in that his goal was

Summary of Findings, and Claims of Other Authors   263

to rid Muslim countries of foreign military and political influence. She tries to explain bin Laden's thinking like this:

> Muslims had become soft and had abandoned jihad because they were afraid of dying. Their only hope was to summon again the courage at the heart of Islam. Hence the importance of the huge martyrdom operation that would show the world that Muslims were no longer fearful. Their plight was so desperate that they must either fight or be killed. Radicals also love the Quranic story of David and Goliath that concludes: "How often a small force has defeated a large army!" The more powerful the enemy, therefore, the more heroic the struggle. Killing civilians is regrettable but, fighters argue, the Crusader-Zionists have also shed innocent blood, and the Quran commands retaliation.[48]

Armstrong goes on to write that, in addition to Osama bin Laden, most of the key members of the group that planned the details of the 9-11 attacks came from privileged backgrounds. They "had studied engineering and technology in Europe" and had not had extensive religious training in Islamic madrassas. Only a fellow named bin al-Shibh "had a deep knowledge of the Qur'an." As to the others, Armstrong writes:

> Unused to allegoric and symbolic thought, their scientific education inclined them not to skepticism but toward a literalist reading of the Quran that diverged (Armstrong spells Quran without an apostrophe) radically from traditional Muslim exegesis. They also had no training in the traditional, so their knowledge of mainstream Muslim law was at best superficial.[49]

Armstrong goes on to advance her thesis that the 9-11 attacks were motivated by politics rather than religion. While I do not have strong objections to her thesis, she often seems to overlook evidence that she presents that indicates that the Qur'an and core beliefs in Islam were part of the daily routines of the terrorists as they prepared for the attacks. "Members became deeply attached to one another, shared apartments, ate and prayed together, and watched endless battlefield videos from

Chechnya. Most important, they identified closely with these distant struggles." [50]

Armstrong relies on Sageman's book and books by other authors to tell us about how the 9-11 terrorists prepared for the attacks in the days immediate before the attacks. At times it seems that she is unaware of how much evidence she is presenting about the influence of their recitations of the Qur'an's verses that promote violence. "The hijackers themselves certainly regarded the 9/11 atrocities as a religious act but one that bore very little resemblance to normative Islam." Armstrong also mentions, as we did in Chapters 1 and 2 of this book, that "A document found in Ata's suitcase outlined a program of prayer and reflection to help them through the ordeal." [51] Armstrong continues, "The prayers themselves are jarring. Like all Muslim discourse, the document begins with the *bismallah*—'In the Name of God, the most Merciful and most Compassionate'—but it initiates an action devoid of either mercy or compassion."

Armstrong repeats well-known accounts of the document:

> While packing, they were to whisper Quranic verses into their hands and rub this holiness onto their luggage, box cutters, knives, ID, and passports. Their clothes must fit snugly, like the garments of the Prophet and his companions. When they begin to fight the passengers and the crew, as a sign of resolution, each one must "clench his teeth just as the pious forefathers did prior to entering into battle" and "strike in the manner of champions who are not desirous of returning to this world, and shout *Allahu Akbar*! For this shout causes fear in the hearts of the unbelievers." They must not "become gloomy" but recite Quranic verses while they are fighting.[52]

Regarding ISIS and Other Contemporary Terrorist Groups

Armstrong contends that ISIS (which she refers to as "IS") and its members only "cherry pick" some of the verses from the Qur'an that suit them, and that their members ignore all the other verses that don't suit them.[53] She also asserts that ISIS and its members are motivated far more by

Summary of Findings, and Claims of Other Authors 265

politics than by religion. She claims that they don't pray or observe the daily rituals of praying five times a day. She also writes that the Charlie Hebdo avengers "were not traditionally devout." All of them had criminal records, she claims. Once again, Armstrong concludes that the "Western media scapegoat" religion as the cause and the basis for terrorists' actions when it is really "politics" at the heart of their violence.[54]

Armstrong also relies on Sageman's book in claiming that "self-starter terrorists" (akin to "lone-wolf terrorists") have very little knowledge of the Qur'an or perhaps even of Islam.

> These freelance terrorists have very little knowledge of the Quran, and so it is pointless to attempt a debate about their interpretation of scripture or to blame "Islam" for their crimes. Indeed Marc Sageman, who has talked with several of them, believes that a regular religious education might have deterred them from lawless violence. They are, he found, chiefly motivated by the desire to escape a stifling sense of insignificance and pointlessness in secular nation-states that struggle to absorb foreign minorities. They seek to fulfill the age-old dream of military glory and believe that by dying a heroic death, they will give their lives meaning as local heroes.... They might claim to be acting in the name of Islam, but when an untalented beginner claims to be playing a Beethoven sonata, we hear only cacophony.[55]

Overlooking Armstrong's occasional rather snide and elitist remarks, her ethnocentrism, and her mixed metaphors, I believe that she has a very questionable image of what she derisively calls "self-starter terrorists." If it is valid, it does not apply to Mohammed Taheri-Azar based on everything I know and describe about him in several earlier chapters. From my many conversations with him, I believe that Taheri-Azar still is a very devout Muslim who practices his faith each day, praying five times a day, fasting, and observing all commandments as fully as he can, even though he is in prison. He is extremely knowledgeable about Islam and the Qur'an. All the evidence that I am aware of indicates that he was this way for at least one year before he committed the vehicle-ramming attack that led to his arrest, conviction, and sentence to many years in prison.

Armstrong's "Afterword"

In her "Afterword," Armstrong again repeats her theme that religion is not inherently violent.[56] She mentions that "in the Hebrew Bible, some turned violent, others did not." She also writes that "when Muslims attack churches and synagogues today, they are not driven to do so by Islam." [57] And then, a few pages later, she writes that "modern religious violence is not an alien growth, but is part of the modern scene." On the final page of her Afterword I found what seems to be her suggestion regarding the future:

> Somehow we have to find ways of doing what religion—at its best—has done for centuries: build a sense of global community, cultivate a sense of reverence and "equanimity" for all, and take responsibility for the suffering we see in the world. We are all, religious and secular alike, responsible for the current predicament of the world.[58]

Some Additional Comments on Armstrong's Claims

There is no doubt that Karen Armstrong knows a lot about the history of many religions. She writes with obvious confidence and she often articulates "Western" viewpoints on religious violence. Her book includes hundreds of footnotes and general references to books that she mentions as support for her assertions. Speaking for myself however, I do not find her book to be of much value in helping us understand portrayals of violence in the holy books or in helping us prepare to deal with political and religious violence in the decades ahead.

Furthermore, Armstrong often claims to know the interior states of mind of people. She does this with statements such as this one: [59] "These political objectives were certainly uppermost in Bin Laden's mind in the immediate aftermath of 9/11, although he also would invoke the divine will." [60]

My final comment is this: Even though it is not essential to my purpose, when Armstrong repeatedly tells us that "religious wars" actually are more political than religious, she seems to be telling us what they mean to her, or perhaps to international relations in their consequences. In doing this, she seems to be overlooking what the wars are to those who fight in them—the ordinary fighters—and to their victims, if not to their leaders. It might well be essentially "political" if a person fights, kills, or dies because he or she wants his country or his unit to defeat some other nation, faction, or enemy military force. That is a matter of power—of imposing one's will very violently on another person, group, or nation. But isn't it more "religious" than "political" if and when a person fights, kills, injures, or is injured or dies because he or she believes that a deity, God, or Allah demands it, or will reward that person with eternal life, paradise, or some desirable other-worldly destiny? And isn't it also more "religious" than "political" if and when that person believes he or she will be condemned to hell by a deity or deities if he or she fails to obey a commandment to fight and to be willing to die without regret? Now regarding the victims, if the victims die because of their religious beliefs or while protecting their mosque, temple, synagogue, or church, isn't this more "religious" than "political?"

Philip Jenkins' *Laying Down the Sword: Why We Can't Ignore the Bible's Violent Verses*

Philip Jenkins' highly regarded book was published in 2011 by HarperOne, a major publishing house in New York. Here is a brief profile of Philip Jenkins from the dust jacket of his book:

> Philip Jenkins has a joint appointment as the Edwin Erle Sparks Professor of the Humanities in history and religious studies at Penn State University and as Distinguished Senior Fellow at the Institute for Studies of Religion at Baylor University. His books include *The Lost History of Christianity, Jesus Wars,* and *The Next Christendom,* and he has published articles in the *Wall Street*

Journal, the *New Republic*, the *Atlantic Monthly*, the *Washington Post*, and the *Boston Globe*.

Jenkins provides a very informed, carefully-written, and compelling exposition on a limited selection of violent verses in the Qur'an as well as in the Bible, particularly the OT. Among other attributes, Jenkins provides a number of very specific and significant claims about the quantities and qualities of violent verses in these books. He contends that careful, objective analysis reveals that the OT is considerably more violent than the Qur'an and that the nature of violence in the Bible is significantly different than in the Qur'an. Let us consider a number of his claims in light of my own findings, as shown throughout this book.

Jenkins indicates that he based his analysis on the KJV of the Bible and principally on Pickthall's *The Meaning of the Glorious Qur'an*. These are the same versions that I use in my analysis, as I present it here in this book. I could not find in his book a detailed description of his research methods, but it is obvious to me that Jenkins is very familiar with the Bible and the Qur'an, as one would expect from someone with his professional status. By the way, Jenkins indicates that he is usually referring to the OT of the Bible when he refers to "the Bible." [61]

What follows is a presentation of Jenkins' major claims about violence in the Bible and in the Qur'an, followed by a comparison of his findings with mine.

Jenkins' Major Claims about Violence in the Holy Books

1. "The Qur'an offers nothing explicit (to justify suicide terrorism) beyond general exhortations to warfare in the name of God." [62]

2. "While the Bible *reports* violence in the distant past, some argue, the Qur'an *commands* violence here and how. The Bible, in this view, records ancient campaigns against forgotten peoples, which are of interest only to archaeologists, while the Qur'an commands 'Fight infidels!'—an order valid in any age. But such a contrast

Summary of Findings, and Claims of Other Authors 269

is false. However, commentators have read it, it is not obvious that the Qur'an was commanding violence without end against unbelievers, as opposed to warfare against specific Arabian tribes or factions in the seventh century CE." [63]

3. "But if instead we compare like with like, scripture with scripture, rather than how passages have been used by later generations of believers, then the Qur'an is in no sense a bloodier or more warlike text than the Bible—either the Hebrew Bible or the larger text beloved by Christians. Indeed, that Islamic text has far fewer passages demanding to be confronted or accommodated." [64]

4. "If the Qur'an urges believers to fight, as it undoubtedly does, it also commands that enemies be shown mercy if they surrender. Some frightful portions of the Bible, by contrast, order the total extermination of enemies, of whole families and races—of men, women, and children, and even their livestock, with no quarter granted." [65]

5. "The Bible overflows with 'texts of terror,' to borrow a phrase coined by American theologian Phyllis Trible, and biblical violence is often marked by indiscriminate savagery." [66]

6. Jenkins also contends that, in contrast to passages in the Bible, the Qur'an is "lacking in extreme violence." [67] In a very original and sincere effort to support this claim, Jenkins provides a scheme for "Classifying Violent and Disturbing Scriptures." The scheme has three categories of violence: "extreme," "alarming," and "disturbing." [68] By the way, Jenkins concedes that the scheme is "crude" and "highly impressionistic." Yet it seems to me that it is worth our consideration.

Category 1: "Extreme"
Jenkins contends that the Qur'an "has nothing strictly comparable" to any of these three subcategories of violence:

> a. Text calling for direct violence against particular races or ethnic groups.

b. Demands of sanctions for the extermination of racial groups.

  c. Calls to annihilate enemies.

Category 2: "Alarming"
Jenkins writes that the Qur'an has plenty of texts that fit into Category 2 by giving divine sanction to warfare. He explains that "The God of the Qur'an commands his followers to fight their enemies, to defeat and conquer them, and to use violence and subterfuge when necessary."

Category 3: "Disturbing"
Jenkins writes that Category 3 pertains to texts in the holy books "that threaten savage violence or brutal punishment against enemies of faith but only in the supernatural realm."

By the way, Jenkins very openly asks if the "threat of hellfire" in Category 3 "poses a danger of actual violence in the real world." He is very balanced in explaining the two possible contrasting responses. He concludes that the most valid response is that it does *not* pose a danger of provoking violence in the real world. However, in Chapters 1 and 2, I provide testimony from my interviewee, Mohammad Taheri-Azar, that indicates that these kinds of threats about eventual violence of hellfire from a deity can sometimes influence persons like Taheri-Azar to commit acts of violence in the "here and now."

Jenkins also contends that "...moreover the Qur'an's warnings of hell are overwhelmingly directed *not* against infidels or any particular race or sect, but against sinners of whatever creed." He elaborates on this as follows: [69]

> The Muslim inferno is reserved primarily for those who skimp on charity;
> Those who show no kindness to the orphan;
> Those who fail to compete with each other in feeding the poor;

Summary of Findings, and Claims of Other Authors   271

Those who love riches, and seize the inheritance of the weak.

Jenkins also contends that, "None of the Qur'an's warnings of fire and brimstone are too shocking when set aside the New NT." As an example, to support his claim, Jenkins mentions a verse in the Epistle of Matthew about "the tares and the harvest." He adds that "If the hellfire texts are more obvious in the Qur'an than in the Bible, the difference is one of quantity not substance." [70]

> 7. Finally, and as indicated in the epigraph at the beginning of this chapter, as well as at the beginning of Chapter 1, Jenkins somehow concludes that differences among the faiths are minimal regarding violence. "But in terms of the violent and unacceptable faces of their fundamental scriptures, differences between the faiths are minimal." [71]

Some Comments on Jenkins' Claims About Holy Book Violence. I believe that Philip Jenkins' claims are very valuable for their candor and clarity, and that most of them are highly compatible with my findings as presented in this book. Many of my findings confirm and even sharpen many of Jenkins' claims and provide additional evidence in support of his observations. There are a few exceptions, however, in which I believe a few of his claims are somewhat mistaken. Let us consider a few of his major claims once again.

1. Regarding "suicide terrorism," Jenkins writes that "The Qur'an offers nothing explicit beyond general exhortations to warfare in the name of God."[72] I agree that there are no passages in the Qur'an that mention suicide terrorism or any terms or phrases equivalent to it. I did not find any passages in the English language versions of the Qur'an that imply that "suicide terrorism" is acceptable in Islam. And yet there are plenty of verses in the Qur'an that go beyond "general exhortations to warfare in the name of God," contrary to what Jenkins claims. Here are just a few of them, as presented in the Qur'an and in Chapter 2 of this book.

*Then, when the sacred months have passed, slay the idolaters wherever ye find them, and take them (captive), and besiege them, and prepare for them each ambush. But if they repent and establish worship and pay the poor-due, then leave their way free. Lo! Allah is Forgiving, Merciful. (Surah 9: 5)

*Now when ye meet in battle those who disbelieve, then it is smiting of the necks until, when ye have routed them, then making fast of bonds, and afterward wither grace or ransom till the war lay down its burdens. That (is the ordinance). And if Allah willed He could have punished them (without you) but (thus it is ordained) that He may try of you by means of others. And those who are slain in the way of Allah, He rendereth not their actions vain. (Surah 47: 4)

In these verses, Allah encourages his followers to not only engage in warfare in his name, but also to be willing to be killed in battle (as martyrs) by their opponents in order to defend Islam ("to become martyrs for the cause of Allah"), and thereby to forever gain honor and paradise for themselves. In agreement with Jenkins, these passages do not state or imply that Muslims are allowed to kill themselves by any method or for any purpose, including imposing terror upon their opponents, but they certainly are encouraged to put themselves in harm's way and to not be reluctant to have their lives ended violently by opponents and unbelievers who oppose Allah or Islam.

2. Does the Bible only report violence in the distant past, while the Qur'an commands violence "here and now"? Jenkins writes that "such a contrast is false." He goes on to explain that "...it is not obvious that the Qur'an was commanding violence without end against unbelievers, as opposed to warfare against specific Arabian tribes or factions in the seventh century." [73]

I believe that Jenkin's is partially correct in this claim, but that his claim needs to be refined, based on my findings as presented in Chapters 2, 3, and 4. There are plenty of verses in both the OT and the Qur'an that portray violence in the past tense. There also are considerable numbers of verses in both of these books that portray violence in the present tense. But there also are considerable numbers of verses in both the OT and in the Qur'an that demand, threaten, or promise violent actions without limitations regarding time. There also are many verses that convey that violence will occur in the future. Very common examples of this are the many verses in both books that promise violence on Judgment Day for those people who violate the commandments of God or of Allah, or that anger God or Allah in any number of ways.

Here are a few of the examples that also are presented in Chapters 2 and 3, first from the Old Testament and then from the Quran.

> *If a man have a stubborn and rebellious son, which will not obey the voice of his father, or the voice of the mother, and that when they have chastened him, will not hearken unto them:
>
> Then shall his father and his mother lay hold of him, and bring him out unto the elders of his city, and unto the gate of his place;
>
> And they shall say unto the elders of his city, This our son is stubborn and rebellious, he will not obey our voice; he is a glutton, and a drunkard.
>
> And all the men of his city shall stone him with stones, that he die: so shalt thou put evil away from among you; and all Israel shall hear, and fear. (Deut. 21: 18-21)
>
> *For every one that curseth his father or his mother shall be surely put to death: he hath cursed his father or his mother; his blood shall be upon him.
>
> And the man that committeth adultery with another man's wife, even he that committeth adultery with his neighbor's wife, the adulterer and the adulteress shall surely be put to death. (Lev. 20: 9-10)

274   Violence, Terror, Genocide, and War

Other examples abound in the OT, as presented in Chapter 3. These include verses that demand the killing of those who engage in homosexuality (Lev. 20: 12), blasphemy (Lev. 20: 16), anyone who "despiseth my statutes" (Lev. 26: 15-16), and any of one's relatives who tempt you to worship gods other than the God of Israel (Deut. 13: 6-10).

> *When thou comest unto a city to fight against it, then proclaim peace unto it.
>
> And it shall be, if it make thee answer of peace, and open unto thee, then it shall be that all the people that is found therein shall be tributaries unto thee, and they shall serve thee.
>
> And if it will make no peace with thee, but will make war against thee, then thou shalt besiege it:
>
> And when the Lord thy God hath delivered it into thine hands, thou shalt smite every male thereof with the edge of the sword:
>
> But the women, and the little ones, and the cattle, and all that is in the city, even all the spoil thereof, shalt thou take unto thyself; and thou shall eat the spoil of thine enemies, which the Lord thy God hath given thee. (Deut. 20: 10-14)

Notice that these verses do not demand or approve of genocide by Israelite military forces against all of their captives. While these verses command that Israelite military forces "smite every male," the verses explicitly state that the women, children, cattle and "all that is in the city" shall be taken as spoil by the Muslims and for the use of the Israelite military forces. The verses do not demand or allow for the killing or extermination of all of the captives. They do not constitute genocide. And yet, as presented in Chapter 3 of this book, there are other sets of verses in the OT that seem to come much closer to constituting demands for genocide or near genocide by victorious Israelite military forces against their captives.

Summary of Findings, and Claims of Other Authors 275

*Samaria shall become desolate; for she hath rebelled against her God: they shall fall by the sword; their infants shall be dashed in pieces, and their women with child shall be ripped up. (Hosea 13: 16)

*But I will send a fire on the wall of Gaza, which shall devour the palaces thereof. (Amos 1: 7)

*But I will send a fire upon Judah, and it shall devour the palaces of Jerusalem. (Amos 2: 5)

*The Lord will be terrible unto them: for he will famish all the gods of the earth; and men shall worship him, every one from its place, even all the isles of the heathen. Ye Ethiopians also, ye shall be slain by my sword. And he will stretch out his hand against the north, and destroy Assyria; and will make Nineveh a desolation, and dry like a wilderness. (Zeph. 2: 11-13)

*Thou are my battle axe and weapons of war: for with thee will I break in pieces the nations, and with thee will I destroy kingdoms. (Jer. 51: 20)

*Woe unto the inhabitants of the sea coast, the nation of the Cherethites! The word of the Lord is against you: O Canaan, the land of the Philistines, I will even destroy thee, that there shall be no inhabitants. (Zeph. 2: 5)

As indicated in Chapter 3, there might be some question as to whether these verses demand genocide of all captives, rather than just the total destruction of the cities of the captives. Notice that these verses are in the future tense—not the past tense. Also notice that they refer to places and kingdoms (Saudi Arabia and Jordan are current kingdoms) that continue to exist in the 21st Century: Gaza, Ethiopia, Assyria, Jerusalem, and others.

Now, regarding the NT, as indicated in Chapter 4 of this book, I did not find any verses that portray or convey genocide against any clan, "race," tribe, or nation except for the verses, similar to those in the OT, that portray God exterminating Sodom and Gomorrah and all of the living things on Earth except Noah, his family, and mated pairs of animals on the Ark, during the flood (2 Pet. 2: 5-6).

Now, regarding the Qur'an, somewhat contrary to Jenkins' claims, there are plenty of verses in which commands for violence seem to be without regard to time. There also are verses about warfare that do not limit Muslims to fighting against "specific Arabian tribes or factions of the Seventh Century." Here are just a few examples that were presented in Chapter 2:

> *O ye who believe! Retaliation is prescribed for you in the matter of the murdered; the freeman for the freeman, and the slave for the slave, and the female for the female. And for him who is forgiven somewhat by his (injured) brother, prosecution according to usage and payment unto him in kindness. This is an alleviation and a mercy from your Lord. He who transgresseth after this will have a painful doom. (Surah 2: 178)

> *Fight in the way of Allah against those who fight against you, but begin not hostilities. Lo! Allah loveth not aggressors. And slay them wherever ye find them, and drive them out of the places whence they drove you out, for persecution is worse than slaughter. And fight not with them at the Inviolable Place of Worship until they first attack you there, but if they attack you (there) then slay them. Such is the reward of disbelievers. (Surah 2: 190-191)

> *Lo! Those who disbelieve Our revelations, We shall expose them to the Fire. As often as their skins are consumed We shall exchange them for fresh skins that they may taste the torment. Lo! Allah is ever Mighty. Wise. (Surah 4: 56)

> *But they who deny Our revelations and scorn them—such are rightful owners of the Fire; they will abide therein. (Surah 7: 36)[74]

*Lo! They who persecute believing men and believing women and repent not, theirs verily will be the doom of hell, and theirs the doom of burning. (Surah 85: 10)[75]

Therefore, I believe Jenkins' claim should be revised as follows:

Both the OT and the Qur'an have verses which do not limit to the past or the present time demands for violence by followers against opponents or against miscreants of their own religion or faith.

3. Jenkins presents a number of claims when he writes that, if we make valid comparisons of comparable verses in the two books, "...then the Qur'an is in no sense a bloodier or more warlike text than the Bible—either the Hebrew Bible or the larger text beloved by Christians."

There actually are a number of claims here in this one sentence quote from Jenkins' book. "Bloodier" and "warlike" are two distinct variables, it seems to me. As indicated throughout this book, an action can be "bloody" without being "warlike," as is the case when a person injures himself or herself, or one family member "bloodies" another family member, either intentionally or not. It is also true that an action can be "warlike" without being "bloody." Historically, governments and military forces have taken "warlike" actions, such as invading another country, or firing weapons upon an enemy force, without causing any bloodshed. Furthermore, as I have shown several times in Chapter 3 of this book, there are quite a few passages in the OT that are extremely "bloody" in their violence but that are not associated with warfare. For example, some verses demand that parents have their disobedient sons stoned to death by elders in their community. And, as shown regarding the Qur'an, many of the passages about battles and war are not "bloody." There are exhortations by Allah for his followers to engage in battles, when necessary, to stop persecution by unbelievers and idolaters, but they do not portray actual violence or bloodshed.

Second, Jenkins mentions that both the OT and the "larger text beloved by Christians" as bloody and as warlike as the Qur'an. Apparently, Jenkins means that the "larger" text consists of both the OT and the NT. As shown in Chapter 4 of this book, the NT has relatively few verses that convey "bloody" violence, and almost all of those verses refer to the torture and crucifixion of Jesus. Furthermore, the NT has very few verses that refer to or portray military battles or war.

Regarding the Qur'an, as shown in Chapter 2, the Qur'an can seem to be more "warlike" than the OT because verses about wars and battles are somewhat concentrated in about twelve of its 114 surahs and because a few of the surahs have titles in Arabic and in English that seem to refer to battles or to warfare. Recall that Chapter 2 identifies these twelve "war and battle surahs." And yet, in none of the twelve surahs do more than 28% of the verses refer to or portray military war or battles. Furthermore, in none of these twelve surahs do more than 24% of the verses convey violence. Going further, only about 13% of the verses that portray physical violence associate that violence with battles or warfare. The surah that is most often claimed to be "warlike," "violent" and "bloody" is Surah 8. Its common title in Arabic is *al-Anfal*; often it is translated into English as "Spoils of War" (by Pickthall) or "Battle Gains" (by Haleem). And yet, even this surah is not predominantly warlike, violent, or "bloody." The word "blood" as in blood-letting does not even appear in the surah. Furthermore, only 24% of its verses refer to or portray violence. Only 28% of its verses are about military war or battles. And only about 13% of its verses about wars or battles portray physical violence in those wars or battles.

And so, regarding Jenkins' claims, I believe that Chapters 2, 3, and 4 of this book show that the Qur'an is relatively and considerably more violent and warlike than the OT, but that the OT is considerably more violent and warlike than the NT, both quantitatively and qualitatively. Nevertheless, absolutely, but not proportionately, the OT has the most verses that demand, describe, threaten, or promise lethal violence and warfare than does the Qur'an or the NT.

Summary of Findings, and Claims of Other Authors 279

4. Is the Bible more genocidal than the Qur'an? As presented earlier in this chapter and also in a section of Chapter 1 of this book, Jenkins' makes several claims in the following statement:

> If the Qur'an urges believers to fight, as it undoubtedly does, it also commands that enemies be shown mercy if they surrender. Some frightful portions of the Bible, by contrast, order the total extermination of enemies, of whole families and races—of men, women, and children, and even their livestock, with no quarter granted.

Yes, Jenkins is correct here regarding both the Qur'an and the *Old Testament*—but not the New Testament. As shown in Chapter 2 of this book, quite a few verses in the Qur'an often urge believers to fight for specific reasons, and the Qur'an also has verses that command that Muslims must show mercy to enemies who surrender. Jenkins also is mainly correct in writing that some portions of the Bible "order the total extermination of enemies, of whole families and races—of men, women, and children, and even their livestock, with no quarter given." Here, once again, is one of the examples presented earlier in this book:

> *And they utterly destroyed all that was in the city, both man and woman, young and old, and ox, and sheep, and ass, with the edge of the sword. (Josh. 6: 21)

I have only three objections and refinements to these statements of Jenkins. The most important one is that the verses that demand extermination (genocide) are found only in the OT—not in the NT. Earlier in this chapter, Table 27 indicates that I found at least thirty verses in the OT in which God is portrayed as the perpetrator of genocide or God demands that his Israelites totally exterminate their opponents and everything belonging to their opponents including children, livestock, residences, and settlements. Also consider that in the often-repeated account of "Noah and the flood," verses portray that it is God who is the genocider of every living thing on Earth except for Noah, his family members, and mated pairs of many species of animals. Can we assume that, as portrayed in the passages like this one from the OT, God has exterminated all the tribes, clans, families, and nations of human beings, including all Israelites except Noah and his family members? And, if so, then isn't the God of the Israelites the very first genocider in Biblical history? If this is the case, is it any wonder that there are so many other verses in the OT that portray the God of the Israelites as demanding that his followers commit genocide against various tribes and nations of non-Israelites?

> *And all flesh died that moved upon the earth, both of fowl, and of cattle, and of beast, and of every creeping thing that creepeth upon the earth, and every man. All in whose nostrils was the breath of life, of all that was in the dry land, died. And every living substance was destroyed which was upon the face of the ground, both man, and cattle, and the creeping things, and the fowl of the heaven; and they were destroyed from the earth: and Noah only remained alive, and they that were with him in the ark. (Gen. 7: 21-23)

However, regarding Jenkins' use of the term "race," I have not found any verses in English language versions of the OT, the NT, or the Qur'an that use the terms "race" or "races" and that demand the extermination of them. I believe that this is important to note. In the OT, many verses identify tribes, nations, and cities that are to be exterminated. This includes the Cherethites (Zeph. 2:15), the Assyrians and residents of Nineveh (Zeph. 2: 12-13), and the residents of Sodom and Gomorrah (by God) (Gen. 19: 24-25). Perhaps Jenkins uses the term "races" very loosely as a synonym for a tribe, nation, or settlement. If so, this is unfortunate and can be misleading if it leads readers to think that the OT is "racist" in this regard.

5. Does the Bible "overflow with texts of terror" and is "biblical violence marked by indiscriminate savagery"? It seems to me that, as presented in Chapter 3 and 4, even if we limit our focus to the OT, it is an exaggeration to claim that the OT "overflows with texts of terror." As shown in Table

Summary of Findings, and Claims of Other Authors 281

27 earlier in this chapter, the word "terror" as violence occurs only about sixteen times in the OT. And if, by "terror," Jenkins means "to instill horror, great fear, or dread into one's victims or enemies," then only a relatively small percentage of verses do this.

Now as to Jenkins' claim about "indiscriminate savagery," it seems to me that Jenkins rather unwittingly combines several different variables in this claim. The level of "savagery" in violent acts can vary from one act to another, as can the level of "discrimination" in savage acts of violence. It also seems to me that, while a lot of the violence in the OT is very savage, as shown in the previous example about genocide, a lot of the violence described and demanded in the OT is *not* indiscriminate. For example, in Verses 18-21 from Chapter 21 in Deuteronomy, parents are told to have "elders of the city" stone to death any of their sons who are "stubborn," or "rebellious," or who are "gluttons" or "drunkards." This is not "indiscriminate." Nor is it as savage as it could be if, for instance, it required that the sons would be tortured mercilessly for days before they were killed, and the killing would include savage acts by wild beasts, as well as by human beings. In the OT, only a small percentage of the verses that portray violence demand that everyone and every living thing be killed. Then again, none of the verses in the Qur'an or the NT do this.

By the way, Jenkins also claims that, in the Qur'an, the violence is directed most often at all miscreants, regardless of religious orientation, not towards non-believers or non-Muslims. Jenkins lists the four categories of miscreants (e.g. traducers of innocent women). While Jenkins is correct about these four categories of miscreants, in Chapter 2, I show that the victims of violence in the Qur'an usually are not miscreants regardless of faith, but that they are "unbelievers," "idolaters," and "polytheists." This is true in about 80% of the verses in the Qur'an that identify victims of violence. In only about 20% of the verses are the victims people who will be punished for their misdeeds, without regard to their faith.

6. Are the differences minimal between and among the faiths regarding violence? [76]

It seems to me that, while Jenkins might be accurate if he means that the differences among *the religions* of Judaism, Christianity, and Islam are minimal, both his book and mine demonstrate quite emphatically and clearly that there are many significant differences *in the "holy books"* of these three religions regarding violence, both quantitatively and qualitatively. One of the many significant differences is that there are no verses in the Qur'an that portray genocide, just as Jenkins claims. He also claims that the violence in the OT often is "marked by indiscriminate savagery." These claims seem reasonable to me when they are taken relatively and in contrast to the Qur'an and the NT. Therefore, I feel compelled to conclude that Jenkins is mistaken if he is implying that differences are minimal *among the holy books* of these three faiths regarding violence, the perpetrators of violence, the victims of violence, and the justifications for violence.

To state one of my major findings once again: based on the evidence provided in Chapters 2-4, and in various tables throughout this book, the Qur'an has considerably more verses that portray violence than the Old Testament and the New Testament, proportionate to size. Even more striking are the qualitative differences in violence as portrayed in the three holy books. In contrast to the Qur'an and the New Testament, violence portrayed in the Old Testament is far more offensive, lethal, bloodier, destructive, and genocidal. The vast majority of the violence is demanded, threatened, committed, and justified by the supreme deity—God in the case of the Israelites. The violence portrayed in the Qur'an is less so in all these regards. Violence in the New Testament is almost absent, except for descriptions of the crucifixion of Jesus in the Epistles of Matthew, Mark, Luke, and John and for quite a few images, dreams, or fantasies of violence in the final book, Revelation.

And so, in sum, I believe that my findings confirm and strengthen some of Jenkins' claims while they also provide important refinements to some of his other observations and claims.

A Conclusion Regarding the Claims of Other Authors

By way of a conclusion to this chapter, it seems to me that most of the authors whose publications have been described here provide insights about religious violence and the holy books that are compatible with mine, as I present them in Chapters 1-4. The only exceptions are authors Robert Spencer and Rabbi Jonathan Sacks. It also seems to me that all of the authors could have done more to explain how contemporary acts of violence relate to the holy books. They also could have provided us with more incisive recommendations about reducing the risks of religious violence in the decades ahead. In the next chapter, Chapter 6, I offer some of my own recommendations and explanations as to why they may be helpful in the years to come.

Notes

1. Jenkins, *Laying Down the Sword*, 74.
2. Spencer, Robert. *The Complete Infidel's Guide to the Koran*. Washington, D.C.: Regnery Publishing. 2009. 232.
3. Op. cit., 2.
4. Op. cit., 3.
5. Ibid.
6. Op. cit., 5-7.
7. Op. cit., 7.
8. Op. cit., 40.
9. Op. cit., 226-228.
10. Op. cit., 230.
11. Ibid.
12. Sacks, Rabbi Jonathan. *Not in God's Name: Confronting Religious Violence*. NY: Schocken Books. 2015. 1.
13. Op. cit., 3.
14. Op. cit., 265.
15. Op. cit., 262-263.
16. Juergensmeyer, Mark. *Terror in the Mind of God: The Global Rise of Religious Violence*. Berkeley: University of California Press. Revised Edition. 2003. 66.
17. Op. cit., 67.
18. Op. cit., 70.
19. Op. cit., 82.
20. Op. cit., 20-21.
21. Op. cit., 21.
22. Op. cit., 22.
23. Op. cit., 23.
24. Op. cit., 138.
25. Op. cit., 30.
26. Op. cit., 147.
27. Op. cit., 149.
28. Ibid.
29. Op. cit., 110.
30. Op. cit., 225.
31. Op. cit., 125.

Summary of Findings, and Claims of Other Authors   285

32. Op. cit., 141.
33. Op. cit., 157.
34. Op. cit., 143.
35. Op. cit., 235.
36. Op. cit., 243.
37. Op. cit., 248.
38. Op. cit., 66.
39. Stern, Jessica. *Terror in the Name of God: Why Religious Militants Kill.* NY: Ecco/HarperCollins Publishers. 2003. xiv.
40. Op. cit., xv.
41. Op. cit., xv.
42. Op. cit., xv.
43. Op. cit., 296.
44. Ibid.
45. Armstrong, Karen. *Fields of Blood: Religion and the History of Violence.* NY: Random House. 2015. ii.
46. Op. cit., 144-145.
47. Op. cit., 184-185.
48. Ibid.
49. Op. cit., 381.
50. Op. cit., 382.
51. Op. cit., 383.
52. Op. cit., 381.
53. Op. cit., 403-405.
54. Op. cit., 405.
55. Op. cit., 391.
56. Op. cit., 393.
57. Op. cit., 396.
58. Op. cit., 401.
59. Op. cit., 385.
60. Ibid.
61. Pickthall, *The Meaning of the Glorious Qur'an*, vii.
62. Jenkins, *Laying Down the Sword*, 6.
63. Op. cit., 10.
64. Op. cit., 74.
65. Op. cit., 12.
66. Op. cit., 6.
67. Op. cit., 75.
68. Op. cit., 76-80.

69. Op. cit., 80.
70. Op. cit., 82.
71. Op. cit., 12.
72. Op. cit., 6.
73. Op. cit., 10.
74. Op. cit., 64.
75. Ibid.
76. Op. cit., 12.

Chapter 6

Suggestions for Reducing Religious Violence Worldwide

You might recall from Chapter 5 that some other authors made some suggestions for reducing religious violence in the years ahead. Most of these authors seem to focus on only the U.S. After reviewing their suggestions, I offer ten approaches beyond what they have suggested.

WHAT HAVE THE OTHER AUTHORS SUGGESTED?

Here is a concise review of what the authors in Chapter 5 suggested for reducing religious violence in the years ahead.

Robert Spencer's Suggestions

As shown in Chapter 5, author Robert Spencer provides three very candid and bold recommendations for U.S. government: (1) He calls for "a dramatic change in U.S. policy towards Islam and Muslims." He writes that "officials should refuse to accept the deceptions and half-truths that U.S. based Islamic groups routinely offer regarding the Koran's violent teachings." (2) He wants U.S. officials to "monitor mosques and Islamic schools in America, demanding that they institute large-scale, transparent programs, open to full and comprehensive inspections, that teach against the doctrines of violence, subjugation, and hatred that we have examined in this (his) book." Spencer says that "immigration of Muslims into the United States should be halted" and those prospective immigrants should be screened for Jihadist sentiments.

Rabbi Johnathan Sacks' Suggestions
Recall that Rabbi Sacks claims that members of all religions need to recognize that God is never violent in Genesis, the Torah, or the "Christian Bible." He writes that God has never endorsed violence. Human beings have created violence and have perpetuated it, often claiming that their violence is "in God's name." Human violence started with Cain and Abel and its basis is "sibling rivalry." Sacks avers that all forms of human violence will diminish if we just acknowledge that violence is based on sibling rivalry. With this in mind, Sacks has five suggestions for reducing religious violence. He says that "Jews, Christians, and Muslims must stand together, in defence of humanity, the sanctity of life, religious freedom and the honour of God himself." He wants to put the "same long-term planning into strengthening religious freedom as was put into the spread of religious extremism." He also wants "an international campaign against the teaching and preaching of hate." He says that "We need to recover the absolute values that make Abrahamic monotheism the humanizing force it has been at its best: the sanctity of life, the dignity of the individual, and so many other core values." Rabbi Sacks also wants us to "insist on the simplest moral principle of all, the principle of reciprocal altruism, otherwise known as tit-for-tat." He adds that "as you behave to others, so will others behave to you."

Suggestions for Reducing Religious Violence Worldwide

Mark Juergensmeyer's Suggestions

As indicated in Chapter 5, Mark Juergensmeyer identifies five possibilities regarding the future of religious violence. He writes that three of these possibilities rarely succeed: "destroying violence," "terrifying terrorists," and "violence wins." He claims that a fourth possibility—separating religion from politics—occasionally works, but he does not tell us how this is to be done. He is most inclined towards the "fifth possibility"—"healing politics with religion." He contends that this can happen "when religious activists have perceived governmental authorities as having a moral integrity in keeping with or accommodating of religious values." He adds that "in some instances when religious violence has been quelled, religion has literally been subsumed under the aegis of governmental authorities." He says that this can occur "when both government and religion provide society with 'high-mindedness' but also a concern with the quality of life rather than just an emphasis on power and possessions."

Apparently, Juergensmeyer believes that measures such as these will reduce or eliminate the opportunities for terrorists to use "performance violence" to make "symbolic statements" that will horrify so many citizens so deeply that they will cripple or topple existing governments in favor of sectarian or theocratic ones.

Jessica Stern's Suggestions

Jessica Stern contends that religious terrorists must be opposed, fought, and neutralized with a number of rather hardline tactics. She writes that "The religious terrorists we face are fighting on every level—militarily, economically, psychologically, and spiritually. Their military weapons are powerful, but spiritual dread is the most dangerous weapon in their arsenal.... We need to respond-not just with guns—but by seeking to create confusion, conflict, and competition among terrorists and between terrorists and their sponsors and sympathizers."

Karen Armstrong's Suggestion

As indicated in Chapter 5, Karen Armstrong's analysis of the history of religious violence and wars by Jews, Christians, and Muslims leads her to contend that most of the violence is for political purposes (to seize power or to weaken the power of others)—not for religious purposes, per se. She indicates that quite a few recent terrorists who claim to be Jewish, Christian, or Muslim actually are nearly or wholly ignorant of the contents of the holy books.

In addition to this, many violence-oriented leaders and followers either ignore most verses in the holy books of their religions or they select and focus on only a limited number of inflammatory verses that seem to justify their violence. And so, for Armstrong, what we need is more religion and deeper appreciation of how religions and the holy books can encourage non-violence. She writes:

> Somehow we have to find ways of doing what religion—at its best—has done for centuries: build a sense of global community, cultivate a sense of reverence and "equanimity" for all, and take responsibility for the suffering we see in the world.

Armstrong adds that "We are all, religious and secular alike, responsible for the current predicament of the world."

Philip Jenkins' Suggestions

As indicated in Chapter 5, in his book *Laying Down the Sword*, Philip Jenkins provides considerable evidence that both the Old Testament and the Qur'an have plenty of passages that portray or refer to many forms of brutal violence by God and by Allah. He also reports that much of the violence portrayed in the Hebrew Bible is more shocking than what is portrayed in the Qur'an. This is especially apparent in many verses in the Old Testament in which God demands that his Israelite followers commit genocide against many different clans and settlements in the Middle East, and that Israelites also stone and kill other Israelites who are disobedient, insulting, adulterous, or inclined towards other religions.

Suggestions for Reducing Religious Violence Worldwide

Jenkins admits that some of the violent passages in the Old Testament and the Qur'an have influenced some people, such as Osama bin Laden, to engage in violence, including acts of terrorism. But Jenkins insists that these passages have never been sufficient to cause people to be violent. According to Jenkins, in order for violence to occur, there must be "particular circumstances" that arise. There must be "particular conditions in state and society" in order for violence to occur. Unfortunately, Jenkins does not identify these kinds of conditions, although it is easy to guess that he would agree that many years of oppression, a sense of relative deprivation, invasions, brutality by adversaries, and violence-oriented charismatic leaders are some of the conditions he has in mind. Jenkins' implicit suggestion might be that we must first assure that those kinds of conditions in state and society do not occur. In the conclusion to his book, Jenkins writes that:

> However bloody texts may be, however explicit, their mere existence will not lead to actual violence unless and until particular circumstances arise. At that point, the texts can rise once again to the surface, to inspire and sacralize violence, to demonize opponents, and even to exalt the conflict to the level of cosmic war. But without those circumstances, without those particular conditions in state and society, the violence will not occur.... Some of what we call "religious violence" may well be authentically religious in its character, but we must find its origins in places other than the basic texts of the faith.[1]

As with so many of the authors, except perhaps for Robert Spencer, I wish that Philip Jenkins would have used his vast knowledge of religion, history, and current events to provide us with more specific, detailed, and instructive suggestions for reducing violence.

FURTHER SUGGESTIONS

While the authors have been very sincere, they provide very few detailed, practical suggestions, and they do not tell us how the suggestions can be implemented. For this reason, in the next and final section of this book, I will go beyond the suggestions of these other authors by offering ten approaches that might help us disassociate violence from religions and their holy books so as to reduce the risks of violence, terror, genocide, and war. Here are the ten approaches:

1. Ignore the holy books.

2. Emphasize the non-violent passages.

3. Delete the violent passages.

4. Embrace one (or more) of the holy books in its (their) entirety.

5. Focus on the less violent holy books of other religions.

6. Create new holy books or "update" those that exist.

7. Acknowledge and sustain other religions that restrain violence.

8. Create new religions.

9. Acknowledge and encourage those people and groups throughout the world that reduce the likelihood of violence.

10. Improve our monitoring and responding to people, groups, and organizations that misrepresent verses in the holy books.

Now let us briefly consider each of these approaches, their feasibility, and the likelihood of them increasing in the decades ahead.

Ignore the Holy Books
It seems as though this is easy to do for many people—but not for all people—and not for some very influential people. Probably it is what many of the world's more than seven billion people do each day, either intentionally, unconsciously, or because they couldn't care less about these "holy" books. Many of these people probably do not consider these

books to be "holy." Some people consider the books to be irrelevant anachronisms that no longer matter. Other people probably believe that the books actually are major sources of conflict, divisiveness, and violence between people who believe their verses convey eternal imperatives and truths, and people who don't believe any of this. And, of course, while an estimated 3.5 billion people identify themselves as Christian, Muslim, or Jewish, the remaining more than 3.5 billion people in the world's population do not identify with these religions. Many of them probably pay little or no attention to the verses in these three books. Included here are members of other "world religions" including Buddhism, Hinduism, Sikhism, Shintoism, and Baha'i; members of the many thousands of folk religions; and many atheists and agnostics.

Of course, one problem with ignoring any one or more of these three books is that there are significant numbers of powerful people, groups, and organizations that consider these books to be extremely relevant, instructive, and even imperative to them and to many millions of "ordinary" people in many nations and regions of the world. There are countless religious and political leaders, influential authors, and news commentators in many of the more than two-hundred nations of the world who do *not* ignore the holy books and many of the passages in them. For example, consider that passages from these books are recited at the inauguration ceremonies and the funerals of government leaders in many of the nations in the world, including the United States, Great Britain, Canada, Australia, New Zealand, and many of the nations in Europe, South and Central America, and the Middle East. Also consider that passages of one or more of these books are recited at the weddings and funerals of many millions of "ordinary" people each year in many nations of the world. Furthermore, as indicated in Chapter 1 of this book, some passages in one or more of these three books often are referred to and are used by people who were, are, or will become violent propagandists, provocateurs, recruiters, and criminals. The late Osama bin Laden was only one of many of them.

And so, to modify an old rubric, "We can ignore the holy books, but we do so at our own risk."

As to the decades ahead, it is not at all obvious to me that the influences of these three books are diminishing now or that they will diminish significantly in the decades ahead. Millions of new copies of these three books are produced on paper and in electronic formats each year and distributed and sold throughout the world. Some estimates indicate that there are at least 2.5 billion printed copies of the Bible and more than 800 million printed copies of the Qur'an in homes, libraries, and religious institutions throughout the world. Over 100 million copies of the Bible are sold or given away each year worldwide. It is estimated that the Bible is available to more than 90% of the world's population, and it is available in more than 2,000 languages and dialects. Regarding the Qur'an, it is reported that it is now available almost everywhere in the world, that it is printed in more than one thousand languages and dialects, that the Saudi Kingdom prints and distributes more than 30 million copies a year, and that its sales in the U.S. are rapidly increasing to more than one million copies each year.[2]

It is also worth considering that fundamentalist political and religious movements have re-emerged in many regions of the world since 1978. That is when the fundamentalist revolution in Iran toppled the Shah and brought Ayatollah Khomeini back into power from his many years of exile in France. It seems to me that what was believed to be a worldwide trend, often referred to as "the secularization of modern societies" (a phrase popular among many social scientists in the 1960s), has stalled or reversed since then in quite a few societies, particularly in the Middle East, Northern Africa, and Indonesia.

And so, it seems that it is prudent to acknowledge that many millions or even billions of people not only do not ignore these three books but that they find great value and direction in them. If only for this reason, governments, police forces, and other agencies of social control cannot afford to ignore them.

Suggestions for Reducing Religious Violence Worldwide

Emphasize Only the Non-Violent Passages in the Three Books

It seems to me that this is exactly what has been done and is being done so often by so many defenders and advocates of Judaism, Christianity, and Islam. One example of this is the case of Rabbi Jonathan Sacks, as presented in Chapter 5. While some of these people might be in what is referred to as "psychological denial," my sense is that many more people who do this are just not interested in violence, or they abhor it. Other people overlook violent passages because they are much more interested in one or more of the many other topics that are presented in the holy books—"holiness" is just one of them. Other topics of great interest include the nature of God, the origins of Earth and of humankind, major events in the development of the religion, and commandments about sexual behavior, marriage, divorce, eating, drinking, death rites, and a possible afterlife, among other topics. And it seems that some people who emphasize only the non-violent passages in the three books do so in order to sustain their belief that their own religion has evolved and become much less violent than it was many centuries ago.

My sense is that this approach will become even more common in the decades ahead for many religious leaders and for religious members of the general public in many societies. One of the reasons for this is that people will become more educated and acceptant of social science research that convinces them that, over the many centuries, and taken as a whole, many human societies and religions actually *have* become less violent. Of course there have been horrible exceptions to this trend, including the violent exploitation of some societies by others during the European colonialization of North and South America, Africa, and the Far East; the Nazi Holocaust; the massive killings during WWI and WWII; the genocides in the former Yugoslavia and in Rwanda in the 1980s; and the current efforts of radical Islamic terrorist groups such as ISIS and ISUL to exterminate various ethnic and religious groups in Syria, Iraq, and Kurdistan.

Delete the Violent Passages in the Holy Books

Unless this is done voluntarily and openly, this approach would constitute censorship, wouldn't it? And of course, deleting any verse is strictly prohibited by Islam and by several verses in the Qur'an, as well, as shown in Chapter 2 of this book. Any deletions from the Qur'an also are prohibited by every sect of Islam of which I am aware. This approach also seems to be very dishonest unless editors of the newly redacted editions explicitly acknowledge that violent passages have been deleted, and their reasons for doing so. Also consider that it could be very difficult to reach agreement about which verses *are* violent or *portray* violence. Of course, in Chapters 1 and 2 of this book, I provide definitions of violence and I explain the criteria I used to determine which verses in the three books portrayed or referred to violence. In the Appendix of this book, I explain further the methods that I used to determine whether a verse portrays violence and in what ways it does so. So, I do not believe that this is an insurmountable problem with this approach.

This approach also could be used to delete from the three books many other topics that might be objectionable to some people, such as the topics of inequality, poverty, Satan, sin, sexual behavior, male dominance, nature, disease, rituals, and the sacrifice of animals. Taken to the extreme with this approach, we would have a rather lengthy array of foreshortened Bibles and Qur'ans, each of which has been "liberated" from verses that are objectionable to someone about something!

As to the future decades, I will not be surprised if this approach becomes more popular, particularly in Judaism and Christianity with the Old Testament and the New Testament. One incentive for this might be that new sects will emerge in these religions that will object to passages that are violent and to passages that seem to cast aspersions on other religions and belief systems. Sects such as these probably can find countries that will not enforce the standard copyright laws that cover the Bible in the U.S. and Europe. This will enable these sects to produce their own electronic and print versions of the passages that are amenable to them from the

Old Testament and the New Testament and then sell and distribute them to their own members and perhaps to other people worldwide.

Personally, I encourage this approach as a "liberated" innovation that might allow more people to tolerate religions, so long as the original, unexpurgated versions of the three books are not destroyed and they remain readily available to members of the public throughout the world.

Embrace One (or More) of the Holy Books in Its (Their) Entirety

It seems to me that many active, true believers in Judaism, Christianity, and Islam fully embrace the book or books considered to be holy in their religion. This is why they refer to their choice as being "The Holy Book." It also seems to me that some very open-minded and liberal scholars, religious leaders, and members of the public accept all three of the books as being valuable. The books might even be considered to be more or less equivalent in the moral codes they advocate and in their images of God, Allah, human beings, sin, and Judgment Day. Some religious leaders, including the late Pope John Paul and the current pope, Pope Francis, seem to have accepted all three books as being inspired by God and as providing valuable moral guidelines and commandments in common, such as to worship only one god, to honor one's parents, and to not engage in adultery. Some of the religious scholars discussed in Chapter 5, such as Philip Jenkins and Mark Juergensmeyer, seem to accept all three books in their entirety for what they have in common and for their value in providing narratives about the key events in the history of each of the three religions. This is also the case with an increasing number of very influential non-governmental organizations whose purpose is to increase inter-denominational dialogue and reduce political constraints on religious freedom. Examples include the International Association for Religious Freedom of the United Nations, the Institute for Global Engagement, the International Coalition for Religious Freedom, and the Institute for Religious Tolerance, Peace, and Conflict Resolution.[3]

Regarding the next few decades, I would not be surprised if this approach becomes less popular. Reasons for this can include the increasing educational levels of people in so many nations and places around the globe, the increasing emphasis on individual freedom of thought and choice, and increasing awareness by many of the world's people of ideological and political differences within each of the religions and how their leaders interpret the verses in the holy books. Yet another reason can be that there are many other sources, forms, and types of printed and electronic material that many people throughout the world will find to be much more entertaining and less complex and demanding than the verses in these three books. And besides, in their original forms, and in many of their contemporary editions, these three books lack stimulating visual and auditory material—in contrast to so many other books and cultural products. My understanding is that visual material, other than print, is prohibited inside the Qur'an by all or most of the governing bodies in Islam. Furthermore, while I have seen some short, abbreviated versions of some of the famous "Bible stories" that include illustrations for children, I don't believe that I have ever seen any graphic or multimedia versions of the Old Testament or the New Testament for adults, other than perhaps for some maps of "the Holy Land" and photos or drawings of famous religious sites such as the "Wailing Wall" in Jerusalem.

In any case, it seems to me that, in the decades ahead, many people will be much less inclined to put all of their faith, trust, and time into any one source of information, including one or more of these three books. Of course, this prediction assumes that we will not experience the emergence of expansive, totalitarian, theocratic states that force their populations to practice Judaism, Christianity, or Islam and to read and recite their holy books in mass, public gatherings.

Emphasize the Less Violent Holy Books of Other Religions
From a sociological perspective, rather than a theological perspective, I have found that the "holy" books of some religions, including Baha'i, are far less violent, both quantitatively and qualitatively, than the Old

Testament and the Qur'an in terms of the number of verses that convey violence and the kinds of violence portrayed, if any. Here are some of the books that are reported to be highly revered by many members of other religions. Of course, I am *not* claiming that all of these religions and their revered books are less violent than Judaism, Christianity, Islam and their holy books:

- Hinduism: Among the books considered "holy" by many Hindus are the *Shreemad, Bhagavad Gita,* the *Upanishads,* and the *Veda.*
- Buddhism: *Tripitaka*
- Sikhism: *Guru Granth Sahib*
- Baha'ism: *Kitab-i-Aqdas*
- Confucianism: *Book of Rites,* the *Analects,* and *Mencius*
- Jainism: *The Agamas*
- Shintoism: *Kojiki*

Also, as shown in Chapters 4 and 5, I found that the New Testament has much less violent content proportionately than the Old Testament and the Qur'an. Except for the final book in the New Testament, Revelation, I have not found passages in the New Testament which portray violence, terror, war, or genocide in a positive way. Nor have I found verses that portray God, Jesus, or most of the disciples or prophets committing, demanding, or threatening violence, terror, war, or genocide against anyone.

My sense is that this approach will become considerably more popular in many areas of the world in the next few decades so long as educational levels continue to increase globally, and we avoid nuclear war, wars on the scale of WWI and WWII, extreme scarcity of material goods, and both natural and human-made disasters which create widespread chaos and conflict within and among human societies.

This is also an approach that I encourage, not because of any personal animosities towards Judaism, Christianity, or Islam or their holy books. I think that this approach could increase the number of highly tolerant religious orientations and attract many more people to the non-violent moral codes of a wide range of religions, both the so-called "major religions of the world" and also the thousands of religions and quasi-religious belief systems that are sometimes referred to a "new religious movements." [4]

Write and Distribute New "Holy" Books or "Update" Those That Exist

This approach could be valuable and worthwhile so long as the new books place greater constraints on violence and they are more effective in discouraging violence. Perhaps the exceptions would be violence as a last resort to save one's own life, as an innocent person, or the lives of other people who are innocent and defenseless. Admittedly, this approach might be intolerable to steadfast members of Judaism, Christianity, and Islam who believe that their own holy book is not only "holy," but is also complete, perfect, and unalterable. Then again, for some Muslims, perhaps the authors and editors of a new, additional "holy" book for Islam could emphasize that Muhammad died non-violently of disease and rather prematurely at age sixty-two. Had he lived longer, he might have received many more recitations from Allah that would have provided many more passages that restrain violence and promote more tolerance within and among religions. Perhaps similar reasons could be given for creating additional "holy" books for Christianity and Judaism. New holy books also might emphasize what the three religions have accomplished in peaceful international, inter-faith, and intra-faith relations in the centuries since the Old Testament, the New Testament, and the Qur'an were compiled. In addition to this, established religions could increase their emphasis on key concepts of anti-violence that already exist, such as the religious principle of *ahimsa* in Buddhism, Hinduism, and Jainism, as explained in Chapter 1 of this book.

As to the future, it seems to me that this approach is plausible and worth supporting. New holy books, and "updated" and "appended" holy books can be informed by new discoveries in science and medicine, and by the global electronic exchange of information and insights. It seems to me that this approach constitutes what we might call "additionalism" rather than the often-criticized practice of "revisionism." As such, it might be considerably more tolerable to fundamentalists and conservatives than some of the other approaches.

Acknowledge and Encourage Other Religions That Can Restrain Violence

There are many other religions, new religious movements (NRMs), and quasi-religions, some of which might be more effective than Judaism, Christianity, and Islam in restraining violence, terror, war, and genocide. This is not the place to try to establish which ones are, or could be, more effective in doing so. Some of these entities have their own "holy books." Some do not. But it seems worthwhile to consider how these entities relate to violence in the contemporary world and whether they might be encouraged to be more effective in restraining violence.

For example, according to Wikipedia, "Some scholars have estimated that NRMs now number in the tens of thousands worldwide, with most in Asia and Africa. Most have only a few members, some have thousands, and very few have more than a million." NRMs refer to "new religious movements." This is "a comprehensive term used to identify religious, ethical, and spiritual groups, communities and practices of relatively modern origin." They might be original creations, or they might be factions or fringe elements of wider religions.[5] Recently I looked at a list of "new religious movements" that appeared on the Internet. I counted more than nine hundred of them. The list included their most common names, their founder(s) (if acknowledged), the year they were founded, and the wider religious, ethical, or philosophical entity to which they are related if any. Here are just a few examples from the list:

- *Adonai-Shomo*; Frederick Howland; 1861; Adventist Communal
- *The African Church*; Jacob Coker; 1901; Anglican Communion
- *Agni Yoga*; Nicholas Roerich; 1920s; Theosophical
- *Ancient Order Rosae Crucis*; H. Spencer Lewis; 1915; Rosicrucianism

- *Baha'i Mirza;* Husayn Ali Num; 1863; Middle East Baha
- *Eckankar;* Paul Twitchell; 1971
- *Scientology;* L. Ron Hubbard; 1955
- *The Salvation Army;* 1865
- *Subud;* Muhammad Subuh; 1933; Sufism (Sufist Islam)
- *Tolstoyan Primitivism;* Leo Tolstoy; 1901; Pacifism
- *Unitarian Universalism;* 1961
- *The Way of the Livingness;* Serge Benhagon; 1999; Theosophical
- *Women's Federation for World Peace;* Hax Jahan; 1992; Unification Church

Create New Religions and Hybrid Religions That Restrain Violence

My sense is that human beings will continue to do this in the decades ahead, just as they have for thousands of years. Unfortunately, not all of the religions that they have created restrain violence anywhere near as much as possible. Let me suggest that one of the "hybrid" religions that I have become familiar with recently is contemporary Yazidi (Ezidi). It is the predominant religion of the Yazidi (Ezidi) ethnic minority people of northern Iraq, with thousands of refugees now resettled in Germany and the United States. The Yazidi religion has its origins in Zoroastrianism, as I understand it from published sources and from the members of a Yazidi family that recently immigrated to Providence, Rhode Island as religious refugees, escaping slaughter by ISIS in Iraq. Over the last two thousand years, the Yazidis have integrated elements of Judaism, Christianity, and Islam into their religion. It is now called a "syncretic religion" by some religious scholars, and it is reported to be strongly opposed to almost every form of violence.[6]

Acknowledge and Encourage People and Groups Throughout the World That Reduce the Likelihood of Violence

This all-inclusive approach could be very compatible with the current trends towards increasing cultural diversity and inclusion, individual freedoms of belief and expression, and with expanding democratic institutions within and across nations. At the same time, however, this approach towards increasing tolerance should not diminish the role of international agencies, such as the United Nations, in emphasizing that no religion or any religious book has legal standing that exempts people or agencies from being arrested and prosecuted for any and all acts of violence, except possibly as a last resort in instances of immediate, situational self-defense. In other words, international laws that prohibit violence, terror, genocide, and war supersede any and all codes, commandments, or prescriptions in religions and religious materials that threaten, encourage, demand, or attempt to justify violence.

Improve Our Monitoring and Responding to People, Groups, and Organizations That Misrepresent Verses That Seem to Threaten, Demand, Glorify or Try to Justify Violence in the Holy Books

Fortunately, the Internet allows us to monitor and respond to a lot of misrepresentations of violence, terror, genocide, and war in the books of many religions, including Judaism, Christianity, and Islam. On the other hand, the Internet also allows many more people and agencies to disseminate misrepresentations of violence in religions and in the books that they cherish. But it seems to me that these are one of the benefits and one of the costs of "free speech" and the use of publicly and privately-funded media to exercise and transmit "free speech."

Let me also suggest that one of the purposes of *this* book is to exercise this approach. That is to say, among other things, I have monitored and responded to some of the people, groups, and organizations that have misrepresented verses in the three holy books. And I trust that you have done so as well, along with me.

SOME FINAL THOUGHTS AND SENTIMENTS

I would like to believe that the supreme beings and deities of all religions are loving, caring, helpful, and wise towards human beings. They might be this way, but as an ordinary human being, it is not for me to say. This is why this book is *not* about the nature or reality of God, Allah, gods, other deities, or any supernatural forces. I have not dealt with this topic in this book. This book is about *portrayals and references* to violence, terror, genocide, and war in three holy books. This includes consideration of how supreme beings, deities, and humans are *portrayed and referred to* regarding physical violence against human beings in three of the holy books—the Qur'an, the Old Testament, and the New Testament. I also would like to have found that portrayals of supreme beings and deities in the holy books would convince us that they are indeed thoroughly loving, caring, helpful, and wise towards us and that they are thoroughly non-violent. Sadly, I have not found this to be the case. The portrayals are considerably more varied than that.

Allah, God, Yahweh, and any other supreme beings and spiritual forces might well be thoroughly caring, loving, compassionate, helpful, and merciful—rather than being occasionally rather angry, wrathful, vengeful, and violent. I certainly hope so. Unfortunately, over thousands of years of recorded history, human beings have not always portrayed them or referred to them in positive, comforting, and helpful ways, from what I have experienced in my life and from the many books and articles I have read.

I am glad that portrayals and references to supreme beings in the Old Testament, the New Testament, and the Qur'an often are compassionate and helpful towards at least some human beings. Often those graces seem to be restricted to people who believe in only one particular god and obey that god only as portrayed in the holy book of that person's choosing. On the other hand, as shown so often in Chapters 2, 3, and 4 of this book, portrayals of supreme beings in holy books occasionally are rather harsh, threatening, and even violent towards non-believers and

Suggestions for Reducing Religious Violence Worldwide

those who do not obey a particular religion's commandments, whether consciously, intentionally, or not.

All three holy books portray plenty of positive graces in their supreme being. But all three holy books also occasionally portray what many human beings, myself included, find to be very troubling qualities in their supreme beings.

And Finally

Finally, and with some regret, I feel obliged to remark that, based only on portrayals of violence in the Old Testament, New Testament, and Qur'an, it can be considerably easier for contemporary devout Christians than their Jewish and Muslim counterparts to avoid being desensitized and dehumanized towards violence. It also can be easier for them to not engage in selective perception regarding violence, to avoid cognitive dissonance regarding violence, and to even pay much attention to violence when it is portrayed in the New Testament, as infrequently as it is.

I say this with special admiration for people devoted to the Old Testament and to the Qur'an who are nonetheless able to "put into context" the occasional, violent portrayals, so to speak, as well as for those who gain far more from the many verses that are non-violent than from those that are violent.

One of my final suggestions is that we honestly and objectively admit that there are significant differences in the quantities and qualities of physical violence as portrayed in the holy books. Another suggestion is that we also honestly and objectively recognize that portrayals of violence constitute only a small amount of the verses the holy books, certainly less than twenty percent. And a third suggestion is that we consider that one of the reasons the holy books are "holy" to so many people in the world is that so many of their verses inspire so many people to behave in other less destructive ways and to believe in other qualities, graces, and behaviors that are far more enlightened than violent.

Notes

1. Jenkins, *Laying Down the Sword*, 251-252.
2. Sources: Google search: https://www.google.com/search?source=hp&ei=s1U2W4_UDs6gzwLuuYbYCg&q=annual+sales+bible+koran." The Economist. December 19, 2007.
3. Google search: https://www.google.com/search?q=ngos%2Bfreedom%2Breligion.
4. "New Religious Movements." Wikipedia. https://en.wikipedia.org/wiki/new_religious_movements.
5. Ibid.
6. Hafiz, Yasmine. "No, They Aren't Devil Worshippers: The Yazidi's Misunderstood Religious Beliefs." *The Huffington Post*. September 06, 2016. https://www.huffingtonpost.com/2014/08/13/yazidi-religious-beliefs_n_5671903.html.

Appendix

Systematic Content Analysis and Coding Procedures

The following procedures of systematic content analysis and coding were used to produce much of the quantitative and qualitative data, as well as the empirical findings presented in this book.[1] Systematic coding procedures were based on the published work of Ole Holsti (1969), Klaus Krippendorf (1980), and Robert Philip Weber (1990). These were the same procedures used to produce the primary data in my previous book, *War, Terror & Peace in the Qur'an and in Islam: Insights for Military and Government Leaders.*

1. For context regarding the Qur'an, I read the introductions, footnotes, and indices to the Qur'an and to its surahs (chapters) as presented in the translations of the Qur'an by Mohammed Marmaduke Pickthall and by M.A.S. Abdel Haleem. Regarding the Bible, I read the introductions, footnotes, and indices to each book in the Old Testament and the New Testament in the massive, 2,000-page *King James Study Bible* as well as *The Jewish Study Bible* (Tanakh Translation).

2. I read every word in every phrase, passage, verse, and surah in Pickthall's English translation of the Qur'an four times; twice in 2002, once in 2015, and once again in 2016. I did the same thing, twice, with Haleem's English translation of the Qur'an; once in 2015, and once again in 2016. During the period between 2015 and 2017, I read every word in every phrase, passage, verse, and chapter in the Old Testament and the New Testament. I compared hundreds of the verses that portray or refer to violence in the "Christian" Bible with comparable verses in *The Jewish Study Bible* in order to determine whether the verses differ significantly in their portrayals of violence. I noted several cases where there were significant differences but there were very few of these cases.

3. Coding: While completing these readings, I marked with a yellow marker every instance when the following keywords and their synonyms appeared. With a red pen, I underlined the phrases and sentences directly associated with each of these keywords and synonyms. Keywords: annihilate, exterminate, assault, attack, siege, seize, defend, repulse, torment, fight, injure, cut-off, wound, terror, terrorize, capture, bind, torture, smite, behead, slay, kill, doom, destroy, burn, drown, bury, fire, battle(s), war(s), warfare, truce, treaty, peace.

4. Using the definition of physical violence established for this study ("severe or injurious treatment or action characterized by extremely rough, harsh, destructive physical force"), I then determined whether the keywords and synonyms, in conjunction with the words, phrases, and sentences associated with them, portray or refer to physical violence in the past, present, or future; by or against any human beings, their material creations, property, or settlements. When this was the case, I noted these instances and I recorded this information on code sheets in such a way as to be able to count every instance, and to determine who is portrayed as advocating, demanding, describing, threatening, promising, or committing physical violence, by whom, against whom, when, where, why, and with what consequences. I also coded whether these instances of physical violence are portrayed as being associated

Systematic Content Analysis and Coding Procedures

with military battles, war, or warfare. Additionally, I noted whether physical violence was intended to exterminate not just the members of military forces but all the members of specific tribes, settlements, ethnic groups, societies, or nations.

Throughout the chapters of this book, there are hundreds of examples of passages and verses in the Qur'an, the Old Testament, and the New Testament that meet these criteria, as well as examples that do not meet these criteria. I also provide explanations as to why this is the case. Additionally, often I provide comments on the historical context of various verses, as interpreted by various authors.

Since the year 2002, when I started doing the reading and coding for a book published in 2004, *War, Terror & Peace in the Qur'an and in Islam: Insights for Military and Government Leaders*, this research has taken *thousands* of hours of my most conscientious effort to be accurate, empirical, inductive, objective, and honest.

To the best of my knowledge, this is the most objective, systematic analysis that has been published in English of portrayals of violence in these three, extremely influential books that are considered to be "holy" by billions of people throughout the world.

Anyone interested in replicating my research is encouraged to contact me and request copies of my data and further details on my coding and analytic procedures.

Notes

1. There are many computer software programs that are designed to assist researchers in completing a systematic content analysis of textual materials, including textual materials in books, documents, and recordings of speeches and conversations. These programs can quickly count the number of times words such as "kill" and "battle" appear in books, including the Qur'an and the Bible. However, I have found that the programs are much less reliable and useful in determining whether words such as "kill" and "battle" are used metaphorically (e.g. to "kill sin," "to battle against temptation"), or literally (e.g. "he killed all of them," "the battle killed every one of the enemy soldiers"). The programs also are very limited and unreliable in identifying the sources, targets, and consequences of violent acts, as specified in textual materials. They do not provide the acute, precise, context-sensitive, and highly engaging, future-oriented analysis that I try to provide in this book.

BIBLIOGRAPHY

An asterisk (*) denotes primary sources used in this book.

Al-Rasheed, Madawi and Marat Shterin. (Eds.) *Dying for Faith: Religiously Motivated Violence in the Contemporary World.* London: I.B. Tauris. 2009.

Arberry, Arthur J. *The Koran Interpreted.* NY: The Macmillan Company. 1955.

Armstrong, Karen. *Fields of Blood: Religion and the History of Violence.* NY: Random House. 2014.

Aslan, Reza. "Cosmic War in Religious Traditions." Chapter 15 (Pp. 260-268) in *The Oxford Handbook of Religion and Violence.* NY: Oxford University Press. 2013.

Montgomery, Ben. "Before Orlando Massacre, Killer Omar Mateen Visited Parents One Last Time." *Tampa Bay Times.* Page 1. June 14, 2016.

Avalos, Hector. *Fighting Words: The Origin of Religious Violence.* 1st Edition. Amherst, NY: Prometheus Books. 2005.

Barker, Dan, and Richard Dawkins. *God: The Most Unpleasant Character in all Fiction.* NY: Sterling Publishing Company. 2016.

Craig, Tim, Max Bearak, and Lee Powell. "Shooter Omar Mateen's father says he's saddened by massacre, calls gunman 'a good son.'" *Washington Post*, June 13, 2016.

Eller, Jack David. *Cruel Creeds, Virtuous Violence: Religious Violence across Culture and History.* 1st Edition. Amherst, NY: Prometheus Books. 2010.

Esposito, Joseph L. *Islam: The Straight Path.* Third Edition. NY: Oxford University Press. 1998.

Esposito, John L. *Terror in the Name of Islam.* NY: Oxford University Press. 2003.

Feldman, Robert S. *Social Psychology.* Englewood Cliffs, NJ: Prentice Hall. 1995.

Fregosi, Paul. *Jihad in the West: Muslim Conquests from the 7th to the 21st Centuries.* Amherst, NY: Prometheus Books. 1998.

Gerson, Michael. "Neuroscientist Andrew Newberg on the Brain and Faith." http://www.WashingtonPost.com/wp-dyn/content/article/2009/04/14/AR2009041401879.html.

Gopin, Marc. *Between Eden and Armageddon: The Future of World Religions, Violence, and Peacemaking.* NY: Oxford University Press. 2000.

*Haleem, M. A. S. Abdel, *The Qur'an.* NY: Oxford University Press. 2010.

Hall, John R. "Religion and Violence from a Sociological Perspective." Chapter 25 (Pp. 363-375) in *The Oxford Handbook of Religion and Violence.* NY: Oxford University Press. 2013.

Harris, Sam. *The End of Faith. Religion, Terror, and the Future of Religion.* NY: W. W. Norton & Company, Inc. 2005.

Hassner, Ron E. and Gideon Aran. "Religion and Violence in the Jewish Traditions." Chapter 4 (Pp. 78-100) in *The Oxford Handbook of Religion and Violence.* NY: Oxford University Press 2013.

Hess, Richard S. *The Old Testament: A Historical, Theological, and Critical Introduction.* Alda, MI: Baker Academic/Baker Publishing. 2016.

Holsti, Ole R. *Content Analysis in the Social Sciences and Humanities.* Reading, MA. Addison -Wesley. 1969.

https://en.wikipedia.org/wiki/list_of_designated_ terrorist groups.

https:// en. Wikipedia.org/wiki/Domestic_terrorism_in_the_United States.

https://en.wikipedia.org/wiki/Jewish_Religious_terrorism.

https://en.wikipedia.org/wiki/Christian_terrorism.

https://en.wikipedia.org/wiki/Army_of_God.

https://www.armyofgod.com/EricRudolphHomepage.html.

https://www.nbcnews.com/news/us/news/Colorado-clinic-shooting-psychologists-call- suspect-robert-dear-delusional.

Bibliography

https://www.google.com/?govs_rd_terrorist+organizations.

https://en.wikipedia.org/wiki/Al-Qaeda.

https://www.herld-sun.com/orange10-716750.html.Herald-Sun.2006-03-24.

https://en.wikipedia.org/wiki/Ahimsa.

http://abclocal.go.com/wtvd/story? Section=local&id=3992674. "Taheri-azar Writes to Eyewitness News." American Broadcasting Company. 2006-03-14.

http://www.danielpipes.org/blog/576.DanielPipes.org.2006-03-14.

http://www.dailytarheel.com/media/paper885/documents/jzjo063s.pdf. The Daily Tarheel. Mohammed Reza Taheri-azar letter Meditation II and III.

https://google.com/?gws_major+nidal+malif+hasan.

https://en.wikipedia.org/wiki/Rizwan_Farook_and_Tashfee_Malik.

https://en.wikipedia.org/wiki/Zachary_Adam_Chesser.

https://en.wikipedia.org/wiki/Naser_Jason_Abdo.

https://en.wikipedia.org/wiki/Faisal_Shahzad.

https://en.wikipedia.org/wiki/Najibullah_Zazi.

http://Quran.com. "The Noble Quran."

https://www.google.com/?gws.most+violent+books+in+the+Bible+Koran+holybooks.

http://Resources.org/Bible/NT-Statistics.

http://Catholic-resources.org/Bible/OT-statistics.

https://www.google.com/annualsales/Bible+Koran.

https://www.google.com/NGOs+Freedom+Religion.

https://en.wikipedia.org/wiki/new_religious_movements.

http://www.huffingtonpost.com/yazidi-religious-beliefs.

https://www.google.com/Nineveh.

Jefferis, Jennifer L. *Religion and Political Violence: Sacred Protest in the Modern World.* NY: Routledge. 2010.

*Jenkins, Philip. *Laying Down the Sword: Why We Can't Ignore the Bible's Violent Verses.* NY: HarperOne. Harper Collins Publishers. 2011.

Jones, James W. "Religion and Violence from a Psychological Perspective." Chapter 27 (Pp. 385-397) *The Oxford Handbook of Religion and Violence.* NY: Oxford University Press. 2013.

*Juergensmeyer, Mark. *Terror in the Mind of God: The Global Rise of Religious Violence.* Revised Edition. Berkeley: University of California Press. 2003.

Juergensmeyer, Mark, Margo Kitts, and Michael Jerryson (Eds.). *The Oxford Handbook of Religion and Violence.* NY: Oxford University Press. 2013.

Juergensmeyer, Mark. "Religious Terrorism as Performance Violence." Chapter 17 (Pp. 280-293) in *The Oxford Handbook of Religion and Violence.* NY: Oxford University Press. 2013.

Juergensmeyer, Mark. "Christian Violence in America." The Annals of the American Academy of Political and Social Science. Vol. 558. July, 1998. Pp. 88-100.

*Krippendorf, Klaus. *Content Analysis: An Introduction to Its Methodology.* 3rd Edition. Thousand Oaks, CA: Sage Publications, Inc. 2013.

Laquer, Walter (ed.). *Voices of Terror: Manifestos, Writings and Manuals of Al Qaeda, Hamas, and Other Terrorists from Around the World and Throughout the Ages.* NY: Reed Press. 2004.

Al-Qaeda Manual. Pp. 403-409 in Walter Laquer's *Voices of Terror.* 2004.

Osama bin Laden. "Jihad Against Jews and Crusaders." Pp. 410-412 in Walter Laquer's *Voices of Terror.* 2004.

"September 11: The Letter Left Behind." Pp. 413-429 in Walter Laquer's *Voices of Terror.* 2004.

Lawrence, Bruce B. "Muslim Engagement with Injustice and Violence." Chapter 6 (Pp. 126-153) in *The Oxford Handbook of Religion and Violence.* New York: Oxford University Press. 2013.

Bibliography

"Terrorist Organization Profile, Army of God." National Consortium for the Study of Terrorism and Responses to Terrorism. College Park, MD. October 5, 2011.

Nelson-Pallmeyer, Jack. *Is Religion Killing Us? Violence in the Bible and the Quran.* Chicago, IL: Trinity Press. 2003.

Newberg, Andrew and Mark Robert Waldman. *How God Changes Your Brain: Breakthrough Findings from a Leading Neuroscientist.* NY: Ballantine Books. 2010.

Perahzur, Ami and Arie Perlinger. *Jewish Terrorism in Israel.* NY: Columbia University Press. 2009.

*Pickthall, Mohammed Marmaduke. *The Meaning of the Glorious Koran.* Eleventh Edition. NY: Mentor Books. The New American Library. 1955. (Originally published in 1930 by George Allen & Unwin, Ltd. London.).

Rodinson, Maxime. *Mohammed.* Translated by Anne Carter. NY: Pantheon Books. 1971.

Ross, Floyd H. and Tyrette Hills. *The Great Religions by Which We Live.* Greenwich, CT: Fawcett Publishing, Inc. 1959.

Sacks, Rabbi Jonathan. *Not in God's Name: Confronting Religious Violence.* NY: Schocken Books. 2015.

Schwartz-Barcott, T. P. War, *Terror & Peace in the Qur'an and in Islam: Insights for Military and Government Leaders.* Carlisle Barracks, PA: Army War College Foundation Press. 2004.

Schwartz-Barcott, T. P. "Conversations with Ali." Unpublished essay. March 31, 2017.

Spencer, Robert. *The Complete Infidel's Guide to the Koran.* Washington, D.C.: Regnery Publishing. 2009.

Steffen, Lloyd. "Religion and Violence in Christian Traditions." Chapter 5 (Pp. 100-126) in *The Oxford Handbook of Religion and Violence.* NY: Oxford University Press. 2013.

Stern, Jessica. *Terror in the Name of God: Why Religious Militants Kill.* NY: Ecco/HarperCollins Publishers. 2003.

The Economist. December 19, 2007. "Bible Versus the Koran."

**The King James Study Bible.* Nashville: Thomas Nelson Publishers. 1988.

**The Jewish Study Bible.* Tanakh Translation. Adele Berlin and Marc Zvi Brettler (Eds.). NY: Oxford University Press. Jewish Publication Society. 2004.

The Living Webster's Encyclopedic Dictionary of the English Language. Chicago, IL: English Language Institute of America. 1975.

Weber, Robert Philip. *Basic Content Analysis.* Thousand Oaks, CA: Sage Publications, Inc. 1985.

Zimbardo, Philip. *The Lucifer Effect: Understanding How Good People Turn Evil.* NY: Random House Trade Paperbacks. 2008.

About the Author

Timothy Philip Schwartz-Barcott grew up near the coal mines, coke ovens, and steel-making factories of Monessen and Latrobe, in western Pennsylvania, in the 1940s and 1950s.

He graduated from Miami University, Oxford, Ohio, in 1964, with majors in philosophy and military science. In 1965-66, he served as a Marine Corps infantry and ground reconnaissance officer with the 3rd Reconnaissance Battalion and the 2nd Battalion, 3d Marines, in Vietnam.

In 1975 he received a Ph.D. in sociology from the University of North Carolina, Chapel Hill. Since then he has conducted academic research and has taught sociology, criminology, and social psychology courses at the University of Delaware, Brown University, the University of Connecticut, the University of Rhode Island, and Providence College.

His research articles have been published in *The Sociological Quarterly*, *Footnotes of the American Sociological Association*, *Teaching Sociology*, the *Marine Corps Gazette*, and other journals and anthologies.

His books include *War, Terror & Peace in the Qur'an and in Islam: Insights for Military and Government Leaders*; *After the Disaster: Re-creating Community and Well-being at Buffalo Creek Since the Notorious Coal-Mining Disaster in 1972*; *Concerning Caputo: Africa and Acts of Faith as Art, Science, and Much More*; and *Let There Be Light: Five Stories*.

His next book reports on his study of the transmissions of happiness and unhappiness from the ancestors through to the descendants of Presidents Ronald Reagan to Donald Trump.

He lives with his family, a golden retriever named Miss Peachy, and a variety of other pets and semi-wild animals on what remains of a two-hundred-year-old farm in rural Rhode Island.

Index

Abdo, Naser Jason, 24, 33
abortion, 8–9, 247–248
Abouhalima, 245–246, 254
Abuse, 93, 253
Abyssinia, 50
Abyssinians, 81
Acts, xvii, xix, 5, 8, 55–56, 58–59, 78, 94, 99, 103–104, 124, 133–134, 136, 138, 155, 164, 166, 193, 198–202, 223, 245, 247–248, 250–251, 254–255, 258, 260, 270, 281, 283, 291, 303, 310
Acts of the Apostles, 193, 198–201
adulterer, 68, 85, 134, 156, 180, 196, 218, 234, 273, 290, 297
adversary, 63, 145, 151, 153, 155, 207, 222, 226, 291
Afghan, 34
Afghanistan, 27, 32
aggression, 58, 63, 126, 129, 276
Ahimsa, 16–17, 25, 300
al-Awlaki, Anwar, 12–13, 15, 33–34
al-Qaeda, 4–5, 11–15, 20, 22, 24, 28, 33–34, 62, 86, 260
al-Rasheed, Madawi, 181
al-Shabaab, 11
al-Zawahiri, Ayman, 14
Algeria, 7
Alpha 66 and Omega 7, 4
Amalek, 129, 165, 167
ambush, 165
America, 6, 13, 15, 24, 31–32, 235–236, 260, 288, 293, 295
American, 1, 6, 23–25, 33, 90, 226, 231, 257, 269

Ammonite, 142, 225
Amorite, 109–111, 113, 120, 135–136, 141, 168, 173–174, 222
Amos, 128, 158–159, 168, 173, 175, 275
anger, 96, 128, 189, 241–243, 304
animal, 17, 36, 96–98, 100, 102–103, 105, 108, 120, 134, 167, 187, 241–242, 276, 280, 296
Animal Liberation Front, 4
annihilate, 164–165, 225, 243–244
Antipas, 217
Arab, 35, 269, 272, 276
Arabia, 32, 35–36, 118, 275
Arabic, 34, 38–39, 74–75, 81, 85, 278
Ark, 98–99, 103, 105, 242, 276, 280
Arkansas, 249
Arlington, 12, 15, 33
Armenian, 164
armor, 141–142
army, 3, 36, 52, 144, 207
Army of God, 7–9
arsenal, 259, 289
arson, 6, 8
Artan, Abdul Razak Ali, 14, 29
Aryan Nation, 4
ashes, 163, 212
assailant, 81–82
assault, xvii, 248
Assyria, 92, 156, 161, 173, 229, 275
Assyrians, 157, 280
attack, xx, 6, 8, 11–13, 30, 32–34, 75–76, 80–82, 87, 119, 244, 248, 251, 260, 262–264
avenge, 131

axe, 91, 154, 174, 275
Babylon, 144, 147, 152–155, 157, 173
Babylonian, 161
Badr, 48, 70, 73, 76, 222
Baghdad, 14, 36
Balkans, 2
Ballantine, 25
battle, 2–3, 19, 36, 46–49, 59, 65, 70, 72–76, 83–84, 86–88, 91, 95, 99, 105–107, 110, 118–119, 127, 135–136, 138, 140–143, 146, 151, 154, 160, 162–163, 170, 174–175, 192, 195, 200, 221–222, 227–229, 244, 249, 259–261, 264, 272, 275, 277–278, 308–310
battlefield, 22, 28, 263
beast, 91, 154, 156, 174, 207, 212, 217, 241–242, 281
beat, 3, 123, 199, 205
Bedouin, 35–36
Belgrade, 3
Berkeley, xviii, 245, 284
besiege, 160
Bin Laden, Osama, xvii, xx, 12, 14, 21–22, 28, 81, 232, 262–263, 291, 293
Birmingham, 8–9
Black Liberation Army, 4
blasphemy, 255
blood, xvii, 142, 175, 207, 277–278, 291
body, 18, 298
Boko Haram, 11
bomb, 246
Bosnian, 3, 164
Boston, 268
bound, 117, 129, 131–132
break, 72, 150
Bridgeport, 34
Britain, 11, 23, 293

British, 232, 252
brutal, 49, 138, 165, 225, 229, 270, 290–291
Buddhism, 16–17, 245, 293, 299–300
Bulgarian, 3
bull, 130
burial, 148
burn, 11, 21, 27, 44, 52, 57, 60, 62, 69, 83, 113, 116–117, 133, 135, 151, 189, 221, 229, 235, 277, 308
butcher, 14, 29
Byzantine, 36
Cairo, 247
California, xviii, 33, 245, 284
Cambodia, 164
Canaan, 92, 94–95, 107–108, 115, 127, 136, 138–140, 161, 275
Canaanite, 163
Canada, 6, 293
captive, 121–122, 138, 274–275
carcass, 91, 153–154, 174
carnage, 251
Carolina, 9, 15, 25, 31, 90
Catholic, xi, 10, 94, 130
cattle, 80, 99, 117–119, 132, 229, 235, 242, 274, 280
Chabad-Lubavitch Movement, 7
chains, 147, 213
challenge, 139, 144
Charlotte, 31
Charlottesville, 15, 33
Chechnya, 264
chemical, 8, 81, 87
Chesser, Zachary Adam, 15, 24, 33
Chronicles, 143–144
circumcision, 100, 203
Colombia, 4
Colorado, 11, 24
Columbus, 29
Combat, 13, 19, 36, 164, 189
commit, 6, 8–9, 20–21, 35, 51, 54,

Index

commit (*continued*), 82, 84, 92, 104, 110, 112–113, 121, 126–128, 141, 156, 164, 167, 170, 173–174, 188, 190–191, 195, 200, 202, 212, 221, 246, 251, 254, 266, 282, 299, 308
condemn, 7, 165, 209, 212, 262, 267
conflict, 89, 95, 102, 106, 157, 175, 207, 249
confront, 3, 23, 49, 109, 269
Connecticut, 34
conquest, 24, 140, 166
consequence, 17–18, 52, 109, 128, 267, 308, 310
conspiracy, 33, 257
convicted, 9, 11, 15, 28, 33, 245, 247–249, 253, 255, 257
counterterrorism, 12
coup, 41
Covenant, The Sword, and The Arm of the Lord, The, 4, 249
cow, 40, 42, 49, 62
crime, 8, 253, 257, 265
criminal, 293
Croat, 164
crucify, 16, 22, 28, 32, 186, 188–191, 193, 195, 198, 205, 217, 222, 278, 282
crusade, xx, 7, 260, 263
curse, 61, 69, 96, 124, 134, 155–156, 163, 207, 229, 273
cut, 16, 32, 189, 191, 196
cyanide, 257
Cyrus, 144
damage, 137, 168, 190, 192, 247
Damascus, 36, 100, 128, 154, 158, 162, 168, 173, 243
danger, xx, 225, 230, 259, 289
Daniel, 100, 243
Darwat, 246
Dear, Robert Lewis, 11
death, 7, 9, 18, 32, 72, 92, 98–99,

death (*continued*), 101–102, 106–108, 112, 117, 121, 123, 129, 132–134, 136, 138, 141–143, 153, 179, 181, 205, 207, 242, 250, 255, 263, 265, 267, 273, 280, 300
decades ahead, xx, 19, 42, 54–55, 60, 70, 76, 81, 84, 87, 93, 127–128, 138, 146, 152–153, 155, 158, 160–161, 170, 173–174, 182, 217, 223, 236, 251, 266, 273, 275, 289, 296, 300, 308, 310
defeat, 109, 140–141, 143–144, 166, 170, 243, 263
defend, 248
defense, 80, 84, 138, 231–232, 247–248, 262
Delaware, 247
demonic, 20, 258
destroy, 39, 43, 54–55, 80, 84, 91, 99–101, 103, 105, 109–114, 117, 127, 132, 136–138, 140, 146–147, 155, 160, 162, 167, 200, 205, 212–214, 243–244, 279–280, 297
destructive, 39, 41, 43, 102, 146, 251, 282, 305, 308
Deuteronomy, 92, 106, 108–109, 111–113, 115–117, 119–122, 124, 129, 229, 235, 273–274
disaster, 225, 299
disease, 42, 49, 296, 300
dismemberment, 10
divorce, 40, 295
dominate, 36, 50–51, 72, 86, 170, 227
doom, 41–43, 49, 57, 69–70, 77, 83, 127, 142, 189, 194, 196, 200, 205–206, 211–212, 221, 276–277, 308
dread, 259, 281, 289
drown, 188, 308
drunkard, 102, 281

Durham, 25
Earth Liberation Front, 4
earthquake, 40, 80
Ecclesiastes, 149
Egypt, 95, 97, 102, 104, 116–117, 124, 127, 129–132, 146, 152–155, 157, 165, 173, 175, 213, 246
enemy, 1, 40, 50, 55, 59, 63, 72, 91, 109, 118–119, 121, 135, 144–148, 151, 154, 158, 166, 174, 226, 231, 244, 249, 269–270, 274, 279, 281
England, 7, 11
enrage, 157
Esposito, Joseph L., 27
Esther, 145
Ethiopia, 161, 173, 175, 275
Ethiopians, 92, 161, 229, 275
Europe, xx, 11, 23, 164, 246, 260, 263, 293, 296
European, 6, 295
evil, 69
execute, 120, 137–138, 157, 165, 182, 201, 203, 206
exile, 79, 138, 144, 147, 216
Exodus, 11, 129–134, 249
expel, 5, 87, 166
exterminate, 1, 87–88, 163, 222, 226, 242, 269–270, 274, 279–280
extremist, xx, 232, 238, 240, 251, 254, 288
Ezekiel, 128, 155–157, 168, 173, 175
Ezra, 144, 173, 175
Fairfax, 33
Famine, 92, 161, 229, 275
Farook, Syed, 24, 33
Fawkes, Guy, 7
FBI, 12, 14, 30–31
fear, 18, 39, 41, 75, 80, 92, 102, 110, 117, 121, 145, 148, 153, 155, 162, 251, 264, 273, 281
feud, 142

fight, 13, 16, 32, 63–64, 71, 135, 139–141, 147, 163, 206, 255, 259–262, 264, 267, 276, 289
fire, 18, 30, 41, 43, 57, 61, 65, 67–69, 77–78, 100, 105, 113, 115–117, 127, 140, 146, 148, 151, 153, 157–159, 162, 169, 189, 192, 194, 196, 205, 207, 212–213, 221, 229, 235, 243, 257, 261, 271, 275–276, 308
flame, 41, 43, 69, 169
flesh, 98–99, 153–154, 163, 213, 241–242, 280
flood, 80, 87, 146, 167
Florida, 10, 14, 248
force, 66, 78–79
France, xx, 11, 294
fratricide, 98, 214
French, 250
fundamentalist, xx, 11, 247, 256, 294
funeral, 293
fury, 156, 225
Gaza, 36, 128, 154, 158, 162, 173, 175, 275
Genesis, 97–105, 129, 241–244, 280
genocide, 138, 164, 167, 170, 177, 279–280, 295
gentile, 158, 194, 199
Germany, 246, 254, 302
oat, 102
Gomorrah, 99–101, 104–106, 167, 174, 212–213, 243, 276, 280
gunman, 30
Gunpowder Plot, 7
gun, 259, 289
Habakkuk, 160
Haggai, 161
Haleem, 34–35, 38, 41, 46, 64, 70, 72, 74–76, 90, 278, 307
hamas, 11, 245, 260
Hammurabi Code, 189

Index

hang, 82, 87, 121, 138, 142
Harvard, 256
Hasan, Nidal Malik, 12–13, 15, 33–34, 90
hate, 32, 77, 87, 111, 114, 145, 158, 179, 236–237, 239, 288
heads, 8, 122, 141–142, 148, 151, 173, 202, 234
heal, 152, 252, 289
heathen, 92, 147, 161, 229, 275
Hebrews, 207
hell, 9, 11, 57–58, 60–61, 75, 77, 205, 246, 267, 270, 277
hellfire, 84, 127, 189, 192, 195–196, 221, 270–271
Hezbollah, 11, 14, 30
hijack, 21
Hittite, 120, 168, 174
Holocaust, 164, 295
homicide, 28
Hosea, 157–158, 166, 168, 175, 275
hostile, 17, 80
hurt, 17, 27, 145
Idaho, 7
inflict, 138
injure, 6, 10, 12, 18, 30–31, 39, 57, 102, 190, 267, 276–277
innocent, 9, 34, 124, 243, 263, 281, 300
insult, 63, 85
intimidate, 219
intrude, 250
invade, 95, 136–137, 144
Iran, 31, 173, 294
Iraq, 4, 11, 13, 32, 160, 295, 302
Iraqi, 160
Irish, 4, 245, 252
Isaiah, 150–153, 156, 159, 168, 173, 175
ISIS, 5, 11, 14, 20, 30, 62, 66, 86, 160, 260, 264, 295, 302

Islamic, 4, 11–12, 23, 29–30, 32–33, 59, 230–231, 235–236, 246–247, 256, 263, 269, 288, 295
Israel, 6, 24, 67, 92, 95, 106–108, 115, 117, 121, 123–124, 132–133, 136–137, 139, 141–143, 151, 153–157, 161, 163, 165, 168, 174–175, 179, 273–274
Israeli, 6, 137, 175, 252
Israelite, 44, 60, 67, 84, 92, 95, 107–120, 126–127, 131, 135, 137–141, 143–144, 146–147, 150, 152–159, 161–163, 165–170, 173–175, 229, 243, 279–280, 282, 290
ISUL, 11, 20, 62, 260, 295
James, 209
Jenkins, Philip, 1, 22–23, 25, 28, 38, 44, 90, 118, 166, 177–178, 181, 226, 230, 267–272, 276–282, 284–285, 290–291, 297, 306
Japanese, 250
Jeremiah, 8, 91, 153–154, 174, 275
Jerusalem, 91, 128, 140–144, 154–157, 159, 162–163, 173–174, 194, 275, 298
Jew, 78, 141, 201, 205
Jewish, xx, 4–6, 13, 24, 77–80, 87, 94–95, 102, 104–105, 130, 147, 150, 164, 175, 186, 190, 203, 207, 225, 238, 241, 243, 245, 290, 293, 305, 307–308
Jewish Defense League, 6
jihad, 15, 24, 230–232, 262–263
jihadist, 90, 232, 235–236, 288
Job, 41, 145, 246
Joel, 158, 168, 175
John, xi, 8–9, 11, 27, 188, 191, 193, 195–196, 214–219, 221, 248, 261, 282, 297
Jonah, 40, 128, 159, 173

Jordan, 110–111, 115, 275
Joshua, 91, 136–138, 279
Jude, 212–213
Judges, 139–140
Juergensmeyer, Mark, xvii, xx, 3, 5, 7, 24, 181, 230, 244–256, 284, 289, 297
Kach, 5–6, 245
Kahane, Rabbi Meir, 5–6, 245
kill, xvii, 6, 10–16, 30, 32–34, 52, 56–57, 100, 104–106, 111, 114, 122, 141–144, 149, 166, 174, 181, 187–189, 202, 209, 222–223, 225, 230, 233, 237–238, 242, 248, 258, 263, 267, 272, 274, 276, 281, 310
Kings, 99–100, 105–106, 113, 136, 140, 142–144, 147, 154, 157, 167, 174
knife, 264
Kosovo, 2–3
Ku Klux Klan, 4, 7
Kurdish, 164
Kurdistan, 4, 13, 295
Lamentations, 8, 155
Lashkar-e-Taiba, 11
law, 13, 107, 118, 129, 133–136, 236, 249, 265, 296, 303
Lebanon, 256
leprosy, 179
lethal, 19, 60, 85, 116, 121, 159, 173–175, 188, 190, 229, 278, 282
Leviticus, 129, 134–135, 229, 273–274
liberate, 4, 296–297
Libya, 4
lightning, 80, 87, 147
lion, 157
livestock, 1, 36, 174, 226, 244, 269, 279
locust, 54
London, 11, 90

Luke, 9, 193–196, 198, 282
Macedonian, 203
Malachi, 163–164
Malik, Tashfeen, 12, 15, 24, 33, 90
Manchester, 11
Manhattan, 6
manual, 47, 201
Mark, xvii, xx, 3, 5, 7, 24–25, 181, 190–196, 230, 244, 282, 284, 289, 297
marriage, 108, 119, 203, 295
martyr, 66–67, 209–210, 272
massacre, 6, 13, 30
Mateen, Omar, 14, 30–31
Matthew, 179–180, 187–189
May 19th Communist Organization, 4
McVeigh, Timothy, 257
Miami, 10
Micah, 159–160
militant, 256, 285
military, 19, 36–37, 46, 48, 50, 75–76, 84, 86, 105–106, 108, 124, 129, 132, 136, 138–139, 142–143, 160, 165–166, 173, 175, 192, 195–196, 200, 221–222, 230, 233, 244, 251, 255, 259–260, 262–263, 265, 267, 274, 277–278, 289, 307, 309
miscreant, 42, 68–69, 77, 84, 122–123, 189, 192, 277, 281
missiles, 87
Moab, 101, 107, 143–144, 155, 158, 169
Moabite, 110, 225
Mosul, 160
Muhammad, 27, 35–37, 48, 50, 52, 55–56, 58–60, 64–66, 70, 73, 75–77, 82–87, 216, 223, 231–232, 300, 302
murderer, 21, 142, 238, 241, 248

Index

Muslim Brotherhood, 11
Nahum, 160
Nashville, 177
Natan-Zada, Eden, 6
Nazareth, 208
Nehemiah, 144
Netherlands, 231
New York, 24–25, 90, 177, 284–285
9/11, xvii, 12, 22, 28
Nosair, El Sayyid, 6, 245
Numbers, 129, 135–136, 302
Obadiah, 128, 159, 161
Obama, Barack, 13
offense, 85, 205
offensive, 84, 138, 175, 244, 262, 282
Ohio, 14, 29
Oklahoma, 256–257
Olympic Games, 9
1 Chronicles, 143–144
1 John, 214
1 Kings, 142–143
1 Peter, 210–211
1 Samuel, 141–142, 167
opponent, 65, 67, 86–87, 127, 137–138, 142, 252, 272, 277, 279, 291
oppress, 16, 32, 56, 246, 291
Order, The, 4
Orlando, 14, 30
orphan, 59, 68–69, 85
Orthodox, 5–6, 175
Ottoman, 3, 164
outbreak, 81
overthrow, 100–101, 132
ox, 165
pain, 42, 49, 57, 70, 77, 84, 173, 276
Pakistan, 12, 256
Pakistani, 34
Palestine, 4, 32, 261
Palestinian, 108, 137
Pan-Islamism, 13

passenger, 12, 264
peace, 47, 189, 215, 231, 234, 300
Pedahzur, Ami, 5–6
Pennsylvania, 12, 22
Pensacola, 248, 256
Pentagon, The, 12, 22, 81, 245, 251
perish, 242
Perizzites, 113, 120, 139
persecute, 16, 32, 58, 60, 63–64, 84, 88, 95, 129, 182, 198, 201, 203, 207, 216, 223, 276–277
Persia, 128, 145, 173
Persian, 36, 157
Peter, 210, 212, 276
Philemon, 206
Phineas Priesthood, 4, 7
Pickthall, Mohammed Marmaduke, 38–39, 41, 46, 66, 70, 72, 74–76, 79, 81, 90, 278, 285, 307
plague, 99, 129, 131, 154, 180, 218, 225
plane, 21, 81, 252
plot, 13, 33, 102, 142, 157, 257
poison, 257
power, 21, 70, 142, 162, 194, 205, 213, 252, 255, 267, 289–290, 294
prejudice, 237
prisoner, 135
propaganda, 5, 14
Proverbs, 148–149
Psalms, 145–148
Pulse Nightclub, 14, 30
punish, 65, 68, 78, 153, 205, 225, 272, 281
Quraysh, 71
Qutbism, 13
radical, 263
rage, 203
raid, 36, 84
ransom, 102
rape, 101

rebel, 12, 109, 158, 275
refuge, 79, 111, 148
regime, 129
repudiate, 105, 188–189, 192, 238
resist, 136
retaliate, 32, 57, 263, 276
Revelation, 180, 216–217, 219, 248
revenge, 96
revolt, 6
rivalry, 40, 238–239, 288
Rodinson, Maxime, 35
Roman, 5, 36, 180, 198, 207, 216, 261
Romans, 201–202
Rome, 182, 190, 201, 203, 206, 210, 261
Rudolph, Eric, 9
ruin, 68, 78
Ruth, 128, 140, 173
Rwandan, 164
Sacks, Rabbi Jonathan, 230, 237–244, 283–284, 288, 295
sacrifice, 9, 134
Salafism, 13
Salafist jihadism, 13
Salem, 234
Salvation, The, 302
Samuel, 141–142, 167
Satan, 55–56, 59, 85, 202, 296
Saudi Arabia, 32, 275
savage, 270, 281
Schneerson, Menachem Mendel, 7
scourge, 68–69, 179
Serbian, 3
severe, 111
sexual, 104, 108, 121, 134, 149, 295–296
Sharia Law, 13
Shahzad, Faisal, 13, 24, 34
Shannon, Shelly, 8–9
sheep, 91, 137, 165, 279
shoot, 6, 14–15, 29, 33

siege, 143, 154, 308
sin, 54, 109, 116, 120, 123, 139, 157, 159–160, 163, 180
Singh, 245
slaughter, 58, 63, 100, 104, 106, 145, 156, 261, 276, 302
slay, 8, 55–56, 65, 76, 92, 97, 99, 101, 109, 111, 131, 135, 139–143, 153, 157, 161, 165, 190, 207, 214, 217, 229, 272, 275
smite, 100–101, 111, 132, 143, 145, 200
Sodom, 99–101, 104–106, 167, 174, 195, 212–213, 243, 276, 280
soldier, 33, 199, 310
Song of Solomon, 128, 142, 144, 149, 173
Spanish, xx
Spanish Inquisition, 7
spear, 150, 158–160
Spencer, Robert, 225, 230–237, 283–284, 287–288, 291, 301
spoil, 22, 28, 40, 48, 63, 72, 74–75, 83, 87–88, 135, 183, 244, 278
Stanford, 256
Stern, Jessica, 58, 230, 249, 256–259, 285, 289
stone, 205, 207, 277
storm, 169
strike, 81, 87
struggle, 264
suffer, 36, 129, 182, 205, 217
suicide, 34, 64, 82, 87, 124, 141, 188, 268, 271
suspect, 29, 67, 90, 180
swine, 188
sword, 150, 158–160
Symbionese Liberation Army, 4
Syria, 4, 143, 161, 168, 173, 175, 295
Syrian, 142–144, 151
Taheri-Azar, Mohammed, 15–16,

Taheri-Azar, Mohammed (*continued*), 25, 28, 31–33, 90, 232, 255, 265, 270
Taliban, 11, 20, 27, 260
target, 13, 58–60, 62, 85, 87–88, 128, 173, 234, 310
terror, xvii–xviii, 1–2, 6, 19, 22–23, 27–30, 43–44, 49, 54–55, 67–68, 78, 80, 83, 85, 87–90, 93–94, 102, 124, 130, 135, 152–153, 157, 176, 181–182, 206, 222, 226–228, 231, 233, 244, 248–251, 253–256, 260, 262, 269, 272, 280–281, 284–285, 292, 299, 301, 303–304, 307–309
terrorism, xvii, xix–xx, 2–8, 11, 14, 24, 29, 183, 230–232, 239, 248, 250, 252, 256–258, 268, 271, 291
terrorist, 1, 5–7, 11, 14, 19–20, 30, 33, 35, 44, 66, 75, 124, 137, 232, 246–247, 250–251, 254, 256–259, 262–265, 289–290
Texas, 15, 33, 257
threat, 7, 19, 21, 39, 52–53, 63, 73, 87, 92, 94–95, 99, 105, 112–113, 126–128, 144–145, 152, 161, 169, 174, 188–189, 195–196, 200, 218, 221, 234, 242, 270, 273, 278, 282, 299, 303–304, 308
3 John, 214
throw, 194
Titus, 205
Tokyo, 246, 250
tolerance, 297
torment, 207
torture, 207, 242, 281
Turks, 164
2 Corinthians, 205–206
2 John, 214
2 Kings, 143
2 Peter, 210, 212
2 Timothy, 206

uncircumcised, 141
ungodly, 211–212
United Freedom Front, 5
vehicle, 28
vengeance, 138, 147–148, 205, 213, 249
victim, xi, xix, 12, 15, 33, 52, 112, 129, 164, 173, 190, 267, 281–282
victory, 141
violate, 189, 234, 247, 273
violence, xi, xvii–xx, 1–3, 5, 7–9, 12–13, 16–24, 27–28, 30, 33, 35, 38–68, 70–81, 83–89, 91–106, 108–118, 120–128, 130–131, 133–150, 152–164, 166, 170–175, 177, 179, 181–215, 217, 219–223, 225–244, 246–262, 264–266, 268–273, 276–278, 280–285, 287–293, 295–296, 299–305, 308–309
Virginia, 8, 12, 15, 33
Waagner, Clayton, 8
war, xx, 2–3, 19, 23, 28, 35–36, 45, 70, 73–74, 83, 86–88, 93–95, 106, 111, 125, 127, 129–130, 137–141, 143–145, 148, 153–154, 160, 162, 168, 189–190, 192, 195–196, 200, 209, 221, 225, 228–229, 232, 236, 247, 249, 251, 260, 262, 267–272, 276–278, 290, 299, 308–309
warrior, 140, 151, 261
Washington, D.C., 12, 30, 234, 268, 284
weak, 207, 290
weapon, 30, 36, 39, 91, 109, 154, 173–174, 257, 259, 275, 277, 289
Weathermen, 5
Westminster, 7
wicked, 9, 100, 117, 241
wolf, 5, 14, 20–21, 30, 265
World Trade Center, 12, 21, 81,

World Trade Center (*continued*), 244–245, 251
wound, 6, 30, 36, 143, 146
wrath, 18, 96, 116, 161, 201–202, 304
World War I, 295, 299
World War II, 164, 295, 299

Yazidi, 13, 302, 306
Yemen, 13–14
Zazi, Najibullah Zazi, 24, 34
zealot, 5
Zechariah, 162–163
Zephaniah, 92, 161, 229, 275, 280

www.ingramcontent.com/pod-product-compliance
Lightning Source LLC
Chambersburg PA
CBHW071811230426
43670CB00013B/2428